It's not our bank balance, looks, social status or popularity that determines how happy, free and fulfilled we are in life. Finally, what really counts is our state of mind. Subhuti's *Mind in Harmony* introduces us to the art of 'mind-watching', offering us valuable skills for understanding how our minds work. Using an analysis developed over hundreds of years within the Buddhist tradition, we can identify what's going on in our mind, including our moods and emotions, and see clearly what's helpful and what will end in tears.

The book works as a standalone introduction to Buddhist psychology, but it will also be useful further reading for those who enjoyed Sangharakshita's *Know Your Mind*.

Vessantara, author of *The Breath* and *A Guide to the Buddhas*

This is a refreshing approach to the classical Abhidharma material, relentlessly experiential and eminently practical. It offers a way of engaging directly with the sophisticated elements of Buddhist psychology that is immediately accessible and offers a real prospect of transformation. I heartily recommend it to anyone who wants to use Buddhist wisdom to explore and clarify their minds.

Andrew Olendzki, author of *Unlimiting Mind*, senior scholar at Barre Center for Buddhist Studies

Mind in Harmony

Also by Subhuti

Bringing Buddhism to the West: A Life of Sangharakshita
Buddhism and Friendship
Buddhism for Today: A Portrait of a New Buddhist Movement
Sangharakshita: A New Voice in the Buddhist Tradition
Seven Papers (with Sangharakshita)
The Buddhist Vision: A Path to Fulfilment
Bauddha Jivan Kese Jien (in Hindi)

Mind in Harmony

the psychology of Buddhist ethics

Subhuti

Published by
Windhorse Publications
169 Mill Road
Cambridge
CB1 3AN
UK

info@windhorsepublications.com
www.windhorsepublications.com

Cover design by Dhammarati
Author photo © Alokavira / Timm Sonnenschein
Typesetting and layout by Ruth Rudd

Printed by Bell & Bain Ltd, Glasgow

British Library Cataloguing in Publication Data:
A catalogue record for this book is available from the British Library.

ISBN: 978-1-909314-08-5

Contents

About the author

Subhuti was born Alex Kennedy, in Chatham, England, in 1947. He joined the Triratna Buddhist Order in 1973 and has since devoted himself to the practice and teaching of Buddhism. He has played a significant role in establishing both the London Buddhist Centre and the Guhyaloka Retreat Centre in Spain. He has also helped develop the training process to prepare men to join the Triratna Buddhist Order.

Since 2000, Subhuti has been a member of the College of Public Preceptors, to which the founder of Triratna, Sangharakshita, handed on his responsibilities on his retirement. Currently based in North Wales, Subhuti spends part of each year in India, leading retreats and giving lectures.

Author's acknowledgements

My first debt of gratitude, as always, is to my teacher, Urgyen Sangharakshita: whatever understanding of the Dharma I have comes through my contact with him. In particular, his exploration of Buddhist psychology is the basis of everything in this work. Sangharakshita's genius is to make the Dharma, in all its breadth and depth, luminously clear in a way that invites, inspires, and guides direct practice of it. I have done my best to continue in that spirit and my exposition is simply my attempt to communicate his teaching in the way that he has done.

Next come those I myself have taught. This material principally comes out of my experience of trying to get the living Dharma across to people in India, principally during retreats for members of the Triratna Buddhist Order, to which I belong. For a reasonably educated Westerner such as myself, with a comfortable upbringing in this fortunate isle of Britain, this presents quite a challenge. The background people in our movement in India have come from, besides being much less advantaged, is much more traditional, in the sense of being firmly based in the context of the extended family, than I have been used to in my life. That means people are, in a certain sense, less psychologically complex – although there are, of course, often complexities of a different kind beneath the surface. Many of my auditors are also less educationally sophisticated than is common in the West. However, that certainly does not at all mean less intelligent, by any means. The challenge then is to put these rich and complex teachings into terms that are simple and, at the same time, deep. My own understanding has benefited greatly from my hearers' patience in listening to me and from their questions and feedback – what they haven't 'got' being more instructive to me than what they have. As always in teaching the Dharma, I can sincerely say that I have learned far more than I have taught.

Dharmachari Subhamati conceived this book some ten years ago and began the process of bringing it together from transcripts of my talks. Its overall shape and the first half or so owe everything to him. He was unfortunately unable to complete the work because of the pressures of life and the book is the poorer for not having had his guiding hand throughout. I am deeply grateful to him for what he was able to do.

Dharmachari Vidyaruci gallantly took on editing the remaining half and brought the book to the verge of completion. Priyananda, Director of Windhorse Publications, has been the midwife of the work, making the path smooth and, in his enthusiasm for the book, enabling its completion. Michelle Bernard has made sure that all the different members of the team, all busy people, did their job at the right time, and she has done so with quiet patience. Kalyanaprabha has, with her usual elegance and precision, compiled the notes. Vidyadevi has brought to bear her great talent for refining gold from raw words and has produced a polished final version, while Dhatvisvari has skilfully worked it up to a publishable text. Dhammarati has very generously taken time from his weighty responsibilities to design a cover that gives true expression to the spirit of the book.

Many others have also made their own contributions to its appearance. In the creation of this book in particular, I feel myself to be merely a player in a team – no doubt a key one, but not by any means the only one. Beyond the giving of the initial talks, my own contribution has been relatively small and all these others have left their mark on the book and must share with me something of whatever praise or blame it attracts – and whatever *punya karma* is to be gained through its usefulness to others. Let us hope there is much of it!

Publisher's acknowledgements

Windhorse Publications wishes to gratefully acknowledge a grant from the Triratna European Chairs' Assembly Fund towards the production of this book.

We also wish to acknowledge and thank the individual donors who gave to the book's production via our 'Sponsor-a-book' campaign in 2014 and 2015.

Preface

The purpose of *Mind in Harmony* is to describe the mind from the Buddhist point of view. Since Buddhism is never interested in mere conceptual understanding, that means offering a description that can serve as a practical tool for transforming the mind so that it becomes more and more ethical, finds greater and greater fulfilment, and ultimately attains liberation.

Although I have drawn widely on my own understanding and practice of Buddhism in compiling this book, my main source is a body of texts called the Abhidharma (in particular, the Yogācāra version). I have tried to communicate Abhidharma ideas in an idiom that can be understood and made use of today.

In order to make these traditional teachings about the mind as accessible as possible, whilst remaining true to the meaning of the original, I have avoided all scholarly apparatus. This is not a history of the Abhidharma, nor a scholarly account of it, but an attempt at a working manual of the mind. I have tried to find English equivalents for Sanskrit words that are evocative of their true meaning rather than philologically accurate translations – however, I give the Sanskrit on the first occasion the term is mentioned, so that those with some previous knowledge can locate themselves.[1]

Who is the book for? I envisage two kinds of reader.

On the one hand, *Mind in Harmony* should interest anyone who is curious to know what Buddhism has to say about the mind. Readers who already know something about Buddhism in general, and fancy taking the plunge into Buddhist psychology, should find plenty here to stimulate them. I hope that the book will be an accessible introduction to a dauntingly technical subject.

At the same time, I have tried to write a handbook for those who are seriously interested in transforming the mind through systematic training. *Mind in Harmony* does not constitute a system of mind training in itself; no book, on its own, could. But I believe it could be a useful resource for committed Buddhists practising under an experienced guide, and in the supportive framework of a spiritual community. The book is intended for such practically motivated readers, as well as for the curious.

I should add that *Mind in Harmony* is a companion to another book – *Know Your Mind* by my teacher, Urgyen Sangharakshita. Both books cover the same general area. However, while my views on the subject have been more or less entirely shaped by Sangharakshita[2], I believe I have some fresh things to say. Also, while *Know Your Mind* is a wide-ranging survey of the area, based on a Tibetan commentary,[3] I have tried to focus on what is most necessary for practice. In this way, I see the two books as complementary. At the same time, they don't depend on one another, so that *Mind in Harmony* can be read without reference to *Know Your Mind*. I do, however, strongly recommend everyone to read my teacher's book after reading this. I am sure that will deepen readers' understanding and compensate for any inaccuracies in my presentation.

One of the principal inspirations for this book has been a series of retreats that I led in India, in which I presented my understanding of the meaning of the Abhidharma material. We discussed that material, not just in the abstract, but finding ways to apply the concepts to ourselves. Using those concepts as a sort of map, each of us explored his inner world. For example, we discussed and shared our own experience of the skilful and unskilful 'mental events'[4] – all of us trying to articulate what, say, faith meant to us personally, or what aspects in our present experience might correspond to such apparently lofty states as equanimity.

Likewise, we practised frequent confession – usually in small groups – in relation to the unskilful mental events. During our sessions in the shrine room, each of us would sit in silent meditation, searching for the various 'mental events' in the workings of his own mind, and looking for ways to foster the skilful ones and transform the unskilful ones. And in all the activities of the day – walking, sitting, eating, discussing – we trained ourselves to keep watch on our state of mind, shining the light of the Abhidharma on the flux of our inner life.

Most of us found, during the course of each retreat, that we came to know ourselves far better, through using the Abhidharma analysis of the mind. We came to recognize our mental states for what they really were, able both to label them accurately and to understand their ethical significance. And we came to see the patterns of mental states as they rolled through our minds. All this helped us to take a lot more responsibility for our own minds, and indeed to change them.

Of course, I had to acknowledge that studying and reflecting on this material on retreat was one thing, but practising it at home another. The danger is that, when one returns from retreat, where conditions are so supportive and inspiring, to a busy and demanding life, often in India with so many difficulties and burdens, the inspiration and clarity one has gained are soon lost in the rush of events. I therefore started to ask the participants, at the end of each retreat, to come to conclusions about what traits they most needed to work on and how they were going to do so when they got home, suggesting even that they make resolutions that could be followed through with the support of their friends in the sangha. Noticing how people used this material in this respect has also taught me a lot and has informed this book.

This work therefore represents the crystallization of experience over several years of study and retreat-leading on the Yogācāra Abhidharma. I suppose I could have pointed students towards the original texts, but, even among committed practitioners, very few could just pick up the Abhidharma and put it straight to use. That is why I felt it would be of service to others if I could offer them my understanding of it, presented in 'user-friendly' terms, emerging from my experience of it, both in my own life and in my interaction with my friends in the sangha.

At this point, then, perhaps I should stress that this book will be most useful if you are a committed Buddhist practising with others as part of a sangha or spiritual community. Only then will it bear significant fruit from a Buddhist point of view. This material is about more than mere psychological adjustment, coming to terms with oneself and living a happier and more fruitful life – excellent a goal as that is. It is ultimately about liberation from all suffering and ignorance, which comes about when we recognize that what we call 'I' is simply a conditioned phenomenon, constructed in the evolution of consciousness as a means of the organism's survival, but that now must be seen for what it is if we are to be truly at peace. When we come to see that all our mental states are conditioned, we can let go of our attachments and experience what the Buddha called the 'bliss of release'. So to use this material fully and effectively we need to be committed to that goal of liberation, which means committed to Enlightenment itself – and this means we need to be Buddhists.

Furthermore, in order to fulfil this path effectively we need to be rigorously honest, and this is very difficult when we are completely on our own or with people who do not care about such a path. There is so much room for self-deception, and we could even say that our self-identity *is* a kind of self-deception, so that if we are to see through it we need deep and honest communication with others, which is what we get when we are part of a genuine sangha or spiritual community.

Not only do we get honest reflection from fellow members of the sangha; at times they are all that keeps us going on the path. As we try to practise the Dharma more and more systematically, it is very likely that we may feel an almost desperate hopelessness and confusion from time to time as we pass beyond our normal 'comfort zone'. It is the presence of our spiritual friends in the sangha that can keep us going even in these difficult times of deep discouragement.

But finally and most significantly, in the sangha, when it is genuinely a sangha, we will find represented an abundance of those positive mental states we will be studying here, so that we ourselves are influenced and inspired by the uplifted mental states of our fellows in the spiritual community. The Buddha himself, of course, pursued the whole path to Enlightenment on his own, but there is every evidence that he was a completely remarkable and exceptional individual. We should recognize in all honesty that we are not yet of his kind and that we need friends on the path – we need sangha.

Making practical use of the material

We need to learn how to translate our Dharmic aspiration into effective practice, and effective practice must involve our whole lives. The Dharma life[5] has to be lived all the time – it's not a nine-to-five job, with weekends off. It isn't merely about having a certain lifestyle, or regularly doing certain things (although those things are usually very helpful). It is a question of practising the Dharma when we are walking down the stairs, taking a bath, or catching the bus to work. But what does practising the Dharma really mean? In the last analysis, it is a matter of transforming the mind. And to transform the mind we have to know it. A method of mind training that incorporates Abhidharma concepts and methods can, I hope we will find, be a powerful but sensitive instrument, revealing to us very clearly what our minds are like and how they work, and thereby how we transform them. It will help us to discover how we can practise the Dharma effectively all the time.[6]

Even the reading of a work such as *Mind in Harmony* can be a form of Dharma practice. In the Dharma we are always concerned to translate merely conceptual knowledge into direct and immediate awareness. That needs to be our effort with the material contained in this book: we need to start with conceptual understanding and then work towards that direct experience called insight. Through our application of this analysis of mind we need to arrive at true wisdom.

The Buddha, as we will see more fully later, spoke of three kinds of penetration of the truth, which sequentially flow one from another. We start with *śruta mayī prajñā*, which means the penetration or wisdom that comes through hearing. That entails really being clear that one has grasped as accurately as possible what the teaching is. In this case, that will mean reading the descriptions of each mental state contained here and making sure one is clear about what is meant – at this stage, independently of whether or not one agrees with it or has some experience of it. If I have done my job properly you should get that clarity relatively easily, but if you do not you may need to do other research, perhaps going to Sangharakshita's *Know Your Mind* or even back to source materials, such as are available.

Once we know what is actually being taught in the Dharma, then we can begin to think about it, to investigate our own experience, both internal and external, to see whether we can identify it in our own minds. This is *cintā mayī prajñā*, the penetration of the truth that comes through thinking or reflection. It means testing what you've heard in reason, and then applying what you have understood to experience, because in the end all concepts must come back to experience. At this stage you might even ask whether you agree with what is being said or not; and perhaps you could begin to reflect on what significance it has for yourself.

Bhāvanā mayī prajñā, which means the penetration that comes through cultivation, really amounting to the wisdom of direct realization, requires us to take our conceptual understanding into deep contemplation, whether in formal meditation or more informal and spontaneous musing. Here we move beyond simply understanding the words and their meanings, and pass to direct knowledge, not mediated by words and concepts. We see for ourselves the truth of what is being said. Most importantly in this context, we see the conditioned nature of these mental states, that they have no ultimate existence, but simply arise sequentially in dependence on conditions, without any reference to an abiding self-identity. In practical terms, this means that, to make full use of this material, we need to take it into a regular meditation practice.

In order to really put these three penetrations of the truth – hearing, reflecting, cultivating – into effect in relation to the material contained in this book, we need to be practising the Dharma vigorously in every area of our lives. That of course is a large subject that I cannot go into here since it requires a complete exposition of the path.[7] What perhaps is most important here in this respect is not merely reading the book, but discussing it with friends, in the context of sangha. That means going through it in detail and doing something of a collective penetration of the truth through listening and reflecting. If you can find someone who has a lot more experience, who can be a spiritual guide and friend, so much the better.

In that context, you could practise confession, which is one of the most important of Dharma practices. That means freely and frankly acknowledging the mental states that you have, and that underlie all your actions of body and speech. Through confession one gains relief from the pains and even torments of negative states and their expressions, but one also objectifies them and therefore makes it easier to avoid reproducing them in the future. One comes thereby to know the mind more and more fully through confession.

Of course, we should put the main emphasis on reflection upon the positive mental events. I suspect it is unwise (for fairly obvious reasons) to dwell too intently on the negative ones. Each of the negative events is linked to a corresponding positive one, and, according to the Buddha, by nurturing the growth of the positive event, we can drive out the negative one, in the same way that (as the old saying goes) 'one nail drives out another.'

The key to progress is therefore to identify the positive events in one's own experience, to become more and more familiar with them, and to try to sustain them and develop them further. At the same time, the effort to do this brings us to a clearer awareness of any unskilful mental states that we habitually engage in – and a better understanding of what causes them. We then need to reflect on those causes, and find skilful ways to remove them.

I hope that you will be stimulated to undertake this strenuous but rewarding task, perhaps the most rewarding there can be, since it will contribute to making your life rich and fulfilling and of greater and greater benefit to others – and ultimately to the attainment of Buddhahood. May this book be a support for your efforts and may those efforts be crowned with success.

Part 1

The art of mind watching

Chapter 1

....

Going deeper

Introduction

Buddhism is a spiritual path. Anyone who chooses to follow it must from time to time face the problem of how he or she personally (and not just 'one' in general) can make further progress along that path.

The question 'How can I go deeper?' arises not once but many times in the Buddhist spiritual life. It tends to come up first when one gets past the stage of exploration.

The stage of exploration is the period between the dawning of an interest in Buddhism and the point when it becomes central in one's life. For some people, the exploratory stage may be quite short, perhaps only a few months. For most people, however, it is likely to be longer. It might last many years. And that is fine: the pace of spiritual growth cannot be forced, and we all develop in our own way, at our own rate.

During the exploratory stage, our needs are fairly simple and don't vary much from those of other people: we need to develop an outline understanding of Buddhism, explore Buddhist practice (for example, by getting into the habit of daily meditation), and build personal links of friendship with other Buddhists. Each of these three aspects – theoretical, practical, and social – takes time. But eventually, if we persist in our exploration, and if we like what we find, we reach a watershed, a stage when we feel confident – not just from intuition but from experience – that Buddhism offers a real spiritual path. Not only that, but we also feel sure that the path is one that *we* want to follow.

So at this stage we make a decisive commitment – to Buddhism in general and probably to a particular Buddhist tradition and community that will provide the context we need to practise effectively.

To cross the watershed and commit ourselves to Buddhism is a big step, perhaps the biggest we will ever take in our spiritual life, because it makes possible all the later steps. Yet curiously one does not always find that the going gets easier from this point onwards. In fact, it usually gets tougher.

The trouble is that it's only *after* we have made our commitment that we really take the measure of the obstacles that stand in our way. It is like learning a language. You begin by memorizing some basic words and phrases – formulae for greetings and simple functional information. You find it works. Exhilarated, you set your heart on becoming fluent. Only then do you start to realize the magnitude of what you have taken on. There is so much to learn.

In the same way, on the spiritual path, sooner or later we reach a point where we form a truer picture of the scale of the task. At that point, some people feel disheartened; others feel quietly gratified that their spiritual efforts are becoming firmly grounded in reality. But, however we may feel about the long climb we now see ahead, we are likely to perceive the need to start afresh – to reapply the general principles we've learned in a way that is more systematic and more tailored to our personal spiritual needs. In short, we will see the need for a system for training the mind.

This book is not itself a system of mind training, but it offers some of the tools needed to construct such a system for oneself. I want to share with other committed Buddhists certain insights into the mind – insights that, in my own case, have helped me to carry forward the task of self-transformation.

But where do these insights come from? I could answer that they come from the whole of my spiritual practice over forty years and more. However, much of the material in the book has a more specific source. It is the fruit of my exploration of the Abhidharma – often seen as the most dauntingly technical part of the Buddhist canon.

I shall have more to say about the Abhidharma later, but first I want to describe the process by which I myself came to recognize the need for a psychology of ethics. That recognition came from more than one direction.

Firstly, my need for such a system became obvious as I tried to go deeper in meditation, and to relate to other people with more love and patience. Secondly, I began to see the same need in others, as I witnessed the struggles of my friends to come to grips with the problems that each one faced in his or her spiritual life. Finally, it was confirmed by my growing recognition of the importance of harmony in the spiritual community.

The best way I can set the stage for what follows is by enlarging a little on each of these three experiences, albeit simplifying and conflating long and complex processes that took place over many years.

The morality of the private moment

Firstly, I discovered the value of the Abhidharma in my own spiritual practice. I had been a Buddhist for some years, and I could happily say that my spiritual efforts had borne some fruit. On the whole, I had lived in accordance with Buddhist principles, and experienced positive mental states. Nevertheless, looking within, I came to sense a deeper layer of mind that was not wholly within reach of my spiritual ideals, and was even sometimes at odds with those ideals. In order to make further spiritual progress I knew I had to get to grips with this submerged layer.

In my own case, it seemed to be when I was alone that these latent tendencies were most likely to emerge. I therefore found myself reflecting a lot upon what I started to think of as 'the morality of the private moment'.

We all experience situations in which we are faced with a moral crossroads of some sort, but no social pressure – no incentive at all from the outer world – to make the 'right' choice. In other words, we all have moments when we see that we can do something wrong, unobserved by anyone else (or, at least, anyone who might recognize and judge us). A basically honest administrator, for example, might be tempted to fiddle his expenses a little in the full assurance that nobody will ever be the wiser. There are smaller temptations too. For example, staying in somebody else's house and finding oneself alone, one might feel tempted to read a private letter one sees lying on a table. For a serious Buddhist practitioner, the temptations might be even subtler, encompassing things that most people would not recognize as moral issues at all, but that contravene the spiritual principles one is trying to practise. In my case, for example, circumstances and lack of mindfulness sometimes make me exhausted from overwork and, in that state, instead of resting, I may feel tempted to indulge in trivial distractions like computer games.

The key to avoiding such difficulties is to guard the mind. And that means, in the first instance, being sufficiently in touch with one's thoughts and feelings to detect the arising of impulses quickly, before they take hold. It also means understanding how they arise (that is, in dependence on what sort of conditions), and how to redirect the energy in them in a more positive direction.

For such reasons I felt compelled to develop a more systematic and thorough approach to training my own mind. I needed to understand better what was going on in my mind and I wanted to do that not from a therapeutic point of view, drawing on modern psychology perhaps, but from an unequivocally ethical and spiritual perspective. I found the Abhidharma a very valuable resource in that effort. It helped me see more clearly both what I had to work *on* and the tools that I had at hand to work *with*. I came to understand my own habits of thought and behaviour, and to see how those habits could lead me into trouble. Consequently, I began to see more clearly what I needed to do.

Making it personal

Such was my own experience. But it didn't take me long to see the wider relevance of my discoveries. After all, I wasn't the only one who needed to 'go deeper'. I saw that many of my Buddhist friends could also benefit from more systematic mind training, especially in India, where I led a lot of retreats and did a lot of Dharma teaching.

This became obvious as I found myself playing a leading role in the Triratna Buddhist Order, the spiritual community to which I belong.[8] I was one of a small group to whom our founder gradually handed on his responsibilities.[9] All of us in the group were well aware that we had inherited a weighty duty, and that fact set us thinking deeply about our order: how could we sustain and enhance its spiritual vitality?

With that question in mind, we embarked on a series of meetings with local groupings of the order. We wanted to find out how people's spiritual lives were unfolding, and how well the order was working as a mutual support system. I myself attended most of the meetings, and I found them very valuable: it was illuminating and sometimes very moving to talk honestly with so many fellow Buddhists about the ups and downs of our shared spiritual quest.

As the meetings progressed, I could see that in some ways our order was in good health. The people I was meeting were sincere, dedicated, and often inspired. They were practising Buddhist ethical precepts, and getting on with their meditation conscientiously. I couldn't help noticing, however, that quite a lot of them – perhaps even the majority – lacked a clear sense of the specific spiritual task that confronted them as individuals. They couldn't answer the question 'What exactly should I – being who I am – be working on in my spiritual life?'

Why were so many people so vague about something so important to them? In some cases, perhaps, because they were too caught up in busy activity; in others, because they had not learned to think clearly. Sometimes each of these causes seemed to reinforce the other, so that it was impossible to say which had come first. But, whatever the cause, the result was the same: here were sincere and serious Buddhists who were 'surviving' spiritually, but not exactly thriving.

The lesson was sobering: even after years of trying to practise the Dharma, we may still be in the dark as regards the real nature of our mental states and how best to transform them. Unfortunately, 'doing all the right things' in a general way is not enough. We may, for example, regularly go on retreats where we get inspired and perhaps have real insights. So far, so good; but, when the retreat is over, we have to go back to everyday life with its stresses and strains, its distractions and temptations. The retreat soon seems like a dream, unless we have brought home from it some specific lessons on how to maintain wholesome mental states in our daily life.

Likewise, we may sit down and meditate every day – perhaps for an hour, or even more – and, of course, that is very valuable. But a daily meditation session, precious though it is, may not change us very much if it isn't integrated into a larger strategy for transforming the mind – a task that doesn't stop when we get up from the cushion, but goes on throughout our life. I can think of plenty of people who have meditated daily for years without ever pinpointing exactly what they need to change in their own behaviour or mental states.

Another example of the same principle: one may understand in theory the need to form spiritual friendships. But I know of people who have realized with dismay, after years of honouring this ideal, that in reality their friendships still aren't very deep. Asking themselves why not, they cannot answer, because they cannot see the traits in their own personality that cause their isolation. In some cases, such people become cynical about the whole ideal of spiritual friendship – which is a great pity.

The lessons of discord

The third area in which I discovered the need for mind training was the spiritual community as a whole.

I had appreciated the importance of the spiritual community – the sangha, as Buddhists call it – from the start of my involvement in Buddhism. I've always known that it is very difficult to live the spiritual life alone. One needs the support and encouragement of guides and companions. More recently, however, I have come to see that the sangha is valuable not just for the support and love it offers us, but also for the challenges it throws in our way.

Even in a thriving spiritual community there will be disharmony. That should not surprise us. In the Buddha's lifetime bitter quarrels sometimes occured within the sangha, despite his presence as an outstanding teacher and living example. The most famous of these quarrels is the clash at Kosambī between two senior monks about a minor breach of monastic rules – a personal disagreement that escalated into a long-drawn-out and bitter quarrel between two factions.[10]

On the whole, the order I belong to is remarkably harmonious. However, like any other large community (as I write, it comprises nearly 2,000 members), it has its share of disagreements, and these include not only amicable differences of opinion, but also personal clashes that give rise to bad feeling.

Sometimes the canonical account of the quarrel at Kosambī can seem eerily familiar to me. Our order has two major concentrations: one in the West, with a majority still to be found in the UK, and the other in India, where a third of our order members live. I divide my time almost equally between India and the West, and have seen many of the difficulties described in the Pali canon[11] played out in both places. I have seen splits at least a little similar to the one described at Kosambī within local groupings of our order in India. Every member of our order belongs to a 'chapter', which consists of roughly five to ten members. Chapter members meet regularly, often weekly, principally to discuss their practice of the Dharma, and especially to confess. In India, what can happen from time to time is that a chapter might suddenly divide into two factions, or two chapters might oppose each other, with everybody lining up behind one or other of the two principal disputants, each of whom feels that the other has made him lose face publicly.

In the West, disharmony generally takes a slightly different form: tensions develop between individuals rather than factions, and especially between a 'difficult' individual and the rest of their chapter. Order member X, for example, might be moody and harsh in their speech. As a result, the other members of X's chapter spend a lot of time skirting around X and avoiding real communication, until finally somebody drifts too close and sparks an explosion. In this way, the chapter goes through long 'dry seasons' punctuated by violent storms. Eventually, people start abandoning the chapter because they feel either bored by the dry seasons or upset by the storms.

Several years ago I held a responsibility in our order that required me to get involved in trying to resolve such cases, both in India and in the West. It was through such efforts to play the role of mediator that

I began to see disharmony as another pointer towards the potential usefulness of deeper methods of mind training.

On the one hand, I could see that friction within the spiritual community was inevitable. People with high ideals are still people – burdened with their share of human limitations and foibles. On the other hand, I saw that I could not simply ignore such clashes. Somehow, it didn't seem good enough just to turn my back on conflict with a shrug, and say, 'These things happen.' On the contrary, I felt a growing conviction that harmony is the essence of a true spiritual community. The continuing effort to transform disharmony into harmony is part of what makes the sangha something more than just a religious club. Indeed, it is the very effort to work with disharmony and transform it into harmony that makes spiritual community possible. Disharmony is not merely an unfortunate accident: it can be the most effective ground for us to practise the Dharma.

In trying to help people sort their quarrels out, I noticed that each party in a dispute always seemed to be preoccupied with *the other person's* behaviour and motives, while paying relatively little attention to their own. The prerequisite for resolving any quarrel was to get each of the warring parties to look at his or her own state of mind, and to recognize the contribution it was making to the disharmony. Once people could do that, they usually began to get things in proportion, and resolve the quarrel.

Through spending a lot of time in both India and the UK, I noticed some interesting contrasts between the distinctive factors that fuelled disputes in each culture. I saw that my Indian friends tended to see ethics in external terms: they criticized the other person's behaviour according to social norms. They assumed their indignation to be righteous, and failed to notice that it was an unwholesome mental state. With Westerners, the problem was often the reverse. They were more adroit at analyzing their own feelings and motivations. At the same time, as compared to Indians, they attached much more importance to individual freedom and much less to fulfilling social duties. They were good at acknowledging their feelings of hurt or anger, but didn't always give due consideration to the impact that their actions had on other people. In short – and at the risk of oversimplifying – the Indians needed more self-awareness, the Westerners more other-awareness.

Whatever the truth of that, one thing was clear: despite tumbling into it from opposite sides, Western and Indian Buddhists were equally capable of falling into the pit of dispute and resentment. Perhaps, then, they could use the same ladder to get out. The ladder would have to be a synergy of psychology and ethics – a framework that permits a deep understanding of one's mental life from an ethical viewpoint. Such a framework would help the Indians to become more aware of the psychological dynamics underlying disputes, while making the Westerners more generously responsive to the claims of others. It seemed to me that this synergy of psychology and ethics was precisely what the Abhidharma offered.

My desire to make my own spiritual practice more effective; my perception of the needs of individual friends and acquaintances; and, finally, my attempts to function as a mediator: in each of these three areas, I found myself drawing the same conclusions: we need to go deeper.

'Going deeper' means converting a sincere but abstract idealism into a hands-on ability to transform one's mental states. And that, in turn, means learning to practise more continuously, and in ways specifically tailored to one's personal mental patterns. In order to go deeper, we need some practical spiritual 'technology' – tools that can help us to relate our Buddhist principles to our mental functioning precisely and consistently.

In a nutshell, then, 'going deeper' depends on two things: firstly, the continual application of effort and, secondly, the spiritual equivalent of a map and compass. Let's look at each a bit more closely.

The bliss of effort

Anyone who has read the Buddhist scriptures knows how often they refer to spiritual effort. The Buddha's very last words to his disciples, as he lay dying, were 'Strive on, with mindfulness.'[12]

'Right effort' is one of the eight items of that venerable Buddhist teaching, the noble eightfold path.[13] Right effort consists of the 'four right efforts'. The first two are the eradication of any unwholesome states currently possessing the mind, and the prevention of any new ones. Eradication and prevention are very important, but not enough. In addition to cutting back weeds and pulling up their roots, we also have to plant good seeds and nurture them. Accordingly, the third and fourth efforts are, respectively, the cultivation of wholesome states not yet arisen, and the maintenance of such states once arisen. Together, these four exertions constitute what the Buddha meant by 'effort'.

The Buddha's exhortations to 'effort' and 'striving' give a mood of urgency to some passages of the Buddhist scriptures – a flavour that is not always to the taste of modern readers. It seems he wanted to impress on his disciples the need to seize a passing opportunity. Life is short and hazardous, and the chance to practise the Dharma is rare. If we want our spiritual life to be fruitful we must try, in the time available to us, to produce a decisive change in ourselves – a fundamental shift in who we are, bringing with it new patterns of thinking, feeling, and desiring. With such a change, we set our steps irrevocably on the road to Enlightenment. Without it, any spiritual gains we make will only be temporary.

To grasp the magnitude of this change is to admit that it won't be easy. The spiritual life can't be lived part-time; we can't squeeze it into the interludes between work, play, and sleep. At each and every moment of our lives, we have to take what we presently are and try to improve it, patiently fostering the emergence of a heart and mind that are purer, wiser, and more compassionate.

Not everybody feels comfortable with this way of talking. Some people find it too goal-oriented. It does not chime with 'letting go' and 'living in the present moment' – phrases that, for many people today, sum up what they find attractive in spirituality. Living as we do in a high-adrenalin, competitive culture, we prefer to think of the spiritual life as an escape from our struggles for success and security, not as a re-enactment of them in religious costume. We prefer to identify the 'spiritual' with relaxation rather than with effort. That is understandable. But how are we to reconcile our predilection with the Buddha's actual teaching, particularly his urging us to 'strive on, with mindfulness'?

That added phrase – 'with mindfulness' – is the key. The traditional emphasis on effort is not a call for the anxious, driven urgency that estranges us from present realities. Effective spiritual effort comes not from anxiety but from faith (*śraddhā*). Faith is not 'goal orientation' in a negative sense, but a deep and authentic love for the spiritual life. It means loving the spiritual life not just as a beautiful ideal, but also in its minute particulars: loving one's daily meditation, for example; loving a simple, uncluttered life; and loving the friends who follow the path with us. It means enjoying the process of change and the task in hand, while not losing sight of their relation to a bigger and more distant goal. Far from being alienated, faith goes hand in hand with a wise patience.

Perhaps most of us are not yet capable of making an effort all the time because we don't yet have enough of this kind of faith. But that needn't worry us. It just means that our first task is to learn how to make such an effort. And that means, to begin with, learning to *want* to. The great secret of making spiritual effort is to nurture the desire to make it – to nurture faith (a subject to which I will return in due course).

One way in which we can think of the four right efforts is as the extension of meditation into every moment of life. That's fine, but thinking that way might make the task seem more difficult – and more exhausting – than it need be. It is also possible, and perhaps more effective, to think of it the other way round: to think of our daily 'sit' as the point at which we can relax and enjoy the fruits of the effort that we make at other times of the day.

It seems that the Buddha himself saw it in this way. In one of his discourses, he describes his continuous effort to nurture wholesome and avoid unwholesome mental states.[14] He mentions that this effort, if taken too far, can produce weariness. When that happens, the effort undermines itself, for a weary mind is more prone to unwholesome states. So whenever the Buddha thought himself in danger of this weariness, he quieted his mind, 'brought it to singleness, and concentrated it'.[15] In other words, he entered into dhyāna – a meditative state – to refresh his mind. The more he practised the four right efforts, the more easily he could enter dhyāna. In this way he was able to find release from the tension of effort, and instead experience the *bliss* of effort.[16]

You might think, 'That's all very well for the Buddha, but I can't do it!' It is true that, for many of us, those blissful states don't come easily. But why don't they? When we meditate on the breath, for example, why do we find it difficult to develop a deep and happy absorption in the experience of breathing, even though we may know – from fleeting glimpses of it – that such absorption is possible?

Individuals being so different from one another, there is no single answer to that question, but I think I know the commonest cause of our difficulties. All too often, our way of life outside meditation nurtures relatively unwholesome states of mind, which impede our development of dhyāna. The more we can learn to make a constant effort *outside* meditation – steering away from unwholesome states and nurturing wholesome ones – the easier and more refreshing our meditation will be.

A spiritual map and compass

In addition to continuous effort, we also need what I earlier called a 'technology' – the spiritual equivalent of a map and compass (or a satnav). We need a way of naming what is going on inside us, so that we can see what we have to change, and how to change it. To do this effectively, we can't just rely on intuition; we need some kind of conceptual framework.

The teachings of Buddhism, as set out in the Buddha's discourses, offer such a framework; but the trouble is that the scriptures are vast, and not organized systematically. They range from one theme to another. In order to go deeper we need something more coherent – something more like a 'manual' of mind transformation.

Buddhism long ago developed such a manual. It is called the Abhidharma. It seems to have been compiled by leading disciples in the period after the Buddha's passing away. Their aim was to gather and systematize the Buddha's various teachings about the mind, which lay scattered – interspersed with other topics – among a large number of orally transmitted sayings.

In carrying out the compilation, the disciples elaborated on the material they had inherited from their master, but their elaboration was in keeping with the spirit of the source. In the original discourses there were already some lists of mental events. The disciples developed and refined those lists. Although the Abhidharma was a late stage in the growth of the canon, it grew organically from the Buddha's words.

Perhaps I should really speak of 'Abhidharmas' in the plural. As the schools of Buddhism evolved and diverged from each other, more than one of them developed an Abhidharma, with the result that several versions have come down to us. They overlap with one another extensively, but there are some differences.

I have based this book primarily – though not exclusively – on the Yogācāra Abhidharma. The reason for my choice was entirely circumstantial: my teacher Sangharakshita once led a seminar on the Yogācāra system, and the transcript was later edited and published under the title *Know Your Mind*. Sangharakshita's prior work gave me a head start in the task of interpretation – an advantage not to be neglected.

To speak of my source as 'the Yogācāra Abhidharma' is really a bit of shorthand. We are dealing here with a tradition that stretches over many centuries. Its original source is the Buddha – the great rain cloud of the Dharma. From him, the current flows down to Asaṅga[17] and Vasubandhu[18] in India in the fourth or fifth century AD, and then onwards to Xuanzang, the great Chinese monk of the seventh century.[19] From those mountain peaks, the waters pass by various streams down to the present. One such stream came via Yeshe Gyaltsen in eighteenth-century Tibet. His *Necklace of Clear Understanding* was published in an

English translation in the 1970s. Sangharakshita took that translation as the text of his seminar.

Each of these Buddhist teachers interpreted the traditions that were handed down to them, but they could not travel in time to interview their predecessors and quiz them on the exact meaning of their words. As a result, the meaning of a concept sometimes seems to metamorphose over time, and this complicates the task of modern readers trying to make sense of the tradition as a whole.

Despite the difficulties, I have tried to distil from the tradition something useful for practitioners today. My approach is therefore to summarize and synthesize, and to arrange the material in a way that seems to make it most readily intelligible and most useful. It is no part of my purpose to trace the evolution of ideas, or catalogue the divergent nuances of the successive phases of the tradition.

Which leads me to a disclaimer: *Mind in Harmony* makes no pretence to be a scholarly study of the Abhidharma. The book has no claim on the interest of academic students of Buddhism or Sanskrit literature, unless they also happen to be Buddhist practitioners. Do not read this book for a systematic, scholarly, and accurate account of what the tradition says. What I am going to set out is based on and inspired by the Yogācāra account of the Abhidharma but is intended as a practical tool that will help people like myself know what is going on in their minds. So I have considerably rearranged the standard ordering of the various lists of mental events and have given them labels that are not intended as accurate translations of the original Sanskrit terms, but rather as expressions of their real meaning, in as evocative terms as I can find. I hope I have nonetheless remained faithful to the spirit of the traditions on which I am basing myself.

As I've already indicated, my choice of the Yogācāra system is partly fortuitous. I wouldn't say that it is more definitive than its rivals, and it makes some surprising omissions. For example, it has nothing to say of a mental state that seems to me a very powerful force in the human soul, namely fear. (In contrast, there are many texts in the Pali canon that deal with fear as a powerful factor in mental life.)[20] Sometimes, too, the Yogācāra system draws distinctions that seem unnecessarily fine.

But, whatever Abhidharma system we chose, we would find similar limitations. Part of the problem is the gulf in time that divides us from the authors of all such texts. Different cultures produce somewhat different casts of mind, so we can't expect a mind-manual produced by one culture to be a perfect 'fit' for minds inhabiting another. The India of 2,000 years ago was a very different place from the world we live in now. (Perhaps, in due course, modern Buddhists will develop their own classification of mental events – one that matches our experience more closely.) But even within a single time and place, there can be no final analysis of something as mercurial as the mind. By its very nature, the mind eludes precise definition. So, whatever its limitations, the Yogācāra system is as good a place to start as any.

The insights that I offer in this book, though largely derived from the Abhidharma, represent my own interpretation of it, as I have already stressed. How could it be otherwise, in the circumstances? Nonetheless, I consider my interpretation 'orthodox' in the sense that it is consistent with basic Buddhist principles, even though it doesn't adhere exclusively to a single traditional orthodoxy. My understanding has been shaped mainly by my teacher, Urgyen Sangharakshita (a believer in the ecumenical unity of Buddhism, and a critic of all sectarian purism),[21] partly by my experience as a practitioner, and partly by my own attempts to communicate this material to others.

I should perhaps mention that my angle on the material, though largely developed from Sangharakshita's, is sometimes slightly different. Readers of *Know Your Mind* therefore shouldn't be too surprised if I sometimes offer them a slightly different interpretation of some aspects of the system and sometimes render Sanskrit words in different ways – ways that scholars might perhaps consider less accurate. One of the dangers of the Abhidharma is that we might take it too literally – as if it were a periodic table of mental 'molecules', along with their possible chemical combinations. But the mind isn't like that. Every moment of consciousness is new and unique. Nevertheless, those moments do fall into typical patterns, which we can learn to recognize. The value of the Abhidharma is that it points out some of the most characteristic and important of the patterns. It draws a map of the mind that helps us first to recognize and then to transform the inner world that is the source of all our doings.

All the various Abhidharmas offer lists of 'mental events' (*caitta dharmas*) that are said to constitute all the possibilities of mental activity. Needless to say, they all arrive at different totals and arrange the mental events under somewhat different headings, which in itself should teach us to be cautious about the enterprise of trying to label something as subtle as the mind. The Yogācāra system we will be following names fifty-one mental events, which it groups under five headings.

The first group consists of what I will call the five constants (sometimes called the omnipresent mental events). These five, which are equivalent to, but not precisely the same as, the five *skandhas* or 'heaps'[22] that make up conditioned existence, are the essential structural components of every mind-moment, which are always present at once in complex interrelationship with each other. We could say that all the other mental events are modalities of these.

The second group are the five intensifiers, elsewhere translated as the object-determining mental events. These five are not always present in the mind and represent successive stages of intensifying engagement with an object of attention, bringing us to a closer experience and a truer understanding of it. Although within the range of everyone at some level, the intensifiers must be cultivated successively to a high degree if one is to gain insight into the true nature of things.

The third group consists of the eleven positives (the positive mental events). These are the ethically wholesome mental factors that lie behind all skilful actions, whether of body, speech, or mind.[23] They are essentially further unpackings of what, as we shall see in the next chapter, the Buddha identified as wholesome thoughts: thoughts of non-sense-desire, non-ill-will, and non-cruelty. The cultivation of these states is our basic task in the Dharma life, since they make possible the unfolding of the whole path all the way to Enlightenment. This cultivation constitutes the last two right efforts: developing unarisen skilful mental states and maintaining those that are already in our minds.

The fourth group, the six afflictions, are the primary unethical mental factors that lie behind all unskilful actions of body, speech, or mind. They are elaborations of the unwholesome thoughts identified by the Buddha: of sense-desire, ill-will, and cruelty. These cause us suffering and lead us to do harm to others and they are immediate barriers to progress on the path. Their eradication constitutes the first two right efforts: eradicating arisen unskilful mental states and preventing unarisen ones from entering our minds.

Finally, the fifth and last group identified in the Yogācāra system is that of the four variables: four functional aspects of a normal mind that can be simply neutral, can turn into afflictions, or can be put to skilful use.

If you don't yet know much about this system, don't worry at this stage about the details of what is meant by these terms; I will be introducing them as we go along. And if you are already familiar with the Yogācāra system, perhaps as outlined in Sangharakshita's *Know*

Your Mind, you may find it useful to refer to the Appendix in this book, which lays out the system as a whole, including the Sanskrit terms, and the ways they are translated in *Know Your Mind*.

If you are familiar with the Yogācāra system, you may spot not only that I am using my own translations of the terms signifying the groups of mental events, but also that I have chosen to tackle them in an unconventional order. I have chosen to do this for three particular reasons, as well as in the general hope of making the whole system clearer. Firstly, there are important connections between the positives and the afflictions, and recognizing these connections makes the task we face much clearer. It is much easier to eliminate the unskilful in the mind when one is aware of it in relation to the skilful. The second reason for the reordering is that in my view the first two categories and the last – the constants and intensifiers on the one hand and the variables on the other – are connected, in so far as they are to do with the way the mind works and can accordingly be put to good or bad use. I have therefore enumerated the variables immediately after the intensifiers. Thirdly, I think that mindfulness has a central role in this whole system, especially in relation to the purification of the mind by discriminating between the skilful and the unskilful, on the one hand, and the intensification of awareness towards insight, on the other: *śamatha* and *vipaśyanā*, in other words.[24] What we usually call 'mindfulness' translates the Sanskrit term *smṛti*.[25] In the Abhidharma lists, that comes under the heading of the intensifiers, and I have translated it as 'attentiveness', which is what it really signifies in that context. However, it seems to me that mindfulness means more than that, and that it requires fuller treatment in this account. I have therefore inserted a consideration of mindfulness at the end of my account of the fifty-one mental events, bringing together elements from elsewhere in the lists, and also something that isn't found anywhere in the lists at all.

I will conclude with a chapter on the psychology of transcendence, because I think it important to acknowledge that an Enlightened mind, the mind of one who has Awakened, works quite differently from our own – although it is still essentially the same mind, in another sense. It cannot therefore fall into the categories of the mental events so far enumerated. Once all trace of attachment to a self-identity is removed, the mind functions in a wonderful and mysterious way, which is really impossible for us to describe. We can find some approach to it, however, so that may be a point of reference for us and an inspiring goal. This we find in the teaching of the five gnoses (*jñānas*).

I hope that gives some idea of where we are going and the inner logic of the route we will be taking. If it isn't very clear to you at this point, it doesn't really matter: just embark on the journey and see where it leads. This book, like the Abhidharma itself, is meant to be a practical tool for the spiritual life. Like any tool, it can be useful, but it won't do our spiritual work for us. History shows us that some Buddhists have made the mistake of thinking that just learning Abhidharma lists constitutes 'knowing the mind'. Let's not repeat that mistake. Not that I want to discourage anybody from learning by heart the lists in this book: I actually think that might be quite a helpful aid to practice, as long as we don't mistake such knowledge for practice, far less for true understanding!

Chapter 2

....

Mind watching

The three big ideas

Mind is fundamental in the Buddhist view of existence. The opening verses of the most famous piece of Buddhist scripture, the *Dhammapada*, make the point immediately:

> Experiences are preceded by mind, led by mind, and produced by mind. If one speaks or acts with an impure mind, suffering follows even as the cartwheel follows the hoof of the ox (drawing the cart).
> Experiences are preceded by mind, led by mind, and produced by mind. If one speaks or acts with a pure mind, happiness follows like a shadow that never departs.[26]

These words go right to the heart of the Buddha's teaching or Dharma. If we examine them closely, we find three fundamental concepts – three 'big ideas' that can transform our lives. The three are closely interwoven – are, in fact, three aspects of a single idea – but we need to look at each one individually.

The first idea is that the mind is the basis of all experience. This does not mean that the 'external world' is a mirage. It means that the situation in which we find ourselves is in large part (though not entirely, as we will come to see through a discussion of karma later in the chapter) the net result of our behaviour, and the ultimate source of our behaviour is our own mind. In other words, the main force governing what happens to us in the present is the thoughts and desires that we have allowed to sway us in the past, whether in this life or in previous lives.

The second big idea is that mental states are of two kinds – pure and impure. It is the predominance of either pure or impure elements in our mental states that determines the kind of experience we have.

The 'purity' in question is an ethical and spiritual purity (and we will see what that means in a moment).

As with mental states, so with outward actions: according to the Buddha, it is the mental state that underlies an action that determines whether it can be called 'good' or 'bad'. This idea is the crucial point at which the psychology and the ethics of Buddhism converge. Evil actions are those that spring from unwholesome mental states; good actions are those that spring from wholesome ones.

The third big idea is that happiness is the product of a pure mind, and suffering the product of an impure mind. The key to happiness is therefore the purification of the mind. This is a long-term job, calling for the progressive extension of purity into deeper and deeper levels of consciousness. When we purify the deepest level of mind, we attain happiness completely and finally, closing forever the door that leads to suffering.

In the final analysis, then, the mind produces its own happiness or suffering, according to the purity or impurity of its states. This is the essence of the three big ideas. The same idea is also expressed in the Buddhist doctrine of karma – a word that nearly everyone knows nowadays, but one that many misunderstand. This is a subject to which I will return later in this chapter.

It is difficult to exaggerate the importance of the three big ideas. Even if we are already familiar with them, we need to absorb them ever more deeply, until they permeate our thinking. If we want to be happy (and who doesn't?), and if we find the three ideas convincing, we are bound to conclude that our main task in life is to purify the mind.

But *how* do we purify the mind? Unfortunately, just wanting to isn't enough. We also need a method. The classical Buddhist method is, in principle at least, quite straightforward: you just pay attention to your mental states, day after day and moment by moment. Through that attention, you become aware of whether your present mental state is pure or impure. Prompted by that awareness, you nurture the pure states and let go of the impure ones. It is as simple – and as difficult – as that.

The technical term for this method is 'the discrimination of mental states' (*dharmavicaya*). But let's give it a simpler, more convenient name – 'mind watching'. In a nutshell, mind watching means the practice (and eventually the habit) of accurately spotting what your mind is up to, sensing its ethical quality, so that you can improve it.

Mind in Harmony

Two kinds of thought

For a classical description of mind watching, we can turn to a Pali scripture called *The Discourse on the Two Kinds of Thought*.[27] Here we find the Buddha reminiscing about a turning point in the early days of his own spiritual quest. One day, while he was still a young man seeking Enlightenment,

> it occurred to me: 'Suppose that I divide my thoughts into two classes.' Then I set on one side thoughts of sense-desire, thoughts of ill-will, and thoughts of cruelty, and I set on the other side thoughts of renunciation, thoughts of non-ill-will, and thoughts of non-cruelty.[28]

The Buddha labels these two categories as 'wholesome' and 'unwholesome' (and they correspond, by the way, to what the *Dhammapada* means by 'pure' and impure'). Unwholesome thoughts are those involving sense-desire, ill-will, and cruelty. Conversely, wholesome thoughts are characterized by the opposite states: renunciation, non-ill-will, and non-cruelty.

There are dangers of misunderstanding here. Let's pause to look closely at the words the Buddha used to express his insight.

Firstly, many of us come to Buddhism from the background of a monotheistic culture where fear and guilt are in the air, even for those who never had a religious upbringing. We may still tend – consciously or unconsciously – to believe that we are 'bad' and that God may punish us. If so, we might feel a bit anxious when we find a Buddhist text apparently urging us to classify our thoughts as either 'good' or 'bad'.

But the stark opposition between 'two kinds of thought' is not what it might seem. As the Buddha knew very well, our mental states exist in a continuum, not in two camps with a high wall running between them. His distinction between 'wholesome' and 'unwholesome' thoughts was pragmatic, not metaphysical. It was simply part of a practical exercise or experiment in mind training. And the criterion for the division was experiential, not given 'from above'. Wholesome means 'conducive to well-being'. All that concerned the Buddha was whether a particular thought, if indulged and dwelled on, would lead in the long run to happiness or to suffering.

This is the essence of mind watching: to see for ourselves how certain attitudes make us happier than others; to see, for example, how we feel relaxed, brighter, and 'cleaner' when we let go of unrealistic desires and tense antagonisms. It has nothing to do with the anxious attempt to guess whether God – hovering somewhere up there, out of sight – approves or disapproves of what's going on in our head.

Secondly, we need not be alarmed that 'sensual desire' is classed among the 'unwholesome' thoughts. We have to understand what the term 'sensual desire' means. It includes the desire for any pleasant experience through the senses (sexual pleasure, while certainly high on the list, is only one of many items on it). However, this doesn't mean there is anything inherently 'bad' about pleasure, whether sexual or non-sexual, or anything 'wrong' with the desire for it. After all, pleasure is pleasant! Which means, necessarily, that it is desirable. To fight against that basic fact of existence hardly seems wise.

The problem is not pleasure itself, or even the desire for it, but the fact that the human mind so easily gets obsessed with chasing pleasant things, or clinging to them, or fretting about not having them. In this way, the mind endlessly sets itself up for anxiety, frustration, disappointment, loss, bitterness, and many other painful states. The phrase 'sensual desire', though a literal translation of the source, is really just shorthand for a more complex concept, which could better be expressed as 'unwisely craving for, or clinging to, sensual pleasure'. From now on, I'll sacrifice literal accuracy, and speak not of 'sense-desire' but of 'craving'.

Finally, we shouldn't let the apparently negative form of the second set of terms – renunciation, non-ill-will, and non-cruelty – mislead us. Although the form of the words may seem to signify mere absences, each actually indicates the presence of something very positive. Non-ill-will is not just a hygienic vacuum but also the experience of loving-kindness (*maitrī*), while non-cruelty includes compassion (*karuṇā*). Similarly, renunciation is not just disenchantment with a lower way of life, but also attraction to a higher one.

Unwholesome states and suffering

So the Buddha decided to divide his thoughts into these 'two classes' – although we would do better to think of it as a spectrum. Towards one end of the spectrum were craving, ill-will, and cruelty. Towards the other end were their respective opposites: renunciation, loving-kindness, and compassion.

He determined that, whatever thoughts arose in his mind, he would try to notice which way they tended to draw him on the spectrum, and to remember the consequences of moving in that direction. In the case of craving, ill-will, and cruelty, he saw that such thoughts produced suffering:

> I understood thus: 'This thought [of craving, ill-will, or cruelty] has arisen in me. This leads to my own affliction, to others' affliction, and to the affliction of both; it obstructs wisdom, causes difficulties, and leads away from nibbāna.' When I considered [these things, the thought] subsided in me. [And so] whenever [such] a thought arose in me, I abandoned it, removed it, did away with it.[29]

This is an important part of mind watching: seeing that unwholesome mental states are always connected with suffering. The connection has two aspects: on the one hand, unskilful mental states bring painful consequences; on the other hand, they are painful in themselves. It is worth looking at each of these aspects.

Let's start with the consequential aspect. It is easy to see that thoughts can lead to action, and action can get us into trouble. If we crave something pleasant, for example, we risk suffering because we might not get it, or having got it we might lose it. Likewise, impulses of ill-will and cruelty, if we act upon them, are likely to make us enemies and expose us to danger.

But of course, the consequential aspect does not just include our own suffering. As the Buddha points out, craving, ill-will, and cruelty have painful consequences not just for us but also for others. If we have any fellow feeling, that fact will weigh heavily on us. In the case of ill-will and cruelty, the danger to others is obvious enough. Less obvious, but evident on reflection, is the fact that, when we desire something too much, we often hurt somebody in our eagerness to get it, or deprive somebody else of the thing that we desire.

The consequential aspect is not the whole story. As we go deeper into our own minds, we learn to recognize that unwholesome states are not just unpleasant in their outcome, but painful *in themselves* – unpleasant in their mere presence. In *The Discourse on the Two Kinds of Thought* the Buddha merely hints at this by mentioning that he saw in impure thoughts not only 'danger' but also 'degradation' and 'defilement'.

Most of us would agree that ill-will is an unpleasant experience – a state of tension, even of torment, in which the mind cannot let go of an object that hurts it. And cruelty – the desire to inflict pain – is clearly even worse.

Yet we may not realize that craving, too, is painful. (Or, if we know it in the abstract, we forget it easily in daily life.) Craving is the longing for a pleasure that we are not yet enjoying. It is a state of privation or lack, and hence of uncomfortable tension. As long as we have some hope of satisfying the craving, we usually fail to notice its unpleasant side, because the anticipation of future pleasure conceals the present pain, as sugar might mask a sharp taste.

Finally, the Buddha's words point to another aspect of the pain connected with an unwholesome mental state. He says, '[I]t obstructs wisdom, causes difficulties, and leads away from nibbāna.'[30] In other words, such states close the door to higher forms of happiness. In this relative sense, too, they are painful. This may not mean much to those who never look for anything more than sense-based happiness. It will mean a lot, however, to those who have begun to taste the serene happiness developed through spiritual practice, and the rapturous and blissful states that can be found in meditation – and from these states catch a glimpse of what complete liberation may mean. We can therefore examine our states of mind with the question, 'Does this bring me closer to the spiritual happiness I'm looking for?'

Reflecting in such ways on their unpleasant consequences, and their intrinsic painfulness, the Buddha found that he could master the thoughts linked with craving, ill-will, and cruelty. When they arose, he could make them subside. Eventually, he could prevent them from arising at all. To impress this idea on his monks, he offered a homely but vivid simile:

> Just as in the last month of the rainy season, in the autumn, when the crops thicken, a cowherd would guard his cows by constantly tapping and poking them on this side and that with a stick to check and curb them. Why is that? Because he sees that he could be flogged, imprisoned, fined or blamed [if he lets them stray into the crops].[31]

The image of a cowherd 'constantly tapping and poking' cows to stop them trampling crops is an apt emblem for mind watching. By keeping his cows away from the planted fields, the cowherd protects the interests of other people, as well as his own.

This kind of mind watching is particularly necessary in the early stages of spiritual practice, when a lot of unwholesome states may still be around in the mind, or at least may arise when one is off guard.

Wholesome states and happiness

But, in addition to removing unwholesome states and preventing them from arising, there is another mode of mind watching – the active cultivation and preservation of those mental states that bring true security and happiness.

When the Buddha noticed wholesome thoughts arising in his mind – thoughts connected with inspired renunciation, loving-kindness, and compassion – he saw that they did not lead to the 'affliction' of himself or others. On the contrary, they aided wisdom and led ultimately to Enlightenment. In other words, such thoughts were pleasant in their consequences.

Not only that, but they were also pleasant in themselves, bringing 'the blessing of renunciation' and a sense of 'cleansing'. Wholesome thoughts are inherently linked to pleasant feelings. The abandonment of ill-will for love and compassion produces a sense of harmony with all that lives, while the abandonment of craving brings an inner peace in which one can happily 'just be' – free from the compulsion to chase external sources of happiness.

The Buddha therefore saw it was good to make an effort to dwell on wholesome thoughts. This led him to a further interesting realization:

'If I think and ponder upon this thought [of renunciation, etc.]
even for a night, even for a day, even for a night and a day,
I see nothing to fear from it. But with excessive thinking and
pondering, I might tire my body, and when the body is tired, the
mind becomes disturbed, and when the mind is disturbed, it is
far from concentration.' So I steadied my mind internally, quieted
it, brought it to singleness, and concentrated it.[32]

In other words, he meditated and entered the state of meditative absorption known as dhyāna. Beneficial as it is to cultivate wholesome thoughts, we can't do it constantly. We also need to refresh the mind at regular intervals by letting go of all discursive thought whatsoever, and dwelling in peaceful meditative states. This is what I spoke of in the last chapter as 'the bliss of effort'.

Having abandoned unwholesome thoughts and cultivated whole-some ones, the final task of mind watching is simply to maintain those wholesome states. To illustrate the point, the Buddha reverted to the image of the cowherd:

Just as in the last month of the hot season, when all the crops
have been brought inside the villages, a cowherd would guard
his cows while staying at the foot of a tree or out in the open,
since he needs only to be mindful that the cows are there, there
was need for me only to be mindful that those states were there.[33]

No need for busy 'tapping and poking' now. It is just a matter of benignly
keeping an eye on the good mental states, to ensure that they don't
wander too far off – or that no thief drives them away while we are
daydreaming or taking a nap.

The force of habit

Summing up the significance of these insights, the Buddha formulated
a general principle:

[W]hatever a bhikkhu [monk] frequently thinks and ponders
upon, that will become the inclination of his mind.[34]

Habit is a powerful force, not just in outward, bodily action, but also in
the inward motions of the mind. The more we allow ourselves to think
in a certain way, the more we will tend to think that way in future.

It is like rain running off a hillside. The water finds the line of least
resistance – perhaps a slight concavity in the ground – flows into it,
and then progressively deepens it into a gully. I've often observed
this in India when the rainy season begins. In the morning, a small
trickle of water might be flowing over a footpath. When I pass back
that way a few hours later, a small stream is traversing the path and
has started to wash away its surface. The next day, the stream is wider
and deeper, and has dug a trench for itself. After a few days I have
to cross by wading up to my knees in the torrent. In the same way,
our thoughts cut trenches, and reshape the topography of our mind.
The deeper a channel is, the more swiftly and vigorously thoughts
will rush down that route in future.

As we shape the topography of our mind, we shape our future.
Because of the intrinsic connection between purity and happiness, a
habitually pure mind will tend to have an increasingly happy experience
of the world. Likewise, a habitually impure mind will find life getting
more and more problematic and painful.

This is the real meaning of the law of karma. Too often, we think
of karma as a system of rewards and punishments, dealing out sweets

or hand-smacks for good or bad behaviour, like an old-fashioned schoolteacher. Some people even imagine that karma operates with perfect symmetry – that if you win a fortune in the lottery, for example, it shows that you must have given an equivalent sum to a deserving cause in a past life.

This view of karma makes it seem remote from our actual experience, in which such neat symmetries hardly ever appear. It also seems to require an invisible hand to contrive the symmetries. In other words, it sneaks God in again through the back door. But the essence of the idea of karma is that our happiness or suffering springs directly from our own thoughts and actions, without the need for a divine judge to supervise the process. Karma is, in a sense, perfectly natural, like the rain running off a hillside.

This isn't to deny that karma might work on a bigger scale than we can presently see, or that it might occasionally produce symmetries. But if we are always looking for neat, regular patterns, we might fail to see the real ones. It is therefore better to think of karma as the process whereby we shape ourselves – and hence our future – through our mental states. We can see that process at work in our lives easily enough if we know how to look for it.

Most of the actions by which we shape ourselves are small and frequently repeated – in a word, habitual. True, we may sometimes perform a single weighty action that radically changes our future for good or ill. Occasionally, too, such a weighty action may be 'out of character'. More typically, though, it erupts as an extreme instance of a pattern that has been gathering momentum for a long time through the force of habit.

That force is truly formidable. We can either let habit shape us accidentally, in blind reaction to events, or we can take responsibility for our habits, and consciously shape *them*. The central task of the spiritual life is to try, gradually and skilfully, to stop our thoughts from cutting unskilful channels, and to make them flow into skilful channels.

Mind watching for beginners

But there is a problem in putting this principle into practice. At first, we can't see our minds clearly enough to know for certain whether a state of mind is wholesome or unwholesome. All too often, we only find out afterwards (perhaps long afterwards), when the damage is already done.

Our blindness to the unwholesomeness of certain mental states is not entirely innocent. Such states have a strong tendency to 'justify' themselves. For example, when we hate someone, we rationalize our feelings by fixing our attention on our enemy's faults, and persuading ourselves that the enemy *needs* to be opposed, *deserves* our hatred. We look away from the fact that hatred, far from being the only possible response, is *our choice*, and a choice that harms us. In such ways, we refuse to see that we ourselves are the authors of much of our suffering. As the *Dhammapada* memorably puts it:

> Those who entertain such thoughts as 'He abused me, he beat me, he conquered me, he robbed me,' will not still their hatred.[35]

One of the main aims of this book is to extend the vocabulary that we have at our disposal for the purposes of mind watching. However, it takes time to assimilate that vocabulary to the point where we can use it freely and intuitively. It is therefore a good idea to start with something simpler – a framework that is more ready to hand.

Fortunately, our sources offer us such a framework – a set of simple yardsticks that we can use as a system of 'mind watching for beginners'. The system consists of four dyads (a dyad is a set of two things or terms). Using these, we can assess our present mental state according to whether it is (i) skilful or unskilful, (ii) praiseworthy or blameworthy, (iii) high or low, and (iv) light or dark. Let's look at each of the dyads more closely.

Skilful or unskilful?

In the first dyad we meet one of the central concepts of Buddhist ethics. The opposition between *skilful* and *unskilful* behaviour runs through all the Buddhist scriptures. By thinking of morality as a *skill*, we remind ourselves that it has nothing to do with obedience to authority. On the contrary, it requires us to take responsibility, to learn, to practise, and to exercise intelligent judgement.

But to speak of ethics in terms of skill also implicitly reminds us that, when we behave ethically, we don't just make a sacrifice for the sake of others, but we also act in our own best interest. An unskilful sailor may or may not harm others but he is in real danger of drowning himself.

How then do we go about classifying our mental states as skilful or unskilful? In brief, by applying what we learned from *The Discourse on the Two Kinds of Thought*: by trying to notice whether our thoughts are coloured by craving, ill-will, and cruelty, or by their opposites; and by remembering that the first triad will cause us suffering, while the second will bring us happiness. We must try to see for ourselves, in our daily life, the way that certain kinds of mental states make us suffer, while others make us happy.

We therefore have to develop a careful attentiveness to our experiences, our feelings, our desires, our choices, and the consequences of those choices. We have to discern the patterns in such things, and reflect on the significance of those patterns. The purification of the mind is a skill – almost an art – something requiring intelligence, training, and long practice.

Praiseworthy or blameworthy?

Secondly, we can consider whether our mental states are *praiseworthy* or *blameworthy*. In other words, we can try to 'see ourselves as others see us' – but not just any others: we need to pay special attention to the viewpoint of those whose moral judgement we respect.

This doesn't mean being dependent on the approval of some authority, or anxiously imagining what others might be saying about us. The fear of being punished or rejected (whether by individuals or by people in general) may help society to maintain law and order, but it doesn't help us to live the spiritual life because it can never be the foundation of an authentic individual conscience.

Having sounded that note of caution, it remains a fact that we need the example and encouragement of other people to practise mind watching effectively. Most of us can't do it very well to begin with. Our spiritual antennae aren't sufficiently sensitive. Here we are brought face to face with the vital importance of spiritual friendship.[36] When we have good friends whom we recognize as spiritually more mature than we are, we gain a new perspective on ourselves.

To practise this dyad, we therefore ask ourselves, 'How would my spiritual mentors feel about this mental state? Would they see it as worthy or unworthy?'

High or low?

Thirdly, we can ask, 'Is this mental state *high* or *low*?' This introduces another important idea: we don't have to rest content with just avoiding unskilful states, or even with cultivating skilful ones. We can also ask ourselves whether our skilful states could be *more* skilful.

Skilful mental states form a continuum that stretches far higher than the point that most of us presently occupy. This is a vital principle in the spiritual life, but many Buddhists don't fully grasp it, and as a result they put up with lower mental states than they are capable of. Too often, we are like lazy gardeners, who keep the garden tidy, but don't bother to make it beautiful.

This doesn't mean giving oneself a hard time for 'low thoughts'. Nor does it mean constantly trying to act out a shallow idea of 'positive mental states' – like someone going around with a fixed smile. That can only produce a sense of strain and, in the long run, an irritable reaction.

The practice of the 'high and low' dyad means cultivating a happy sense that we can go further – that the adventure of the spiritual life endlessly offers us fresh horizons. However good our meditation may be, we can still plumb our inner sources of happiness more deeply. Whatever we've given up so far, we can still free ourselves a bit more from reliance on material things and on 'fixes' of sense-pleasure. However good our relations with other people may be, we can still extend the range and depth of our sympathies. The spiritual life is a path leading onwards, and to walk that path is an adventure and a delight.

Light or dark?

Fourthly and finally, we can assess whether our mental state is *light* or *dark*. A light mental state is one that is illuminated by awareness. This illumination is essentially the recognition of the mental state *as a mental state* – one among a range.

Awareness sheds light on any mental state that it accompanies. It allows us to be in that state without being imprisoned in it. When a mental state is lit by awareness, it holds the potential for spiritual growth, but when it is dark it lacks that potential, and may become unwholesome.

For example, when you are sad, you may be 'darkly' sad: that is, lost in the sadness, forgetful that it is a mood, and inclined to believe that the world's bleak appearance is reality. By contrast, you may throw light on the mood by saying to yourself, 'This is a sad mood; it is painful, but impermanent.'

This doesn't mean trying impatiently to get rid of the mood. The aim is not to fight one's way out of an uncomfortable state, but to see beyond it. The act of seeing beyond will affect the mood, weakening any unskilful tendencies it may have, and strengthening its skilful elements.

We need to throw light not only on painful moods like sadness but also on pleasant ones. When things are going well – when we are experiencing success and pleasure – we feel potent and confident. That may be very nice, but if we don't illuminate the experience with awareness, it can intoxicate us, leading us into a false world, just as much as the painful moods can.

None of this means that moods – whether pleasant or unpleasant – are 'bad things', to be avoided in favour of some zombie-like state, devoid of feeling. Indeed, any mood can reveal a certain aspect of reality (and may, in that sense, be a source of knowledge) provided that we remember that it is only one aspect, not the whole.

In this way, mind watching can have a positive effect on the mind, even without any direct effort to change one's present mental state. By its very nature, awareness transforms our inner life. Even when awareness is not enough to remove an unskilful state, it may at least check its growth. When we set out simply to watch our thoughts, we often find, strangely enough, that the thoughts become more skilful as we watch.

Using the dyads

Before we leave the subject of the four dyads, there is something to be said about how to use them.

Firstly, we must remember that, as I said earlier, mental states exist in a continuum, not in two distinct camps. The two terms in each dyad represent the poles of that continuum, not a pair of opposites. To apply a dyad is not so much to assign a mental state to one class or another, as to detect roughly where it is on the spectrum.

Secondly, we need to be aware of potential dangers in each of the last two dyads – the 'high and low' and the 'light and dark'. The dangers I am referring to are inherent in any effort to alter our mental states, and we may encounter them either in sitting meditation or in mind watching.

On the one hand, we can meditate or mind watch with the aim of raising the level of our present mental state. This corresponds to the 'high or low' dyad. The danger here is that we will overdo the effort and put ourselves under strain, which may eventually drive us to an irritable reaction. Another problem with this approach is that it invites us to pass judgement on ourselves – to deem our efforts successful or unsuccessful – and that can bring problems. A sense of success may intoxicate us with pride, while difficulties may induce a dejected sense of failure. Either outcome reinforces our egoism – our overconcern for our status in relation to others.

On the other hand, we can meditate or mind watch by receptively 'tuning in' to whatever is going on in the mind – just witnessing our present mental state, directly and calmly, without any effort to change it. This corresponds to the 'light and dark' dyad – the principle that awareness on its own is enough to dispel negative states and nurture skilful ones. As we have seen, there is a lot of truth in this, but it is also possible to overemphasize the receptive approach. If we are too tolerant of whatever is going on in the mind, we can end up indulging distracted and even unskilful states.

In meditation and in mind watching, we should adopt a balanced approach that blends the active and receptive elements. We need to use both the 'high or low' and the 'light or dark' dyads, and to follow a middle way between them – acknowledging the actual nature of the mind (allowing its depths and heights to emerge spontaneously) but also making a directed effort to cultivate higher states. In short, sometimes we should strive to change our mental states, and sometimes we should just relax and 'be interested' in them.

The Buddha called these two methods 'striving with determination' and 'looking on with equanimity'. He said that a skilled practitioner could apply either technique according to need:

> He knows thus: 'When I strive with determination, this particular source of suffering fades away in me because of that determined striving; and when I look on with equanimity, this particular source of suffering fades away in me while I develop equanimity.'[37]

In other words, we will find that certain mental states improve more in response to one method than to the other. Accordingly, we all need to be able to use each method as appropriate. As time goes on, we can develop an intuitive balance between 'striving with determination' and 'looking on with equanimity'.

The four dyads provide us with a rough and ready way of gauging the quality of our mental state. But it is not always easy to know whether a mental state is skilful or unskilful, praiseworthy or blameworthy, and so on. The landscape of the mind is sometimes like hill country in thick mist: it is hard to judge whether the path is ascending or descending. We may need a more sophisticated compass than the dyads.

Mind in Harmony

In the following chapters, I will try to provide such a compass. However, the dyads are a good starting point, and, in a way, the detailed analysis of mental events that we will explore in later chapters is just an elaboration of them.

The nature of mind

But before plunging more deeply into the art of mind watching, let us pause to consider a more theoretical question: what *is* mind?

No entirely satisfactory answer exists. Objects can be defined, but mind, far from being an object, is the 'subject' that perceives objects. We cannot even say that mind belongs to a class of non-material objects, for what else is there like mind? The term 'mind' doesn't fit into any broader category, in the way that 'table' or 'chair' can be classed as 'furniture'.

Nevertheless, our aim is to transform the mind, so we need at least a working definition of it. Otherwise we really won't know what we are doing.

According to our sources, mind has three essential characteristics. Firstly, it is transparent ('clear' would be a more literal translation, but 'transparent' expresses the underlying idea better). Secondly it consists of 'cognition'. Thirdly, it is momentary.

To say that mind is *transparent* is like comparing it to a flawless windowpane. You can look through the pane, but you can't see it. Mind is similarly elusive and hard to see. Nowadays, of course, scientists are describing in growing detail the physical processes that they believe underlie mental activity, but a gulf must always remain between the content of such descriptions and the way that consciousness looks from 'inside'.[38]

Some Buddhist texts offer a simile for the transparency of mind. They say that the mind is like space: you cannot see, hear, smell, touch, or taste it. Nor can you measure it.[39] (We can measure *parts* of space, of course, but not space itself.) But perhaps even the metaphor of space is inadequate. Space can perhaps be adequately understood through concepts. But not even concepts can grasp mind, because concepts are themselves the functioning of mind. When mind tries to understand mind, the attempt is like the eye trying to turn around in its socket to look at itself.

We must therefore abandon any hope of finding an object we can call 'mind'. It doesn't exist in the world of objects. We can only know mind indirectly, by what it *does*. (Which is why, in the next chapter, we will be looking at mind in terms of its basic functions.)

Secondly, mind is *cognition*. The word 'cognition' literally means 'knowing'. Usually we distinguish cognition from other mental functions, such as feeling or desire. For example, we can distinguish the act of recognizing a certain person as X from whatever feeling we might have about X.

However, when our sources say the mind is cognition they are using the word in a broader sense than that. The term here refers to the fact that every state of mind must have some *object*. Every mental state is necessarily 'about' something, or 'of' something, or 'for' something. So, in this context, 'cognition' includes not only the thought of an object, but also the feelings, desires, and so on that we have in relation to that object.

In this book, I will often use the word 'object' in this sense of 'something experienced by a mind'. An 'object' in this sense is not necessarily a material thing. It might be a person, a situation, a mood, an abstract idea – or indeed anything that the mind can relate to as a *something*.

To say that mind is cognition is to assert that there is no subject without object. The converse is also true. When an object is present, the subject – the mind – must likewise be present.

Thirdly, mind is *momentary*. This idea underpins much of what we will learn in the coming chapters. According to our sources, the mind is a flow of 'mind-moments' (*citta*), each of which is said to last an infinitesimally small amount of time: a tiny fraction of an eye blink or a lightning flash. Sometimes the measurement is given rather precisely in relation to such phenomena, but I don't think we should take this literally More likely, it is just a picturesque way of saying that mind-moments succeed one another too quickly to be distinguishable to ordinary consciousness, just as the eye can't distinguish the frames in a film.

By regarding the mind as a swift and endless succession of mind-moments, we start to break down our habitual, deluded assumption that we have a fixed self – a core that remains the same under the flow of our experience, an unchanging thing designated by the pronouns 'I' and 'me'. There is no such entity. If we must compare the mind to things in the world of objects, it is a good idea to include in our list of comparisons some dynamic, ever-changing things, such as a stream or a fire.

The idea of mind-moments is not the last word in the analysis of mind. Mind is not a succession of discrete flashes of consciousness, but an unbroken continuum, a flow of experience. (And even this idea is only relatively true, because to speak of a 'flow' is to assume the reality of time, but time is within mind, rather than mind within time ... to make a very big statement in a very few words.) Nevertheless, even if it doesn't perfectly express reality, the idea of mind-moments does take us an important stage beyond our usual naïve belief in an abiding self.

Mind-moments are sometimes called 'primary mind'. As we will soon see, each one includes a variety of elements, but a mind-moment in itself comprises the 'bare illumination' of the object. This means that each and every mind-moment is an act of experiencing something. In that sense, all mind-moments are alike. But in addition to this 'bare illumination', each one also has its specific characteristics. In other words, our response to the 'something' that we experience can take a wide variety of forms.

I will use the general term 'mental events' for the specific characteristics that arise with each mind-moment. Actually, 'mental events' is not a literal translation of the original Sanskrit words (*caitta dharma*), which really mean something like 'things connected with mind'. However, by calling them 'events', we remind ourselves that they are 'happenings', not substantial things. And, of course, they are not discrete happenings, but aspects of the larger happening that is the mind-moment.

The Yogācāra system (which I am following here) lists a total of fifty-one mental events, comprising the basic five together with their variations. (In a way, this is not strictly logical, because it is rather like listing 'eyes' and then enumerating 'blue eyes, brown eyes, green eyes', and so on. However, once we've understood this, there is no problem.) Other Abhidharma systems, while overlapping with the Yogācāra, come up with different numbers of events. However, the systems all resemble one another in their general picture of mind, even where they differ in detail.

The Abhidharma tradition sees each mind-moment permeated by the flavour of its mental events as salt permeates water. In itself, the water is flavourless – a fact that corresponds to the 'bare illumination' aspect of the mind-moment. Yet to the tongue, the salt and the water are mixed indistinguishably. It is only the memory of fresh water that allows us to know the water apart from its saltiness. Likewise, although it is possible (and useful) to make a conceptual distinction between the mind-moment and its mental events, that distinction is never actually found in experience.

In order to go further, we must learn something about the mental events, and this will be our concern in the rest of this book.

Part 2

How the mind works

Chapter 3

··

The constants

The basic functions of mind

Our sources present us with a list of fifty-one mental events. However, five of these are of a different order of importance from the rest, and we must consider them first. These five are the essential mental processes by which we perceive and respond to the world. Without them, there would be no 'mind' at all. I will call them 'the constants' because they are 'always present' (*sarvatraga*) in the mind. All five appear, in one form or another, in each and every mind-moment.

The constants are a version of a 'psychology' that goes right back to the Buddha himself. In the early scriptures, we find numerous references to the five 'heaps' that make up conditioned existence.[40] As time went by, some of the terminology changed, and some of the items in the list were redefined – a process of doctrinal evolution that needn't detain us here – but the five constants are clearly recognizable as descendants of the 'heaps'.

The relation of the mind-moment to the five constants is said to resemble that of a king to his five chief ministers. A king is concerned with every aspect of state business, while each minister is concerned with just one aspect of it – foreign policy, for example, or justice, or defence. This metaphor expresses the functional nature of mind: it is not a thing, but an ongoing *activity*, which can be analyzed into various subactivities.

The metaphor, however, might mislead us. A king could perhaps get by without any ministers, and would, in a sense, still be a king even if he exercised none of his kingly functions. But the mind-moment can't 'get by', or even exist, without the constants, which are integral to it, just as a torso, a head, and a heart are integral to what we mean by 'a body'. The whole may be greater than the sum of the parts, but without the parts there can be no whole.

Let's start with a brief introductory tour of the constants, after which we can look at each one in more detail.

Contact (*sparśa*) is the meeting of a sense-faculty with an object – for example, the eye seeing visual forms, or the ear hearing sounds. Contact is said to be the 'bare illumination' of the object. In other words it is a sort of raw awareness that 'something is there' without any understanding of what it is, and without any response to it.

Feeling (*vedanā*) is the first step in the mind's response to contact. It is the aspect of mind that finds contact pleasant, unpleasant, or neutral.

Interpretation (*saṃjñā*) is where the mind makes sense of the raw data of contact by relating it to past experience. Let's say, for example, that contact presents you with a small, soft, downy, orangey-red sphere with a sweet fragrance; interpretation's job is to search its archives and tell you that this is a peach, and that it may taste delicious.

Will (*cetanā*) is, for instance, the desire (whether acted upon or not) to bite into the peach. In other words, will is the way in which we respond to contact, feeling, and interpretation. Will generally makes us move either towards the object or away from it. The choice mostly depends on the kind of feeling – pleasant or unpleasant – that the object produces in us. (A neutral feeling tends to produce indifference.) Will is a very wide category. It includes most of what we would label with such words as emotion, desire, and volition.

Attention (*manaskāra*) includes what we normally mean by attention – the focusing of our awareness on some particular thing. But this ability to spotlight one feature of our experience is only the 'tip' of attention. In its wider sense, attention designates the unity of the other four constants in a complete *act* of consciousness. It might, for example, take the form of me-happily-eating-a-peach, or me-hungrily-searching-the-fridge. In fact, it might be anything with this basic structure of *me* in relation to *something*.

The constants are, by definition, all present in each mind-moment. Sometimes our sources suggest that they appear in a sequence: contact conditions feeling and interpretation, which jointly condition the responses of will, which determines the focus of our attention. At other times, however, the sources speak of the constants as arising simultaneously. Although it seems to contradict the idea of sequence, this viewpoint also seems necessary because the five constants must somehow unite to form a coherent experience. Otherwise mind would be a dysfunctional jumble. We therefore need to think of the constants in a way that combines sequence with simultaneity – like a chord played on a harp (where the notes sound one after another, but remain in the air as a single multifaceted sound).

The constants are the mind, and mind is the constants. The search for a 'self' can never find anything 'above', 'below', or 'behind' these five interlinked processes. (As we will see later, the other mental events in our list of fifty-one are specific forms or states of the constants.) To firm believers in an eternal spirit, this might sound nihilistic – a reduction of mind to its functions – but in fact the constants substitute a complex and dynamic model of mind for the naïve idea of a fixed self. This is far from being nihilistic because spiritual practice can raise the 'quality' of the constants. At Enlightenment they are transformed into five aspects of transcendental consciousness – the five wisdoms of a Buddha.

Once we grasp that the constants *are* the mind, it becomes clear why our sources class them as ethically neutral. The functions of feeling, perceiving, desiring, and so on are just aspects of our human state. They can't be judged as morally good or bad in themselves. It is not the function as such but *the specific way* we feel, perceive, or desire that leads to our happiness or unhappiness.

Before looking at the constants in more detail, let's pause to remind ourselves that we are breaking down into bits – in a useful but artificial way – something that is really a seamless continuum. Looking at a rainbow, we seem to discern a set of distinct colours. Each colour seems vividly *there*, but, no matter how hard we look, we never find a sharp boundary marking off one from the next. Likewise, we can easily find all five constants in our experience, but never a clear line dividing contact from feeling, or feeling from will, and so on. They all blur into each other.

Despite that blurring, it is meaningful to distinguish them. Designers, decorators, and artists would be badly handicapped if they lacked any concept of colour. Likewise, if we couldn't distinguish between the five constants – or make some similar analysis – we would have no language with which to talk (or even think) about our mental workings from a spiritual perspective. That would badly hamper our efforts to follow the spiritual path.

Let's now look more closely at each constant in turn.

Contact (*sparśa*)

Contact provides the raw material of our experience. It is defined as the meeting of a sense-faculty and an object. Buddhism counts six such faculties. The first five are the physical senses: the eyes, ears, nose, and tongue, together with the tactile sense distributed throughout the body. Each physical sense has its own objects: the eye makes contact with visible things, the ear with sounds, and so on.

In Buddhist psychology, the mind itself counts as the sixth faculty, an internal 'sense' that perceives mental 'objects' – abstract ideas, for example. The mind sense also coordinates the other five senses.

The Buddha called this 'the sixfold sense-base' (*ṣaḍāyatana*). Each 'base' produces its own stream of mental events. For example, visual contact leads to visual feeling, visual interpretation, and so on, while parallel processes go on in each of the other bases (though not all the senses are active to the same degree: smell and taste seem to come to full consciousness only intermittently in human beings).

We must therefore not think in terms of just one 'act' of consciousness taking place at a time, but of several such acts occurring simultaneously, and blending together into a larger act. To revert to the musical analogy, each mind-moment is not one chord, but several chords orchestrated into one.

To say that contact is 'the meeting of a sense-faculty and an object' is not to define it in terms of biological mechanisms. We are dealing with mental events, not physical ones (and, interesting though it might be, we had better not digress into the question of how the two kinds of event relate to each other). The 'meeting' of faculty and object consists precisely in the consciousness that occurs. If no consciousness arises, contact has not taken place. Imagine someone who has fallen asleep with open eyes – something that can happen in a state of exhaustion. Light passes from objects into the lenses of the eyes and strikes the retina. Nevertheless, the sleeper sees nothing. Despite the occurrence of the necessary physical processes (or at least some of them), visual contact is not taking place, for visual consciousness is absent.

But at the stage of contact, this consciousness is very rudimentary. Contact tells us that *something is there*, but as yet we don't know what it is, or what we feel about it. Nor do we know whether it requires our attention, or what we want to do about it.

Feeling (*vedanā*)

Feeling is a crucial aspect of the mind's response to contact. For that reason, it is a very important mental event, about which I will have much more to say in Chapter 5. Yet, in another sense, feeling is very simple. It means the act of classifying contact as pleasant, unpleasant, or neutral.

The third category – neutral – is defined simply as 'feeling that is neither pleasant nor unpleasant'. This certainly seems a necessary option, for not all our experience is enjoyable or painful in any clear-cut way. Nevertheless, the idea of neutral feeling seems to raise a problem. Is there any difference between neutral feeling and the *absence* of feeling? And, if the answer is 'no', why is feeling classed as a constant?

Feeling is the relationship between our desires and what happens to us. Desire is always present. The sixfold sense-base is not a machine, but an entity animated by a wide spectrum of desires, ranging from bodily needs and appetites to the most refined intellectual interests and aesthetic tastes. Whatever impinges on our senses must bear some relation to those desires – even if the relation is one of irrelevance.

To put the same idea another way, the absence of pain or pleasure is just as significant as their presence. For example, if we don't yet feel tired (i.e. in the absence of pain), we may go on working after hours in order to get a job done. If the novel we are reading isn't interesting (i.e. in the absence of pleasure), we are likely to put it down and look for something livelier. In such ways, even neutral feelings condition our choices, and this is why feeling is classed as a constant, rather than just an intermittent feature of mind. A lack of response is a response. Perhaps we might rephrase 'neutral feeling' as 'not interested' or 'not stimulated'.

Feeling, like contact, arises in each of the six sense-bases. However, our sources make an important distinction between physical feeling and mental feeling. In the context of physical feeling, the texts speak of 'pleasure' or 'pain', but in connection with mental feeling the terminology changes to 'joy' and 'sorrow'. What exactly is the difference?

Imagine that you are sitting near the window one day in August, when you suddenly feel a sharp pain in your hand. You have no idea of the cause, but looking down you see that you've been stung by a wasp, which is still feebly clinging to your skin. With annoyance and disgust, you flick the insect from your hand.

The initial pain, before seeing the wasp, counts as physical, because interpretation has not yet identified an object. The body has simply registered a sensation that it finds unpleasant (because of its innate 'wiring'). But then interpretation steps in with an object-perception ('a wasp'). This brings a further, *mental* wave of unpleasant feeling, perhaps stemming from memories of being stung in childhood.

Physical feeling is the body's direct response to contact. The pleasures of eating, orgasm, or a soft bed; the pains of illness, injury, hunger, or the discomfort of being dazzled by bright light: all these feelings are physical at their core, although they are generally accompanied by a mental element too (because the physical sensation is usually preceded or accompanied by an object-perception).

By contrast, mental feelings are those that arise from interpretation – such as the joy of recognizing a familiar and loved face or hearing a beautiful piece of music, or the sorrow of a bereavement.

Of course, even 'mental' feeling has a physical dimension. (The very word 'feeling' indicates something experienced in the body.) For example, the pleasure prompted by the sight of a loved face may be felt as a kind of warmth in the heart area. Physical and mental feeling therefore differ primarily in their source – either contact or interpretation – rather than in themselves. Yet each source gives a distinctive quality to the feeling that it conditions. For example, pleasure and pain are confined to the present moment, while joy and sorrow are often bound up with our perception of time, and are intricately entwined with memory and anticipation.

Interpretation (*saṃjñā*)

Imagine you are walking outdoors at dusk. Suddenly, out of the corner of your eye, you see something scurry out from under a hedge and move across the path in front of your feet. Your steps falter and, for a brief, queasy moment, you think that your footsteps have scared a rat from its hiding place. But, as your eyes catch up with it, you see a flat, lifeless shape, rolling in the wind – a large fallen leaf, brown and gold, loosened from the hedge and blown across the path. Your feeling changes from an initial burst of fear and disgust to relief and even aesthetic pleasure, as interpretation substitutes the second judgement for the first.

Interpretation is the process of examining the data provided by contact, and recognizing it as something in particular. There are two stages. Firstly, you notice the object's basic characteristics (something small, brown, moving across the ground). Secondly, in the store of memory, you reach for concepts that fit those characteristics (a small, frightened living thing). The concepts are at first wordless, but may then produce a verbal 'tag' ('rat'). We can call these two stages discriminating and labelling, although the process is so rapid that they cannot normally be distinguished. Sometimes (as in my example) our first act of labelling is wrong, but, as attention focuses the senses and produces further contact-data (something flat, rolling), that new information may lead interpretation to cancel the first act and substitute a second (a dead leaf).

Interpretation therefore transforms raw sense-impressions into an *object* – a 'something-in-particular'. As I have already said, objects in this sense include not only physical things, but also people, and abstract things like situations and relationships – anything that the mind can mark off from other things as a distinct, intelligible component of its world.

Correctly identifying rats and leaves belongs to the basic workings of interpretation. But interpretation gets a lot more complex than that. Initially, it is simply a question of labelling, but then, as we grow up, we increasingly combine those conceptual labels with other labels, building conceptual structures that explain our experience to us, whether in part or in whole. Our patterns of interpretation ramify into systems of concepts and views, usually on the basis of ideas in the surrounding culture that influence us. All religions, philosophies, and world views are, in the end, forms of interpretation. But whether in simple or in complex forms, interpretation is always at work, organizing the torrent of sense-impressions into an intelligible world around us.

Will (*cetanā*)

We took contact as the starting point of our exploration of the constants. That may have created the impression that mind is a set of responses to stimuli, lacking any initiative of its own. If so, it is time to correct that idea.

We might equally have started our exploration with will. If we'd done that, we would have ended up with a rather different angle on the mind.

Let's go back to the example of the impulse to bite into a peach. That impulse was preceded by contact (the orangey-red, fragrant sphere), feeling (pleasant), and interpretation ('Ah, a peach!'). But what preceded contact? Probably an impulse to investigate the fruit bowl. That was will.

Will is much more than a response to a casual stimulus. Indeed, it is much more than conscious desire. The world does not flow in upon our passive senses. Rather, our mind throws itself into the world. Most of that movement is instinctive and unconscious. Fundamentally, will is the energy that impels consciousness to seek out and involve itself with objects. Being a constant, will never lets up. As some Yogācāra texts put it, the mind 'is always hungry' – always looking for some object to engage with.

The mind's constant hunger is, in itself, morally neutral. It can be channelled towards wholesome or unwholesome objects. The craving that Buddhism names as the source of suffering is only one form of the mind's hunger – one can, one might say, be 'hungry' for the Dharma, 'hungry' for truth or virtue: this is called *Dharmachanda* in Buddhist tradition. Nonetheless, craving is crucially important in shaping our unenlightened existence.

Attention (*manaskāra*)

Of all the constants, attention is the most elusive. The sources say various things about it, and at first it isn't easy to fit the pieces of the jigsaw together. However, they start to fall into place if we assume that attention has two closely linked aspects. At one level, it is a specific mental function (like each of the other four constants). But, at a deeper level, it is the 'structure' of mind in general – something that welds the other four constants into a whole in each mind-moment.

The functional aspect corresponds, more or less, to the meaning of 'attention' in everyday English. It is the act of focusing awareness on some particular object within a wider perceptual field. Imagine, for example, that you are at a concert where a friend is playing the clarinet. Without losing awareness of the orchestra, your ears can pick out the sound of the clarinet as it threads its way through the fabric of the music.

But the act of focusing awareness is only the spearhead of the mind's ongoing confrontation with the world. 'Attention', in its deeper sense, signifies the whole of that confrontation. In any confrontation, of course, there are two sides, and attention is no exception. On the one hand is *the perceived*: in this case, the music, the concert hall, the face of your friend, and so on. On the other hand is *the perceiving*: you, sitting there, listening, and having a certain response – perhaps enjoying the music, or feeling baffled at its complexity; perhaps delighting in your friend's performance, or envying her place in the limelight.

Attention, in this wider sense, is the totality of the subject (the mind) attending to the object (whatever is 'out there'). To focus on a particular object – such as the clarinet – is a mental *act*. But behind that act is an existential *fact*: we can choose to attend to this or that, but we must attend to *something*, because attending is the very nature of the mind.

So it seems that, while the other four constants are parts of a greater whole formed by the mind-moment, attention both is and is not. In the functional sense, attention is one stage in the cyclic sequence of the constants. Conditioned by will, it takes hold of *this* object rather than that. But in the existential sense, attention is a way of talking about the mind-moment as a whole, highlighting its double aspect as the meeting of subject and object.

Here, by the way, we touch on an idea that lies near the heart of Yogācāra philosophy: mind has an inward, perceiving dimension and an outward, perceived dimension. Both dimensions are intrinsic to consciousness, and they are inseparable from each other. As unenlightened beings, we habitually misunderstand them, crudely trying to 'fix' each dimension as a distinct 'something'. In other words, we misconstrue the perceiving aspect as an enduring self 'in here', and the perceived aspect as a solid world 'out there'. That is a mistake, but a natural one in the circumstances: it is an over-literal interpretation of a real feature of consciousness.

There is something paradoxical in the functional aspect of attention, and this paradox is the cause of some disagreement in the ancient texts. Is attention the act of *holding* the mind to an object? Or is it – on the contrary – the act of turning the mind to a *new* object? Neither of these two definitions seems satisfactory because neither allows attention to be a constant. (It is a plain fact that the mind doesn't hold constantly to a single object; but it is equally plain that it doesn't shift to a new object in every mind-moment.)

But once we recognize the distinction between the existential and functional aspects of attention, this problem vanishes. We can illustrate this with an image. Think of the mind as like a monkey moving through trees by swinging from branch to branch. At every moment, the monkey must be holding a branch, or it would fall – a fact that roughly corresponds to the existential aspect of attention (the mind must always attend to *something*). But that continuous state of holding is made up of numerous small acts of 'taking hold', then 'holding on', and then 'leaving hold'. These small acts correspond to the functional aspect of attention – the way the mind moves its focus from one object to another.

Clearly, the act of 'holding on' to a mental object must have some duration. This is why, despite being part of the fleeting mind-moment, attention has some sticking power. It produces 'bursts' of coherence, holding the mind to a particular object for at least a short sequence of mind-moments.

Of course, the sticking power of attention varies a lot from one individual to another. It depends on the nature of one's desires. If your desires are numerous and chaotic, your ability to hold your attention on an object will be weak. For example – to go back to our concert-hall metaphor – after focusing on the sound of the clarinet for a few moments, your thoughts might stray to other preoccupations: perhaps to the work that is waiting on your desk at the office, or a holiday that you are looking forward to, or any of a thousand objects with which your mind has some ongoing concern at that moment.

But, despite the relative weakness of attention in the average human mind, we all have some natural power to sustain and deepen it, and if we choose we can develop that power much further through mental training. Sustained attention can become absorption – a mental event that is indispensable for the spiritual life. We will learn more about that in Chapter 6.

Chapter 4

....

The constants and karma

Karma-creation and karma-result

To grasp the full significance of the constants for our spiritual life, we need to understand the role that each one plays in the workings of karma.

To begin with, let's briefly remind ourselves of the meaning of 'karma'. In Chapter 2, we learned that karma is not some mysterious power standing over us, watching us unblinkingly, devising a punishment to fit each crime and an apt reward for every good deed. Karma is both simpler and more profound than that: it is the way in which we shape our future by shaping our mind.

There is another myth about karma that we had better clear up before going further. Karma is not an all-inclusive causal system. Many people seem to believe that everything that befalls us, for good or ill, can be ascribed to our karma. No doubt karma plays some part in everything we experience, but we inhabit a world in which many causal forces are at work, and karma is only one of them. The laws of nature, the norms of the culture we inhabit, the circumstances of our time and place: all these things contribute to the larger context in which karma must work itself out. The variety of possible forces playing upon us are summed up in the teaching of the five *niyāma*s, five categories into which all conditioned relationships may be grouped according to later commentarial tradition: physical, organic, perceptual, karmic, and Dharmic.[41] Karma is therefore like a seed – a bundle of potentialities. But the plant that grows from that seed – its height, the luxuriance of its foliage, the colour of its blossoms, and so on – will be shaped not only by the genetic 'script' in the seed, but also by the soil in which it germinates and the climate in which it grows.

Bearing in mind that karma is not an all-inclusive system, let's now explore its relation to the constants. To begin with, we must distinguish two fundamental aspects of karma: a cause-process and a result-process.

....

Both are at work ceaselessly. In each moment, we experience the results of past actions, and also perform fresh actions that will produce results in future. Strictly speaking, the word 'karma' (which literally means 'action') refers only to the cause-process, and not (as many people wrongly believe) to the result-process. However, for convenience I'll speak of the two processes as 'karma-creation' and 'karma-result'.

Some of the constants are karma-creation, while others are karma-result. In order to practise mind watching effectively, we need to know which is which – to distinguish the aspects of the mind over which we have immediate control from those over which we do not. Without this wisdom, the practice of mind watching might become an ineffectual struggle or a self-destructive inner war.

What yardstick can we use to work out whether a constant belongs to the karma-creation or to the karma-result process? The key is the last of the three big ideas that we learned from the *Dhammapada*: impure actions lead us to suffering, and pure actions to happiness. This implies that karma-creation will correspond to those mental functions that make up moral choice. Conversely, the aspects of our experience that lie beyond our choice can't be part of karma-creation. In so far as they belong to karma at all (and not to some other causal process), they must be karma-result.

Admittedly, the concept of 'choice' is problematic – a point to which I shall return at the end of this chapter. Meanwhile, let's see how far the concept can take us.

Contact, feeling, and will

Let's start, as usual, with contact. This is karma-result, not karma-creation. What we experience now is a result of choices we made in the past. We can, of course, make new choices here and now in order to set a course for a different and better future, but in the present moment we are more or less saddled with the results of our past choices.

Feeling is likewise karma-result. We have no power to choose a feeling in the present mind-moment. To inhabit a human body is, willy-nilly, to find a punch on the nose unpleasant, and good food pleasant (at least if you are healthy and hungry). It is much the same with mental feeling, too. A Rangers supporter can't really choose to be pleased when Celtic suddenly goes one–nil ahead in the last minute of the match. Contact impinges on us *now* as pleasant, unpleasant, or neutral, depending upon our choices in the past.

The corresponding good news, of course, is that *future* feeling can be modified by our present choices. And, actually, this doesn't apply only to the remote future. As soon as we become aware of a feeling, we can – if we are sufficiently mindful – at least influence the way it develops, even if we can't radically alter it. We do that simply by modifying our attitude.

Contact and feeling, then, are both karma-result. What next? Let's sidestep interpretation for the moment, and go on to will. Will is our emotional and volitional response to contact and feeling. In plain language, will is what we *do*. (However, we must understand 'do' in a very broad sense that includes not just our physical actions, but also the words we speak, and even the fantasies that we entertain in the privacy of our heads and the thoughts that pass through our minds.)

Obviously, then, will is in the domain of choice, and as such it is karma-creation. Undoubtedly, contact and feeling can strongly predispose will to respond in a certain way, but they don't finally determine it. We don't have to run forever in the trench cut by habit. We can always strike out in a new direction, deviating from our habitual course, at least by a few degrees. We can't stop the world thrusting itself on our senses; nor can we stop our reactions of pleasure and pain; but we *can* choose how to respond to them.

For example, we can resist the impulse to distract ourselves from boredom by embarking on a greedy quest for pleasure. We can refrain, too, from getting addicted to pleasures. Likewise, when someone hurts us, the choice is ours whether to respond with rage or with patience.

So far, in our karmic audit, we have accounted for contact, feeling, and will. What about interpretation and attention? These too are classified as karmic, although how they represent 'choice' is not straightforward. To understand why, we need to look at them closely.

Wise and unwise attention

As we saw in Chapter 3, attention has two aspects: an existential aspect and a functional aspect (we called them, respectively, the 'fact' and the 'act' of attention).

Existentially, attention is the mind-moment as a whole, viewed from one angle. As such, it contains within itself both karma-creation and karma-result, so it can't be reduced to one or the other.

What of the functional aspect of attention? This follows will in the sequence of the constants. In fact, on close scrutiny, it seems less like a separate event than an aspect of the operation of will. To engage with a particular object emotionally – whether by liking it or by loathing it – is to focus our attention on it. The functional aspect of attention therefore seems to be part and parcel of will's role of karma-creation.

It seems obvious that we exercise some choice about *what* we pay attention to. True, our freedom here isn't absolute: things often force themselves on our attention, against our will. But, even when that happens, we still have a choice about *how* we attend to them. Any object can be looked at from a variety of mental angles.

Imagine that you've just got home after a hard day's work at the office. A keen film fan, you've been looking forward all day to watching a DVD. You settle down in front of the screen and press the start button. Twenty minutes later, just as you are getting engrossed in the story, the phone rings, and you find yourself listening to your boss demanding your attention regarding an urgent problem. He wants you to get a report ready by tomorrow morning. You see your pleasant evening evaporating before your eyes.

You didn't choose this rude intrusion upon your evening's relaxation, but you *can* choose how to look at it.

For example, you might dwell on the fact that your boss is frustrating your cherished plan to watch a DVD, that he is invading your private life, and disrupting the peace and quiet of which, perhaps, you feel sorely deprived. You might also suspect that he is implicitly accusing you of neglecting your work, and hotly feel the indignity of that insinuation.

More or less any response born of such a mood will have a painful outcome. If you reluctantly cave in to your boss' demands, you will probably feel either depressed or resentful about it. Conversely, if you irritably fend off the intrusion, you won't find it easy to resume your pleasant evening, for, while you are playing the DVD, you will also be playing the conversation over in your head, and anticipating an even nastier one at the office tomorrow morning.

Let's rewind to the point where the phone rang. Suppose you look at the whole thing differently. Naturally, you feel some annoyance at the phone call, but you immediately see that it won't help anybody if you indulge that. Nevertheless, you have no intention of making yourself a doormat. So you relax and take a broad view, but without lapsing into passivity. You listen and ask a few shrewd questions, judging coolly whether the intrusion is warranted. If it *is*, you shrug and reconcile yourself to spending the evening doing whatever is necessary, and console yourself with the idea that you can watch the DVD at some other

Mind in Harmony

time. If the intrusion isn't necessary, however, you explain pleasantly but firmly that you don't need to deal with the problem now; you'll give it careful attention in the morning. You politely end the call, reach for the remote, and enjoy the DVD, untroubled by resentment or by fear of what your boss might say or do tomorrow.

The functional aspect of attention is inherently selective: it means attending to this rather than that. Any object has a range of features, and we can build up a distorted picture of it by attending selectively to some features while ignoring others, or by focusing too narrowly on a detail while missing the bigger picture. In a case such as the intrusive phone call, we can, if we are so inclined, focus our attention on those aspects of the situation that make us feel undervalued, put-upon, and powerless. Such acts of functional attention may be so swift and fleeting that we might hardly be aware of performing them, yet without doubt they are within the realm of choice. We *could* attend to the situation more objectively. In this way, a set of choices at the mental level paves the way for either skilful or unskilful action at the level of speech and body.

Our sources express this aspect of mental life by drawing a distinction between 'wise attention' and 'unwise attention'. Wise attention is the kind that keeps the mind in harmony with reality and leads on to happiness. Unwise attention falsifies things. In the end, unwise attention is seeing things as permanent, when they cannot be, as having substantial existence independent of conditions, when they do not, and as offering lasting satisfaction, when they cannot have that power.[42] Wise attention is correspondingly recognizing directly that each thing that arises in our experience is momentary, is empty of substance, and can grant no more than fleeting pleasure or happiness. Instead of revealing the object to us truthfully, unwise attention presents us with an object that is partially or even mostly unreal – a chimera created by our own craving or ill-will. The more we inhabit a world of unreal objects, created by unwise attention, the more we suffer.

Scholarly readers will know that 'wise' is not a strict translation. The original Pali word *yoniso* has the meaning 'down to its origin or foundation', so we might say 'thoroughly, completely, or methodically'. But why is thoroughness desirable? Not for its own sake, but because it can produce a happier outcome. In other words, thoroughness, in this context, is implicitly a function of wisdom – specifically of the wisdom that understands the workings of karma. For practical purposes, then, it seems more revealing to speak of 'wise' and 'unwise' attention, although 'thorough' and 'careless' attention would be closer to the literal meaning (and quite illuminating in their own way).

Shallow and deep interpretation

It seems obvious that a lot of interpretation is (like feeling) an automatic product of prior conditioning. We have little or no control over it. It simply assigns conventional labels to the items that comprise our shared world. We can't 'choose' to perceive a peach as, say, a tennis ball (and what would be the point?). In so far as it belongs in the sphere of karma at all, this kind of interpretation must be karma-result, not karma-creation.

Admittedly, this sort of interpretation can make mistakes. Even when labelling simple things, we sometimes get it wrong (as when, at first glance, we mistake a leaf blown in the wind for a rat scuttling across our path). More often than not, though, we quickly rectify such errors, and they don't have any moral significance.

However, as labelling tries to deal with subtler and more complex 'objects' – such as the mental states and intentions of other people – it becomes liable to make more significant errors. For instance, when your boss rings you at home, you might 'label' his tone of voice as 'angry' or 'condescending' (i.e. these concepts might arise in your mind, even if you don't attach such words to them). But the truth might be quite different from the way you label the situation: he might just be very agitated about the problem, and not critical of you at all.

The complexities of interpretation don't stop there. Even when it assigns accurate labels, interpretation may or may not reveal to us the full significance of what we perceive. Our sources express this idea by saying that interpretation may be either 'shallow' or 'deep'. Every day – and especially in our interactions with other human beings – we encounter situations that require us to do more than just assign labels. The mind must often perform a complex – even a creative – role to produce an adequate picture of the object that confronts it.

Let's look at an example (a real event, described to me recently). One day, answering the doorbell, you find at your door a homeless woman to whom you have given money a few times before in the street. Dressed in a dirty old coat, she is crouching a couple of yards from the door, half turned away from you. You then see that the lower part of her face is thickly smeared with bright silver paint; and then, that she is clutching a rag stained the same colour. Slowly, it dawns on you that she has been inhaling solvents by spraying paint on the rag, and pressing it to her nose and mouth.

As this interpretation unfolds, it generates a succession of associations: firstly (as the significance of the paint smudges dawns), an impression, tinged with disgust, of somebody who has drifted to the margins of human dignity; then a disapproving recognition of how she uses the money that she begs. Mixed up with all this is a fastidious fear that she might at any moment lurch towards you and get paint on your clothes. Naturally, these thoughts produce unpleasant feelings, which coalesce into an impulse to close the door and shut out the problem.

But before you decide to do that, some further thoughts arrive: it occurs to you (from things you've read and heard) that she has probably been in the habit of inhaling solvents since her childhood, no doubt as a result of neglect or abuse. More or less anyone who started life in such conditions might end up where she is now. Then you wonder why, having rung the doorbell, she wandered a few yards from the door, and turned away. It looks as if she feels ashamed of her state. Your anxiety about paint stains gives way to a sense of the triviality of such a fear in the face of this real suffering.

So what to do? Not a good idea to give her money, evidently, but she might appreciate something to eat and drink. You fetch a hastily made sandwich and some tea in a paper cup, which she consumes while sitting on the doorstep – still wordless – before wandering off along the street towards who knows where. Perhaps the food and drink have simply freed up some money to buy another spray-can. All the same, as a response to suffering, the gift seems more in keeping with the principle of human solidarity than closing the door. And you feel somewhat better for that than if you'd just closed the door.

It seems clear that at this level interpretation ceases to be merely karma-result and starts to play a part in karma-creation. Indeed, it seems to be the crucial nexus in the whole process of moral choice. When presented with a complex 'object' – such as the beggar at the door – the mind frequently offers us a range of 'takes', each with its own implications for action. The takes may differ so widely that, before we can choose an action, we must, in a sense, choose what object to perceive.

By allotting to interpretation a role in karma-creation, are we mistakenly ascribing to it the functions of desire and choice, which really belong – by definition – to will?

Although in the abstract we can distinguish between the 'thinking' and 'willing' aspects of a state of mind, in reality they are often just two aspects of the same thing, like the weight and shape of a pebble. Will always enacts a particular interpretation. (And perhaps interpretation always – or at least often – has volitional implications.) Without the specific 'content' provided by interpretation, will would lack anything on which conscience could pass a moral judgement.

In responding to an intrusive phone call, a beggar at the door, or any complex situation, our first acts of interpretation are likely to spring from our most basic and habitual ways of looking at the world – which may not be the best that we are capable of. But, if we don't act on our first thoughts too impetuously, each succeeding mind-moment may deepen interpretation, bringing subtler and more complex associations into play. These will modify and may even reverse our initial perspective on the situation.

As our interpretation of a situation deepens, the range of responses available to us widens. Instead of reacting from habit or the sheer strength of feeling, we can choose a more thoughtful and creative response.

Seeing and choosing

To draw together the threads of what we've learned, let's recapitulate what happens in a single sequence of the constants, seeing how each stage fits into the double process of karma-creation and karma-result.

Will conditions attention

The mind is always 'hungry', so, in every mind-moment, it reaches out to the world and takes hold of certain objects. Will is the 'reaching out', and attention is the 'taking hold'.

Sometimes we take hold of objects skilfully (with wise attention), but sometimes we take hold of them clumsily (with unwise attention). In other words, we can look at things objectively, or we can falsify them by dwelling too selectively on certain features. The way we take hold of the object will condition the way in which contact, feeling, and interpretation subsequently unfold.

Will and attention therefore belong to karma-creation – the point of the mind's functioning at which choice occurs, the point where we shape our future experience.

Mind in Harmony

Attention conditions contact

Having 'taken hold' of the object in a particular way, we experience fresh sense-impressions. These impressions are the consequence of our 'taking hold' and as such are karma-result.

Contact conditions interpretation

At the basic level, interpretation simply labels an object as x, y, or z. For instance, you identify a voice on the phone as your boss, or the figure at the door as the homeless woman to whom you gave money yesterday. These judgements – automatic, not 'chosen' – are karma-result.

But, at a higher level, interpretation plays a creative role, construing the object as such-and-such – a job it performs with varying degrees of accuracy and depth.

The way in which you took hold of the object at the stage of attention – focusing on some aspects rather than others – strongly influences this higher aspect of interpretation. It is like the old story about the blind men and the elephant. One of them took hold of the trunk and concluded it was a snake; one seized an ear and called it a fan; one clasped a leg and thought it was a tree; and so on. Fortunately, interpretation doesn't always make such fundamental mistakes! But often it does produce an inaccurate or shallow view of the object.

Contact and interpretation condition feeling

Having taken hold of the object in a certain way, you experience physical and/or mental feeling: pleasure or pain; sorrow or joy; or perhaps just indifference. The one you get depends entirely on how the object (as taken hold of and interpreted) relates to your desires. But, in the moment feeling arises, you don't have any choice about it: it is karma-result – the ripening of your past choices.

Of course, the feeling you get now may change later on, especially if it arises from inaccurate or shallow interpretation. (The blind man who thought he had got hold of a fan may have found it pleasant – until the elephant turned and gored him for pulling its ear.) What seems pleasant at first may be revealed as painful later on, or vice versa.

Interpretation and feeling condition will

Feeling – itself moulded by our past desires – tends to reinforce the desires that shaped it. Pleasant feeling draws us towards the object; unpleasant feeling makes us want to escape from the object, or perhaps to destroy it.

Working in tandem with feeling, interpretation proposes a specific relationship to the object – or perhaps indicates several possibilities.

Will conditions attention

Will enacts one or other of the options presented by interpretation. Faced with the boss' querulous demands, for example, we can either slam the phone down or discuss the matter calmly. When a shabby, half-deranged beggar rings the doorbell, we can either mumble 'sorry' and close the door or try to offer something that will help and not harm. Our choice is the moment of karma-creation.

In making that choice, will once more reaches out to the world, and attention takes hold of a new object (or maintains its hold on the old one, perhaps shifting its grip slightly). The sequence begins again.

I have been discussing karma-creation in terms of *choice*. This seems to be the only way of expressing a crucial aspect of Buddhist thought, namely, that we are responsible for our actions – not just for our bodily and verbal actions, but also for the desires and attitudes that underlie them. Other people can help us understand ourselves, and encourage us in the right direction, but in the final analysis nobody else can solve our problems for us, or make us happy.

Nevertheless, there are dangers in the language of choice. To think in terms of 'choosing' is to imply the existence of a 'chooser' – some component of mind that sits 'above' mental states and prefers one state to another, like a king adjudicating the claims of squabbling subjects. But why do our sources describe mind in terms of the five constants? The whole point is to go beyond the idea of an abiding soul or self, and substitute for it a subtler, dynamic model of mind.

Rival views and desires have to fight it out among themselves. The strongest one wins. Our glimpses of wiser perspectives may be too faint and fleeting to help us break from older ones into which long habit has channelled strong feeling. Even if we sense that slamming down the phone or closing the door isn't the best option, we may do it anyway if feeling is too strong to allow any other option.

Still, our better judgements may surface again after the event, when the strength of feeling has subsided, to make us feel ashamed of our choice and resolve to do better next time. Such shame is a wholesome mental state – something to cultivate and welcome as part of the practice of mind watching – which helps to condition our future responses in a more skilful direction.

Meanwhile, we can keep trying to apply wise attention to our experience. As we do that more and more, we increase the chances that, in future, deeper interpretations will arise, and will accumulate the clarity and strength that they need to capture will.

An interesting fact emerges from this picture. Although will and attention are the focus of karma-creation, they don't operate in an ideal, morally neutral space, in which all possible options are clearly visible and ready to hand. We make our choices within a particular 'landscape' of feeling and interpretation – a terrain that has been shaped by our previous choices, perhaps over many lifetimes.

That landscape may either facilitate or restrict our freedom in choosing skilfully. Although we never entirely lose our freedom to choose, the actual scope of that freedom may be small if our powers of interpretation are weak, and if the feelings that attach to certain objects (as a karma-result of our choices in the past) are very strong.

We can't just wish ourselves into a better moral 'space' instantaneously by magic. We must gradually reshape our landscape of feeling and interpretation. Our next task is to examine in more detail what that means.

Chapter 5

··

Modes of feeling and interpretation

The ethical significance of feeling

Feeling is a constant, it is always there. To some extent we can ignore it if we choose, and for a variety of reasons we sometimes do. It is a risky strategy. When we deny a feeling we split off a part of ourselves, and, the more we become estranged from ourselves, the less hope we have of attuning to any larger reality. Sometimes the distortions are only minor. For example, living in an intense sensory environment such as a modern city, with all its pressures and distractions, we may get a bit numb. We can get over that fairly easily – by taking a quiet holiday in the country, for example. But there are other, more serious ways in which we lose touch with feeling. We may get into the habit of inwardly disconnecting from feelings that seem dangerous in some way, perhaps because they tempt us to do things that incur the disapproval of somebody important (our parents, perhaps, in our early years; or, later on, the social group that we belong to).

One of the tasks of mind watching is to make feeling more conscious, to become more aware of the internal voice that says 'Mm, nice ... Ugh, nasty ... Yawn, that's not interesting.' But getting in touch with feeling, though necessary, is only the starting point. Mind watching also calls for a critical awareness of the *quality* of our feelings.

This might seem a surprising idea. After all, we have just seen that feeling is a karma-result, and so, in one sense, we can't make moral judgements about it. That is a valuable lesson. It helps us, for example, to free ourselves from irrational guilt about feelings, to stop blaming ourselves for enjoying things we 'shouldn't' enjoy, or being bored by things we 'should'.

But in another sense we *can* make qualitative judgements about feeling. Feeling is the relationship between our desires and what happens to us, which is why a 'neutral' feeling still counts as a feeling, despite its neutrality. It follows logically that if people vary in their desires – as they obviously do – they are bound to vary in their feelings too. Different people can have very different feelings about exactly the same object. Proverbially, one man's meat is another man's poison, and, as the proverb implies, many such differences are perfectly innocent, 'just a matter of taste'. Sometimes, however, they are ethically and spiritually fraught. It doesn't matter if you find peaches pleasant and oranges unpleasant. But what if you find hurting people pleasant? What if you find a whole race or class of human beings unpleasant?

Because feeling is a karma-result and therefore not something we can control directly, the central strategy of Buddhist mind training is to work on will rather than on feeling. The Dharma teaches us to restrain unskilful desires and foster skilful ones. By re-educating our desires, we indirectly re-educate our feelings. But we can't work very effectively on changing our desires without getting to know our feelings more intimately. The trouble is that we don't always see the real nature of our desires very clearly. By cultivating awareness of feeling we learn more about the hidden contents of will. (We also get feedback on how our spiritual practice is changing those contents.) Mind watching therefore includes keeping a critical eye on our feelings.

It is at the mental level that feeling becomes spiritually significant. This is because mental feeling colours our experience of objects. Mental feeling may be relatively objective or subjective – that is, more or less in tune with the real nature of the object, or out of tune with it. For example, the joy of listening to a great symphony or looking at a beautiful painting is a response to what is actually 'there' in the work, and in that sense the joy has an objective element. By contrast, other mental feelings spring from arbitrary personal associations rather than from inherent meanings. For instance, the sight of a dog might be either pleasant or unpleasant, depending on whether dogs figured in your early life as loyal playmates or savage beasts.

Mental feeling tends to be at its most complex – and most crucial for our mental and spiritual well-being – when it arises from contact with people. Every person we meet sparks off some association within our mind, however slight, and that association always brings feeling with it. These 'gut reactions' may be based on accidents as trivial as the shape of a nose or the tone of a voice. If we don't recognize the subjective and arbitrary nature of these responses, we may end up liking or disliking somebody for no real reason, and perhaps accumulating a selective portfolio of 'evidence' to rationalize our feeling.

Our sources discuss these qualitative differences in feeling in terms of two technical-sounding distinctions. Firstly, feeling may be either 'contaminated' or 'uncontaminated'. Secondly, it may be either 'egoistic' (which is not the same thing as 'egotistic') or 'suprapersonal'. Let's explore the meaning of each of these distinctions.

'Contaminated' feeling

Tibetan tradition tells a story about the great Buddhist yogi Milarepa and his disciple Rechungpa. Having studied for some years with Milarepa in a mountain cave, Rechungpa asks permission to leave for Weu (central Tibet). Milarepa warns him that 'an egg ripens quicker in a warm place', but Rechungpa is determined to go, so Milarepa gives his blessing, and even fondly escorts Rechungpa for a distance, thinking to himself, 'Rechungpa has lived with me for such a long time! After this separation, we may never meet again.' After the parting, Milarepa frankly confesses himself 'a little sad', and declares that, of all his principal disciples,

Rechungpa, my long-time
Companion is most dear,
I think of him and miss him much now he has gone.[43]

When I first encountered this story (in a seminar led by my teacher Sangharakshita), I found it illuminating, and even liberating. It clarified for me an aspect of the Dharma that I had been puzzling about. I knew that Enlightenment was, by definition, the end of suffering. That sounded attractive. But, when I thought about it, the elimination of suffering seemed logically to entail the abolition of feeling. Put that way, it sounded rather cold – and less attractive. Even if such a state were possible, would it really be something to aspire to? But now, here was Milarepa – said to be a fully Enlightened being – confessing something we can only call the pain of loss. Perhaps Enlightenment was not, after all, a cold state without feeling.

The feeling of an Enlightened being is very different from ordinary feeling, however, even when it takes an analogous form. Milarepa is 'a little sad', but not because he is clinging to Rechungpa. We can be sure of that because subsequent events establish it clearly: Rechungpa later returns from Weu, resumes his practice under Milarepa's guidance, and eventually makes a great spiritual breakthrough. At that point, Milarepa actually encourages Rechungpa to go once more to Weu, for he sees that his disciple is now ready to be a great spiritual teacher in his own right.

If there was no attachment, how can we understand the nature of Milarepa's sadness at Rechungpa's first departure? We don't know, but there are clues in the text. On the one hand, Milarepa felt sad *for* Rechungpa, who was not yet ready to strike out alone and would suffer as a result of his mistake (as events in Weu confirmed, but that is another story). On the other hand, Milarepa evidently felt that he himself had lost something. Although he didn't depend on Rechungpa for his happiness, he recognized that some creative possibility had been curtailed, perhaps forever – as if the blossoming of some rare plant had been nipped in the bud. The world – not just Milarepa personally – had been deprived of something good. Milarepa's sadness was, if we can speak in such terms, an objective sadness.

Even without sharing Milarepa's Enlightenment, most of us can probably resonate with the story in our own way. Sadness can take various inflexions, according to our attitude to what we have lost. Sometimes one feels a strong desire to hang on to someone or something, and that intensifies the pain of loss. But sometimes a sense of loss, though no less sharp, can be somehow 'clean': the sadness does not lead downwards into despondency or recrimination. Indeed, it may bring a heightened sense of life's meaning.

Spiritual development does not nullify feeling but purifies it. In our sources, this insight is formulated by the classification of feeling as either 'contaminated' or 'uncontaminated'. Feeling is 'contaminated' by the unwholesome forms of will, the negative emotions that we will catalogue later under the collective heading of the 'disturbances'. The main contaminant of pleasant feeling is craving, while unpleasant feeling is often contaminated by hatred.

As we saw in Chapter 4, the 'carrier' of the contamination is unwise attention. For example, craving for pleasure (and the hope of finding it in a certain object) often makes us focus exclusively on the pleasant aspects of an object, while remaining blind to its faults and limitations. Sooner or later we suffer on account of that blindness. Those who have fallen heavily in love, got hurt, and then fallen heavily out of love will understand the point. Conversely, hatred makes us attend unwisely to the unpleasant aspects of an object, making it seem more and more painful. If you hate somebody intensely, you may reach a state where the mere sound of that person's name is enough to throw you into a rage.

Despite all this, it is possible – and this is a vital point – to have feelings that are free of contamination. If this were not so, there could be no spiritual life. Milarepa's sadness about Rechungpa is an example of an uncontaminated pain. There is also such a thing as uncontaminated pleasure. The most important example of this is dhyāna, the highly concentrated state that we can develop in meditation. Dhyāna is saturated with joy and bliss, but is entirely free of contamination.

Certain Buddhist texts might seem to suggest that one *can* crave or cling to dhyāna. For example, when describing his Enlightenment experience, the Buddha mentioned how he took care not to allow the pleasure of dhyāna to 'gain power over [his] mind' – an apparent hint at the danger of addiction to such states.[44] Yet, in the same passage, he clearly describes dhyāna as 'seclusion from unwholesome states'.

The answer to this conundrum is quite simple: in order to enter dhyāna in the first place, one must at least temporarily relinquish craving. Likewise, no clinging is present while one is actually *in* dhyāna. (As soon as clinging arises, one falls out of dhyāna.) However, one eventually has to 'come down' from dhyāna, if only to function in the world. At that point it becomes possible to crave one's former bliss, especially – and this is the crux – if one has not fully understood the conditions that gave rise to it, and how to reproduce them.

Feeling and 'me'

In addition to distinguishing contaminated from uncontaminated feeling, our sources make a further important distinction – between 'egoistic' and 'suprapersonal' feeling. This refers to the relation between feeling and one's sense of 'me'. Briefly, feeling is 'egoistic' when it is linked with the deluded belief in an abiding self, and 'suprapersonal' when it is free of that delusion.

It is an interesting fact that feeling can be egoistic without being contaminated. Dhyāna, for example, though always uncontaminated, may be associated with a deluded belief in a fixed self. In the early Buddhist scriptures, there are stories about the gods of the 'brahma world', who (although good and happy) are not Enlightened, and are therefore doomed eventually to fall from their heavenly existence into a lower rebirth.[45] The idea of egoistic but uncontaminated feeling was therefore always implicit in Buddhist cosmology. However, it was not explicitly formulated in terms of Buddhist *psychology* until the Yogācāra.

In the unenlightened mind, all feeling is egoistic. Even in wholesome states – when we are calm and wishing well to others – we still think of ourselves as being somehow 'number one' or 'at the centre'. Nevertheless, there are degrees of egoistic feeling. A healthy sense of self may harden into *egotism*, making us increasingly preoccupied with our own feelings. When that happens, egoistic feeling starts to become contaminated too: we get very concerned to defend ourselves against pain, and prone (when we can't keep up the defence) to react to it with depression or self-pity. At the same time, we may feel little for the misfortunes of others (or we may feel an agitated 'sympathy' that really springs from our fear of falling victim to the same misfortunes that oppress others).

In the suprapersonal mode of feeling, in contrast, we don't see any difference between our own feelings and other people's. We simply respond to suffering – whether it is our own or theirs – positively, calmly, and creatively. Of course, we can never have *exactly* the same relation to other people's pain or pleasure as we do to our own. We inhabit our own senses and mind, and not anybody else's. But we can at least become intimately familiar with what it is like to inhabit senses and a mind. Equipped with that familiarity, we can look, listen, and use our imagination; we can build our powers of understanding and empathy. Eventually, we can learn to see suffering in ways that are consistently positive and practical, regardless of whether the suffering impinges on us or on others.

Only a fully Enlightened mind experiences feelings that are purely suprapersonal, but this does not mean that we have to wait until Enlightenment to have any glimpse of suprapersonal feeling. Nor does it oblige us to dismiss all our ordinary human feelings as irredeemably 'egoistic'. Each of us moves towards suprapersonal feeling whenever we experience something of that calm sympathy with other people's suffering that is called 'compassion'.

Our sources thus make it clear that we have to undertake two kinds of purification of feeling. At one level, we have to transform contaminated feeling into uncontaminated feeling, by cleansing the mind of craving, ill-will, and their offshoots. In the context of Buddhist meditation, this is called 'tranquillity' (*śamatha*). At a deeper level, we have to transform egoistic feeling into suprapersonal feeling, which we can only do by giving up our deluded belief in an abiding self. This is the task of a different kind of Buddhist meditation, usually called 'insight' (*vipaśyanā*).

In terms of the constants, we could say that feeling is not only contaminated by unwholesome will but also *distorted* by deluded interpretation. In order to purify feeling, we therefore have to purify both will and interpretation. In the long run, the purification of interpretation will liberate us more decisively, because it precludes the possibility of any future re-arising of contaminated emotions.

Levels of interpretation

As we saw in Chapter 4, interpretation may be either shallow or deep. Deep interpretation takes us beyond the level of conventional labelling towards the real nature of the object. Depth is of course a continuum, but our sources discuss it in terms of three levels. At the shallowest level of interpretation, we simply 'label' things by drawing on a common stock of concepts and words. For example, we recognize a wretched figure at the door as a 'beggar' or a 'solvent abuser'. The labels are correct, and reveal some truth about the object, but in a way they also limit our perception.

As we go deeper, we develop reflective interpretation, the second of the three levels. This allows us to understand something of the object's deeper nature – in particular its impermanence and lack of any fixed essence. We thereby become less dependent on the conventional labels. We recognize, for example, that the concepts 'beggar' or 'solvent abuser', while accurate, don't exhaustively define the entity before us. We have some sense of the past conditions that may make a human being a beggar or a solvent abuser, and the potential future conditions that could make those labels irrelevant.

The third level of interpretation goes further in the same direction, revealing the relativity and impermanence of the object even more radically. Indeed, it goes beyond the conceptual level and allows the mind to experience reality in a direct and intuitive way. But this level can be reached only through meditation. I won't discuss it here, as it will come up again when we discuss the mental event of penetration in Chapter 6.

There is a further way in which our sources classify interpretation, namely, according to the 'world' to which its objects belong. When the mind enters a finer mode of interpretation it thereby enters a finer world, and this may be more literally true than we imagine. Buddhist cosmology speaks of three worlds, arranged in a hierarchy. The first (or lowest) is the world that impinges on us through our bodily senses. Above the sense-world, but accessible to us through meditation, is the archetypal world. Higher still is the 'formless' world.[46]

These three levels of experience are called 'worlds' because Buddhist cosmology regards them as objective realms of existence in which we may be reborn according to our karma – objective in the sense that they present themselves as objects to our minds. Even if we prefer to reserve judgement on the 'worlds' as cosmology, we can learn from them something relevant to the practice of mind watching.

Perhaps we can put it like this. For much of the time we relate to the world from the viewpoint of a physical body, impelled by appetites, the instinct for survival, and the desire to stand out from the herd in some way. In that frame of mind, objects appear to us in a very matter-of-fact way. A horse, for example, is simply a hay-fuelled conveyance to get from A to B, a charming pet-cum-status symbol, or a good bet on the starting line.

But, in loftier moods, we look at things with awareness of their intrinsic meaning and beauty, rather than as physical entities related to our egoistic purposes. How might a horse appear then? Perhaps, if art can suggest an answer, like George Stubbs' Whistlejacket, who bursts out of his canvas at the National Gallery in London with flared nostrils, mane flapping, and hooves drumming the air: not so much a horse as the Horse: a force of nature, wonderful to behold.[47]

Interpretation can go further. Magnificent as Whistlejacket may be, he is still tethered to the world of sense-perception. We see him from a single angle in space, and at one moment in time. Other artists, breaking away from the conventions of realism, have envisioned the horse more freely: simplifying its shape to a few lines charged with energy; abolishing time by combining multiple views in a single image; showing us dream-horses that glow in unearthly hues, or merge with nature in near-abstract patchworks of colour. In short, artists can represent the form of the horse with such fluidity that it almost disappears, and in doing so they reveal something more of the animal's beauty or mystery.[48]

This is only suggestive: I don't suppose we can entirely correlate works of art with Buddhist cosmology. But it may serve to illustrate the idea that in different frames of mind we perceive things in very different ways. When we let go of the limited viewpoint associated with our worldly needs and appetites, we open up to higher levels of meaning. According to Buddhism, we rise first to a level where form becomes purified and ideal. That is the archetypal realm. But if we continue further in the same direction, we may arrive at a realm where things seem 'formless'. This probably does not mean literally 'without form' (which I suspect is strictly inconceivable), but clothed in forms so refined, so subtle and fluid, that they can no longer be pinned down as this or that, or as located precisely here or there, or as existing 'now' or 'then'.

This shift to the higher realms of interpretation is one of the goals of meditation. When meditating upon the breath, for instance, we must start by experiencing it in physical terms. At first, we attend to a mental image of our body with the breath moving in and out of it. Then, as we become more absorbed in the sensations of the breath, we let go of those 'constructed' elements of the experience and instead dwell in the pure sensation, experiencing it aesthetically.

Hand in hand with this purification of the object goes a purification of the subject: as the breath becomes subtler and purer, we feel the quality of our awareness becoming finer and brighter. We no longer experience the body as a material entity with desires and fears, but as a flow of energy, saturated with rapture and bliss. In the technical language of meditation, this is the movement away from the 'hindrances',[49] through 'access concentration' and into dhyāna.[50] The transition is gradual, for even within the sense-world there are various levels, and we must ascend through those until we enter the archetypal world.

As for the shift from the archetypal to the formless realm, I won't attempt to evoke it except by listing the names of its successive levels: 'Infinite space', 'Infinite consciousness', 'No-thing-ness', 'Neither-perception-nor-non-perception'. One can only experience – or at least imagine – this for oneself.

This traditional analysis of interpretation in terms of the three worlds, however strange it might seem at first, boils down to a straightforward and intelligible lesson: when we spend our time concerned narrowly with ourselves (looking at things in terms of what our senses or ego can 'get' from them), we inhabit one kind of world, a very constricted one. But when we look for the truth and beauty in things, we inhabit a much vaster and more beautiful world.

Part 3

How the mind becomes absorbed

Chapter 6

....

The intensifiers

The constants are the fundamental processes through which the mind engages with its world, but, on their own, they aren't enough to explain how consciousness can engage steadily with a particular object, to the exclusion of other objects. As we saw, undisciplined attention has some 'sticking power', but not enough to account adequately for this feature of consciousness. There must be processes by which attention can intensify its relation with certain objects. How does the mind get absorbed, and stay absorbed, in x rather than y? How does it come to bring x into sharper focus – and how does it come to see x as it really is?

As practitioners of meditation, the authors of the Abhidharma were naturally very interested in these questions. They saw the power of concentration as crucial to the attainment of their goal of Enlightenment, so for them there could hardly be a more important feature of mind. Accordingly, they investigated it carefully, and analyzed it in terms of a further set of five mental events, which they called the 'object-determining mental events' (*viniyata caitta dharma*), because these mental events intensify our engagement with specific objects of attention, bringing us into a closer and closer relationship with them and taking us deeper and deeper into them. It is to these five events that we will turn in the present chapter. I will call them the five 'intensifiers'.

The intensifiers, we could say, give the mind its *depth*, whereas the constants define its *breadth*. Let's start with a brief preliminary overview of them, before looking at each one in detail.

The first intensifier is what I will call 'emotional engagement' (*chanda*). Emotional engagement is a more intense and stable form of will – the movement of the mind towards (or away from) an object. It connects us to the object, providing a basis for a deeper involvement with it.

If strong enough, emotional engagement develops into the second intensifier, resolve (*adhimokṣa*). Resolve is the crucial point at which inclination develops into volition – that decisive shift in consciousness by which we choose to do *this* rather than *that*. But resolve is not just an emotional event. It also involves a 'thinking' element (or, in terms of the constants, it brings interpretation into play). This consists of a conviction that a certain action will produce a desired result. Resolve says: 'Doing this will give me what I want, so I am going to do it.' The mental event we are calling resolve is therefore necessary in order to do anything at all, as opposed to just toying with the idea of doing it.

Resolve is perhaps enough to ensure the completion of simple, brief tasks – posting a letter, fetching a spanner from the garage, or reading a short newspaper article. But for bigger tasks (i.e. those that take longer to complete) resolve seems inadequate. The trouble is that new resolves keep arising and overriding the preceding ones. You need the capacity to keep a single resolve in view until it is accomplished, whether it takes hours, days or years. Accordingly, the third intensifier is recollection or attentiveness (*smṛti*), which enables us to carry our purpose forward through time.

The fourth intensifier is absorption (*samādhi*). This is the capacity to focus more and more of our mental energies on our objective, whether it be accomplishing a task, resolving a problem, or concentrating on a meditation subject. Absorption is therefore any strongly focused act of attention that has become steady enough to be relatively unshakeable and that has collected sufficient energy and purpose to achieve its ends. We might call it 'single-mindedness'.

The fifth and last of the intensifiers is 'penetration' (*prajñā*). This is, in the first place, an analytical understanding of something and its relation to other things. If you want to succeed in any enterprise – whether Dharmic or worldly – you need to think about it and analyze it, so that you really know what you are doing. You need to penetrate beneath the surface. Especially this means cutting through appearances, illusions, and confusions to get to the reality of the situation, whether it be in one's personal relations, the accomplishment of everyday tasks, scientific enquiry, the finding of the right word in a poem, or the discovery of the ultimate truth of things.

Readers who are already acquainted with Buddhist jargon may recognize some of the Sanskrit names for the intensifiers, so at this point I had better guard against a misunderstanding. The Sanskrit terms for the last three intensifiers (*smṛti, samādhi,* and *prajñā*) appear frequently in Buddhist texts, and they usually refer to Dharma practices or higher states of consciousness. For example, *smṛti* is often translated as 'mindfulness' and refers to a whole complex of practices. Likewise, *samādhi* usually refers to lofty states of meditative concentration, and *prajñā* to the highest 'transcendental' wisdom. But when used as names for the intensifiers, each of these three words has a much more general meaning, stretching from the most humble and everyday functioning of the mind through to what is required for the attainment of Buddhahood itself. Although some individuals develop them to an almost superhuman degree, the intensifiers can be quite ordinary mental states that every healthy human being experiences every day to some degree. Attentiveness, for example, is simply the capacity to sustain resolve without being thrown off course by distractions. Likewise, *samādhi* is simply the ability to focus intently on something. It isn't necessarily a Dharmic state (just as, in English, 'absorption' doesn't usually carry any Dharmic connotation). A sniper waiting for hours for the brief moment in which his target will appear in the cross-hairs of his telescopic sight is experiencing a kind of *samādhi*, albeit an ethically unskilful one.

This contrast between the 'high' and 'low' levels of the intensifiers highlights an important difference between them and the events we discussed in the last three chapters. The constants – being constant – belong to everyone equally, but the intensifiers do not. Some people have developed them to a much higher degree than others: some are rather distracted and lacking in purpose and drive, while others are very focused. Of course, at the lower levels, the intensifiers have nothing to do with ethics. Some of the world's worst evils are perpetrated by people who are very focused and driven indeed.

If we want to develop the intensifiers, we must remember that they form a progressive sequence. We therefore need to develop the earlier ones before we can get very far with the later ones. For example, you probably won't be able to muster much absorption if you are weak in attentiveness. Arguably, there are exceptions to this general rule. For example, some people seem to have a good intellectual penetration of what is involved in a task, yet lack enough resolve or attentiveness to actually do it. But equally arguably, there is a big difference between a purely theoretical understanding of an activity and the real 'penetration' that comes through actually performing it.

Because the intensifiers are not constants, they are not present in *every* mind-moment to any marked degree. For most of us, there are many moments of the day (and, no doubt, even more in dreams) when the mind just wanders freely. But while the intensifiers may not be present all the time, they play a big part in our mental life. We wouldn't be human without them and would just flit from stimulus to stimulus with little sustained purpose, like a dog smelling his way down the street. Without emotional engagement, we would be zombies. Without resolve, we would be incapable of doing more than reacting to random momentary stimuli. Attentiveness, absorption, and penetration are necessary to any long-term goal. We have to use the intensifiers, for example, to pass an exam, or to improve our tennis game, or to keep up a meditation practice.

Like the constants, the intensifiers are ethically neutral in themselves. They can be used for ends that are morally good, bad, or indifferent. Nevertheless, they have a special importance for the Dharma life. We can't live that life without developing the intensifiers far beyond their average strength, because we have to break through illusions that are built into the way our minds are structured from the very outset so that we can see life as it truly is. That requires an intensity of mental effort that is literally superhuman. We see this most clearly in the practice of meditation, which is really all about greatly strengthening the intensifiers so that we can get closer and closer to a meditative object and eventually penetrate its real nature – seeing what the object *is* in the ultimate sense, and therefore what everything is. The whole of the spiritual life, as conceived by Buddhism, can be represented in terms of the intensifiers.

Let's therefore look at how the five intensifiers operate in the Dharma life, and especially in meditation. I am going to treat them as a progressive path, but we need to bear in mind that they don't always appear in that way. They come into operation, in varying ways, whenever we intensify our experience of any material or mental object.

Emotional engagement, as the first, is the foundation for the others. Indeed, the remaining four intensifiers are, in a sense, no more than emotional engagement focused, sustained, intensified, and applied. Each intensifier is, in a sense, simply the ripening of the previous one. If we compare emotional engagement (the first in the series) to the crescent of the new moon, then penetration is like the full moon, while resolve, attentiveness, and absorption are like the intervening phases.

Emotional engagement

The word *chanda* is often translated as 'interest', but that is far too weak a term, and conveys only the first intimations of the nature of this intensifier. It is really the engagement of our desires – finding something in our experience interesting or attractive, even fascinating, so that we desire to be involved with it more deeply in some way. In the Dharma life, emotional engagement is what draws one's will to the goals of that life. When people drift away from the Buddhist life, it is generally because they lack sufficient emotional engagement in the actualities of Dharma practice, even though they know, in the abstract, that it is the best kind of life and one that they would ideally like to lead.

It should be stressed that emotional engagement can be 'negative': a desire *not* to be involved with certain objects. Indeed, Dharma life requires this kind of negative emotional engagement. We need the spirit of renunciation: a healthy disenchantment with worldly things, a growing distaste for 'contaminated' and 'unreal' objects. This needs to be consciously cultivated if one is to make genuine progress. At the higher reaches of the path of the Dharma one will even feel a kind of revulsion for what had previously been so alluring.

Much more crucially, the Dharma life also requires positive emotional engagement. In broad terms, positive emotional engagement means an attraction to the long-term goals of the Dharma life, so that when you encounter symbols and images of the Buddha, for instance, you feel inspired by them and drawn towards them; when you are studying the Dharma you are doing so with a deep existential desire to understand the nature of things; and when you engage with the sangha, the Dharma community, you do so because you are moved by an aspiration to an ideal form of fellowship. But emotional engagement also includes an attraction to the particular objects that form the stepping stones to those long-term goals. For example, we need to feel emotional engagement in getting to know Dharma friends, in practising ethics, in learning and ruminating on the Dharma, and in developing meditative states.

Getting even more specific, we also need to feel emotional engagement with the objects of concentration prescribed by our chosen meditation practices. This means we need to feel an attraction to each such object – a desire to *be with* that object. For example, in order to do the Mindfulness of Breathing,[51] we must want to *be with* the breath. We need to feel a kind of fascination for the sensations of breathing, an attraction comparable to the desire to pay attention to something aesthetically pleasing – to listen to a fine piece of music, for example, or to feast our eyes on a beautiful landscape. The mere abstract understanding that the practice is beneficial, or even an intellectual curiosity about it, is not enough to help us do it effectively.

But here we come to a tricky question, one faced by many meditators: what if you simply don't find the breath interesting? This is just one instance of a much bigger question: how do you translate a theoretical interest in meditation into a strong desire to engage with a specific meditation object? Many people want to meditate, but simply don't feel very interested in the breath, or perhaps in any of the available meditation objects – mantras, images, *kasiṇa* devices, and so on.[52]

The great secret of meditation, as with all aspects of the Dharma life, is reorienting our emotional engagement to specific meditation objects. This is not an easy task, except for those happy few (perhaps enjoying the fruit of Dharmic efforts in past lives) whose emotional engagement flows easily into such channels right from the start. For most of us, a lot of self-knowledge has to be acquired in order to solve these problems. We have to exercise intelligence and patient skill to retrain our feelings towards the object of meditation.

The first step is to set up the right circumstances, so that our emotional engagement is free to flow naturally into the object of meditation, and – more broadly – into our Dharma practice in general. Here there are two things to consider: environment and lifestyle.

As regards the environment, finding or creating a situation that is conducive to meditation will greatly aid our efforts. This is partly a matter of aesthetics: an ugly environment will blunt our emotional engagement. If you feel repelled by what is around you, you will find it relatively difficult to engage emotionally with any subtle object because your mind will be either agitated or dulled by the background of painful feeling. On the other hand, if you are sitting in a quiet shrine room with a beautiful Buddha image and everything laid out in a tasteful and pleasing way, you are on the way to meditation already.

Unless you are very experienced, a noisy or disruptive environment, such as a crowded street, will make it very difficult to achieve a concentrated state. Although it is possible to use even an unconducive environment as the basis for one's meditation experience, most people don't yet have enough depth and strength to maintain their purpose in such difficult circumstances, so they need supportive conditions.

Secondly, lifestyle makes an enormous difference. Many people (including, strange as it may seem, quite a few Buddhists!) follow a lifestyle of constant stimulation that fosters mental distraction. Indeed, some live in a way that almost amounts to a systematic cultivation of distraction. Consequently, when they sit down to meditate they cannot easily turn their emotional engagement towards the object of meditation. Instead, it drifts off into their habitual distractions.

In order to change our lifestyle, we need discipline. But to apply discipline effectively, we need shrewd sensitivity. If we try to redirect our emotional engagement forcefully and abruptly, by means of a rigid discipline, the effect will probably be the opposite of what we intend: the heart rebels, and we may lose emotional engagement in the Dharma life altogether, at least for a while. Imagine someone who prematurely decides to get up at 5am every day in order to meditate for three hours. On the first day he gets up at 5am, the next day at 6am, the next at 7am, and on the fourth he doesn't get up at all! In fact, he feels increasingly repelled by even the thought of meditation. So we need to discipline ourselves, but in a way that creates a positive association with the changes we intend to make, so that our heart is in sustaining and deepening our efforts.

Friendship, the human environment, one might say, is very important – especially having friends who share our desire to cultivate emotional engagement in the Dharma life in general, and meditation in particular. As human beings we have a natural, instinctive desire to be included and accepted, so if we can't share our interests with the people around us it is very difficult to keep those interests alive, unless our emotional engagement with them is already very strong. This is especially true of something as subtle and difficult as Dharma practice. If the Dharma is not part of the perspective of your friends, it is very easy for it to cease to be part of your perspective too, because we very easily fall in with our friends' attitudes and ideas, without even noticing it. Conversely, if you have friends who are also trying to practise the Dharma, who want to talk about it, and from whom you can receive encouragement and even advice, that helps to keep your motivation alive. But there is more to the value of friendship than its power to support our efforts in the Dharma: mutual delight and goodwill shared with friends, purposeless companionship even, stimulate and enliven one's zest for Dharma practice in all its forms.

The next issue to consider is mental refinement. Very often, the trouble that people have with meditation stems from the fact that their emotional and mental functioning is generally a bit coarse, tied up with the mere business of survival and the superficial gratification of the senses, especially through relatively crude and powerful sensations. Consequently, when they try to meditate, they have no natural affinity with the objects of meditation, which are very subtle, so it is hard to find any emotional engagement with them. If that sounds like you, what you need in your life is more activities that engage you with the world of the senses, but in ways that are more refined, in the sense of being less concerned with strong and crude sensation and less bound up with mere egoistic sensory gratification, with 'my' satisfaction.

This can be quite a simple matter: for instance, just going into the countryside for a few days and immersing yourself in nature has a directly refining and integrating effect, especially if you are generally pent up in a city. Though attempts are made – at times, very successfully – to make cities beautiful, more often than not, urban life is noisy, dirty, crowded, and alienating. In a city, you are surrounded by people, but not really in contact with most of them. Being in such an environment, which is often artificial and impersonal, can have a deadening effect on our sensibilities, so that we forget that we are part of nature, become more disconnected from our feelings, and live more 'in our heads'. But in the beauty of nature we are put in touch with ourselves, with the fact that we too are part of nature. That in itself refines our sensibilities, lessening our need for crude stimulation to awaken our senses, which tend to be numbed by the ugliness and superficiality quite often found in modern urban life.

The cultivation of aesthetic experience through music, poetry, painting, or any of the arts, whether actively or as a spectator, can be a very effective step in the task of refining emotional engagement, gradually raising one's interests and desires so that they have more and more of an affinity with the subtle objects of meditation. For most people it won't help to follow a crash course in the highest kinds of art, with which they don't yet feel any affinity: we cannot usually enjoy something just because we ought to or because it is 'good for us'. It is better to start with what really does appeal to you, and then gradually learn to appreciate what is more subtle, refined, and significant. In other words, aesthetic taste needs to be educated. Here, friends with more experience than we have ourselves can be a great help in guiding us to discover our own genuine appreciation of art and culture that is more elevated than what we are used to.

Lastly, some sort of physical exercise can be significant in developing mental refinement. In the first place, physical well-being has a strong emotional effect, supporting those happier and more relaxed states from which meditation generally takes off. The body is the concrete form of our innermost energies and it is hard for them to flow in new and more subtle ways if physical energies are congealed and coarsened. Physical disciplines that require inward attention, such as some forms of yoga, dance, and even some martial arts, can be very effective ways of cultivating meditative states, and can even be considered indirect techniques of meditation.

We all need to review – and keep reviewing – the ways in which we are trying to 'retrain' our emotional engagement. If we don't do that, the effectiveness of all our Dharmic efforts will be vitiated because there will be no energy for our practice. We can ask ourselves 'What is it that really engages me emotionally?' and be ruthlessly honest about it, not pretending that we are enthused by something on the 'approved Dharmic list' when actually our juices flow in response to quite other things. This kind of enquiry into our real emotional responses requires us to notice when we are emotionally engaged and when we are not: for instance, we might be feeling disconnected and bored by a conversation, but then a particular topic comes up, and we suddenly perk up and start engaging with real animation. Noticing such things, we may come to a greater understanding of where our interests truly lie and thereby be able to use those interests to lead us onto more fruitful and fulfilling ones. The education of our emotional engagement is both an art and a science.

We study and review our emotional engagement in order to try to make a stronger and firmer connection between where our emotional energies actually are at the moment and the ideals to which we aspire but upon which we can't yet bring our full energies to bear. This is where we need intermediaries such as I have been describing. We can't relate to God, to use a theistic metaphor, so we need angels as mediators. Or, to come back to Buddhism, we can't relate to the Buddha,[53] so we need Bodhisattvas.[54] Or if we can't relate to them, we can at least relate to our Dharma friends who are just a bit further on the path than we are. We need to find the next step up, as close to the one we are on as possible, but nonetheless a definite progression. This is one of the principal arts of the Dharma life: finding where we are spontaneously emotionally engaged, but also stretching ourselves a bit in the direction of something more elevated. It is easy to pitch things either too high, in which case we can't engage our emotions, or too low, in which case our emotions, though engaged, remain on the same relatively coarse level and no progress is made.

It isn't at all easy to redirect emotional engagement to the Dharma life and meditation, but with patience and subtlety it can be done. We can't just abruptly break off the present tendency of our emotional engagement and force it into meditation. There has to be a gradual and very delicate weaning – almost a seduction – of the whole emotional life, so that it flows into meditation. What is at issue here is that we are naturally drawn towards pleasure – pleasure is, after all, pleasurable! – so we won't get very far with meditation unless we are able to find pleasure in it. The activities I've described can help to refine our experience of pleasure, preparing us for the even more subtle pleasure it is possible to gain from meditation. But, unless we get at least a taste of that pleasure right from the start of our meditation careers, it will be hard to sustain our emotional engagement with meditation.

If you want to focus on the breath, for instance, it will help to do so aesthetically, not merely functionally. The movement of the breath in the mouth, in the throat, and in the lungs almost always has a very subtle pleasurable sensation that we don't usually notice. This pleasure is not thought, but *felt*. Pleasure – and beauty, which is the source of the highest pleasure – cannot be experienced in the abstract, but only directly felt. By concentrating on what is felt rather than thought, we get closer to an experience of objects as they are, prior to our contaminated interpretation of them, but it is hard to sustain this unless it also gives us pleasure.

Perhaps it helps to recognize that there is a hierarchy of pleasure, stretching from the most immediate pleasures, for instance, of the table or the bed, through those of a delightful landscape or a fine piece of music, to those of lofty experiences in meditation, and then to the highest pleasure of all: 'Nirvana is the highest bliss', says the Buddha.[55] We should never deny ourselves pleasure at a lower level until we have some genuine experience of pleasure at a somewhat higher level. The consequences of premature renunciation are easy to see in the recent revelations of widespread cruelty and perversion among celibates who may well have been genuinely devoted to a religious life.

Initially it is likely to be necessary to enjoy pleasure of the sensory kind, but to try to do so in a more refined way. Meditation, however, can give us access to pleasure that is beyond the senses, which can be enjoyed even if one is in physical pain. This sort of enjoyment gives us more and more zest for yet higher experiences.

Resolve

Emotional engagement is the first and fundamental intensifier, but it is not enough. There are plenty of people who feel quite a lot of emotional engagement in this or that aspect of the Dharma, but in many cases little or nothing comes of it, and they never really make up their minds to pursue the Dharma life. That is very likely to be because they are weak in the second intensifier – resolve. They experience too much wavering about it, and consequently the limited emotional engagement that they superficially feel sooner or later dissipates.

Resolve has two sides: conviction and commitment. If you have really strong conviction, commitment follows almost automatically. Conviction is the cognitive or 'thinking' side of resolve. It is the firm belief that the object really is worthwhile – that it is a means by which you can attain something you want. Strong conviction only arises when we overcome doubt. Of course, there are healthy kinds of doubt that can be Dharmically productive, but here I am speaking of a kind of ineffectual dithering about whether to do something or not: the nagging thought, 'Well, maybe I should be doing something else. Perhaps this isn't really the best thing ... at least for me.' Such doubt in the context of Dharma practice commonly centres on one or more of six factors, as we will see in Chapter 10: doubt about any of the Three Jewels of Buddha, Dharma, and Sangha, or doubt about one's teacher, his or her particular presentation of the Dharma, or the Dharma community one is practising in, these latter three being the immediate counterparts for you of the Three Jewels.

Whatever your doubt fastens on to, you need to identify it and deal with it, because it is corrosive of Dharma effort to the point of destruction. You first need to realize that you are held back from resolution by doubt and then you need to sort out whether that doubt is merely a habitual emotional pattern, or whether there genuinely is some dubitable matter at stake.

Regarding the first, the emotional habit of dithering, some people seem to be congenitally inclined to it, and this tends to manifest as an unwillingness to commit oneself in certain kinds of situation – or, in chronic cases, more or less all the time. Commitment involves effort, standing up to comment and criticism, and the possibility of failure, so it is safer to remain vague when there is any degree of uncertainty – which is, after all, inherent in all aspects of life. This kind of chronic unwillingness to commit oneself needs sorting out in itself; trying to sort out particular issues can be a hopeless task in such cases, because new uncertainties can always be found as old ones are dealt with.

Conversely, it may be that you are feeling the insecurity of doubt because you genuinely haven't made up your mind yet, and then you need to take the time to address that. One needs to be careful not to rush to a conclusion. Some people try to resolve the uncomfortable feeling of being unsure by prematurely impaling themselves upon one horn of the dilemma, and then becoming fundamentalist apologists for that point of view. The true resolution of doubt often involves finding the courage to stay with the doubt until one is able to resolve it at a deep enough level, even if that takes a long time. But one shouldn't remain in doubt for *too* long. Give yourself a period in which you have the circumstances you need to address your doubts, and try to avoid tackling them on an emotionally reactive basis. A good friend may be a great help in this: someone who is not biased, who has their own commitment to the Dharma, but who is prepared to make the effort to help you find out what you really think and feel.

I suspect that many of us are not aware of the extent to which a lack of resolve is undermining our Dharma practice. Of course, the problem could lie at a deeper level; it may be a lack of emotional engagement. But if you know that emotional engagement is present and you have some real interest in what you are trying to do, then perhaps the problem is lack of resolve.

This most obviously shows itself in the practice of meditation. We probably all know how, on some occasions, one can spend a whole meditation session just trying to decide whether to do the practice or not. One has superficially decided to do it, but actually one's heart isn't in it. If this is happening (assuming that you know yourself to have emotional engagement to some degree), you need to examine your resolve. If you find that you are not getting concentrated, you could try asking yourself, 'Am I really convinced that this is a good thing to do and the best way to do it?' If the answer is 'No' or 'I'm not sure', the next step is to work at developing confidence in the practice and making up your mind to pursue it.

Such then is the first aspect of resolve: the absence of doubt – in other words, conviction. Removing doubt, convincing yourself, allows your emotional engagement to flower into the second aspect of resolve: *commitment*. Having worked through your doubts, and convinced yourself, you then dedicate yourself to acting upon that conviction.

Attentiveness

Resolve on its own is not enough for a task that requires persistence over time. It certainly isn't enough for the task of Dharmic growth, which is lifelong (and perhaps longer). One may have a strong attraction to practising the Dharma, one may even commit oneself to it, yet still lack the 'mental muscles' needed to sustain that commitment indefinitely in the face of competing (non-Dharmic) objects of emotional engagement.

This is quite humiliating, as many of us know from personal experience: you feel strongly motivated to complete some task, you

Mind in Harmony

dedicate yourself to it, and then ... you find yourself doing something else! Your mind has just drifted away. The problem might lie in a lack of emotional engagement and/or resolve. But it may reveal the lack of a certain mental faculty that could make even one's present quantum of emotional engagement and resolve stretch much further. Many of us simply haven't learned how to sustain our mental focus. Consequently, we give in too easily to distraction, especially when our circumstances and lifestyle offer a lot of it. In this situation, we need to develop the third intensifier – attentiveness.

In the context of meditation, attentiveness means simply holding one's mind to the practice, even if not yet in any very intense way. (That will require the next intensifier – absorption.) Attentiveness is just a sort of 'remembering not to forget' – the capacity to keep steering back towards the object of meditation without ever wandering too far from it, or for too long. This sort of attentiveness usually blossoms naturally out of the growth of emotional engagement and resolve: we feel interested in the object, and committed to it, so on the whole we stay with it, even if not always in a strongly focused way.

I suspect that lack of attentiveness is the problem that most often lets committed meditators down. Often they have enough emotional engagement to generate a fair degree of resolve, but there is a lack of mental discipline, a habitual tendency to dwell in a scattered state of mind. It is tempting to suggest that we live in an age in which people are more easily distracted and have shorter attention spans than in the past, due to the ubiquitous use of technology such as social media for instant stimulation. Certainly, if we are using technology for these purposes we should try not to do so in a distracted way. But I am agnostic about whether people are really becoming more superficial because of technology. We are in a major cultural transition, and it remains to be seen what effect this will have on people's minds. I do, however, have some concerns about the high degree of abstraction that technological media impose upon us, by which I mean that in using them we are less directly connected with immediate, concrete, sensory experience. Technologically mediated tasks can often require a high degree of concentration. This may not, however, be the kind of drawing together of all our mental energies that is required for the practice of attentiveness, but rather a focusing of a narrow band of consciousness and an alienation from the broader field. We need to watch our own experience honestly and critically in these situations.

So how do we cultivate attentiveness in meditation? The key to success lies mostly in what we do *outside* meditation. Many people fondly imagine they will be able to sit down and meditate when they wish, whatever else they have recently been up to. But when we try to meditate we find ourselves face to face with all the mental habits that we have unintentionally cultivated in our daily life. When we meditate, we can't use some 'special mind' that we reserve just for meditation; it's our ordinary mind that we must work with, the one that we have been using all day (not to mention yesterday, last year, and our whole life). The moment we try to apply our everyday mind to meditation, all its habits come home to roost. You can't expect to be successful in meditation if you've spent the twenty-three hours since you last meditated in a distracted and superficial way. In fact, you will probably find it quite difficult. You won't have much sense of purpose, and, if you have been feeding your mind with negative thoughts, feelings, or images, that is what it will be distracted or tainted by; or perhaps your meditation will simply consist of the random playback of all the images you have ingested.

As much as possible you therefore need to make the environment of your life supportive of meditation: not too much distraction, a reasonable degree of solitude, time for reflection, surroundings that are as attractive as is possible in the circumstances, and companionship that encourages greater seriousness of purpose, while at the same time being enlivening, pleasurable, and playful. Attentiveness in daily life is not so much a question of learning a technique, watching the breath, or doing things slowly, though all those things can help; it is more a question of shaping your life so that it promotes more mindfulness. Some degree of structure for your activities can be necessary, a certain framework for your day that you are able to vary when appropriate, but that supports a reasonable degree of focus and concentration. Also important is time that is entirely unstructured, in which you deliberately don't make yourself do anything, but just allow the tasks or issues before you to come to your mind.

Perhaps most important of all is one's ethical conduct. Unskilful conduct requires a kind of split in consciousness, because one is not allowing oneself fully to acknowledge what one is doing when one is harming oneself or others, which is what unskilfulness is. That means that the mind behind unskilful actions is divided and therefore cannot become concentrated beyond a certain point. And there is an additional issue. In the background of one's mind, there will be a sense of disquiet, even an element of disgust with oneself, which, unless it is made conscious and resolved, can become extremely debilitating. We will look at this more in Chapter 7 when discussing remorse.

What you generally concern yourself with, your habitual preoccupations, will condition the mind with which you come to meditation. If that mind has little integration or depth, meditation will just be a struggle to concentrate. That struggle can of course be fruitful, but if you have to struggle to regain that depth each time you meditate you won't make much progress and will easily become dispirited.

Attentiveness represents a fairly strong engagement with the object: it means holding the object quite steadily before you. As the third of the five intensifiers, it occupies a crucial and central position in the process. We can think of it as the half-moon phase, from which point the illuminated side of the moon starts to predominate over the part veiled in shadow. To the extent that we can develop attentiveness, we leave the unwholesome states behind, because our mind is now turned so steadily towards the object that those states can't get a strong grip on us. That means we no longer taint the meditative object with the afflictions,[56] so we are starting to see an uncontaminated object.

Admittedly, at this stage we are not going beyond the mind's ordinary relationship to the object. In other words, we are still relatively separate from the object: we experience ourselves as 'here' and the object as 'there'. There is still a definite distinction between 'me' and 'it'. Nevertheless, when we reach this 'half-moon phase' we become quite deeply involved with the object. An important advantage flows from this fact: we can now start to use our knowledge of the intensifiers more consciously and systematically in the meditation practice itself. For example, if you notice that your mind is wandering, you can ask yourself, 'Have I got enough resolve? Am I sufficiently convinced?' If you find that you are not, then you can go back a step and ask: 'Is emotional engagement flowing? And if not, how am I going to get it flowing?' Once you have generated more emotional engagement, you can then go forward again to resolve, and once you have strengthened resolve, you can build attentiveness.

In this way, we can consciously use the intensifiers as conceptual tools to analyze what is going on in our meditation, or indeed in our general mental life, and to see which parts of the structure needs reinforcement. The basic principle is: if a certain factor is weak, start by checking the *preceding* factor and, if need be, nurturing that factor.

Absorption

With absorption, the fourth intensifier, subject and object enter a new kind of relationship. Of course, I am now referring not to absorption in general, but to absorption at meditative strength (although that is still just a higher level of intensity of the same intensifier). In meditative absorption, subject and object enter a more intimate dialogue.

When we enter this stage, the object we experience is no longer the gross physical object located in ordinary space and time, but a subtle or purified object. If you perceive this subtler form of the object, that means you have become a subtler subject. A subtle subject and object relate to each other much more intimately and fluidly. They interpenetrate each other to some extent.

As we saw in Chapter 5, in discussing interpretation, Buddhism teaches us that meditative absorption shifts the mind into a different world. It is, in effect, the mind's elevation above the world of the senses (*kāmaloka*) and its entry into the meditative world of purified form (*rūpaloka*).

Meditative absorption is not just a refinement but also a unification of the mind: it absorbs not just part but the whole of our mental energy into the object. In this sense, absorption is an unmistakable step up from attentiveness. With attentiveness, only the conscious mind attends to the object, but with absorption all the energies of the mind, including those that are normally unconscious, come into play.

We have been concentrating on absorption in the context of meditation, but an important question arises: can we bring meditative absorption to bear upon objects outside our meditation practice? It seems that we can. The great Chinese commentator Xuanzang, for example, confirms this quite explicitly: he speaks of absorption as absorption in whatever your mind attends to.[57] This means that it is possible to be in a state of meditative absorption while thinking reflectively (or even performing relatively simple tasks). In such a state, one's thoughts don't come and go in a fragmented, distracted way, but unfold in an ordered, 'organic' sequence, and form a coherent, luminous whole. In this way, we can practise mind watching at the level of meditative absorption.

Conversely, we can, when necessary, bring reflective thought into our meditation. Indeed, this sort of thinking-with-meditative-absorption is actually necessary for some kinds of meditation practice. It is the ideal state in which to do any practice that requires the mind to range over a variety of objects, or to explore the ramifications of a conceptual object, rather than focusing intently on a single, non-conceptual object (such as the breath). Such is the case, for example, with the Mettā Bhāvanā – the 'cultivation of loving-kindness' – a practice in which you think of a variety of people, and call to mind their qualities.[58] It is also necessary in *vipaśyanā* ('insight') meditation, in which you contemplate (for instance) the impermanence of things, or their inability to satisfy egoistic desire, or the lack of any fixed, inherent 'being' in our own experience.[59]

Penetration

Meditative absorption is infinitely extensible: we can become more and more deeply absorbed in the object. Traditionally, this process is charted in the classification of the concentrated states called the dhyānas.[60] But in this gradual convergence, subject and object are like two lines that draw closer and closer to one another, yet never meet within a finite distance. In absorption there always remains a barrier between self and other, even though that barrier is highly attenuated – like a clear pane of glass dividing you from a scene, the glass betraying its presence by a faint smudging or reflection.

In order to remove this last barrier, we need to bring in a factor higher than absorption. This 'factor' is the last of the five intensifiers, penetration (*prajñā*) – an analytical intelligence that is now backed by the weight of all our energies, unified and refined by absorption. With that integrated and purified mind, we reflect upon the object of absorption, and so see its true nature, especially in the light of the three characteristics (*lakṣaṇas*) of conditioned existence.[61]

That is, we see that the object arises in dependence on conditions, and is therefore impermanent. For the same reason, it lacks any abiding substance or 'own being'. We therefore cannot help but see that the object is incapable of satisfying any subjective emotional need, so it would be absurd either to crave it or to hate it. This is a special kind of penetration. We could call it *transcendental* penetration of the object, because it transcends both the contamination of the object and its egoistic interpretation. However, since penetration at this level goes so far beyond our normal experience of this intensifier, from now on, I will differentiate it by using the term by which it is more usually known: transcendental wisdom. We should nevertheless keep in mind that transcendental wisdom is penetration at its pinnacle of intensity.

One might, for example, develop a strong focus on the breath and then allow a certain amount of reflection on the character of that breathing, using one of the three characteristics of conditioned existence. You could consider that the breath is impermanent (*anicca*), that it changes moment by moment, never staying still; or that there is no such thing as the breath (it is *anattā*), in so far as what you are experiencing is not a thing but a flow of sensations, arising dependently. Or else you can recognize that one day your breath will stop and you will die, and that clinging on to life must therefore give rise to suffering (*dukkha*).

It is important that one doesn't just concentrate on the characteristics, but also on the 'gateways to liberation' (*vimokṣa mukhas*) that are their positive counterparts. So, at the same time as concentrating on the impermanence of the breath, you see the impossibility of pinning it down – you see the 'signless' (*animitta*), the breath as unnameable, beyond the possibility of your knowing it with the conceptual mind; and you cultivate a sense of wonder at the extraordinary richness of each breath as a breath. Likewise, when concentrating on the breath's *anattā* aspect, you see it as 'empty' (*śūnya*) of any fixed being or identity, and see that the fact that it has no fixed identity means that it is open, illimitable. And contemplating the suffering of clinging to the breath gives rise to the 'wishless' (*apraṇihita*), a sense that there is nothing you need, nothing lacking, nothing to be sought after or chased.

Transcendental wisdom is the sword that cuts through the veil of views – cuts through the delusions that maintain our belief in a 'real' independent subject and object. It is therefore the apogee of the whole process mapped by the intensifiers. But it is not so much the product of that process as the final step in it, the final rounding to the full moon that began to wax with the crescent of emotional engagement.

We can therefore see how the five intensifiers, while neutral (and thus capable of being used for bad ends), nevertheless also offer a way along which we can travel to the ultimate truth: we develop emotional engagement in the object, form a resolve to pursue it, learn to stay with it persistently through attentiveness, absorb our mind deeply in it through absorption, and finally achieve penetration of its real nature.

Most of the time we don't pay proper attention to our experience. For one thing, what we are paying attention to, in our unenlightened state, is never a real but always a contaminated object – that is, an object distorted by craving or hatred (or by the various subsidiary negative emotions that stem from these two). And for another thing, even if we could clear those defilements away, the object would still be – at least to some degree – an egoistic or *unreal* object. In other words, what we perceive is not the object itself but our false idea of it, especially as falsified by notions of its permanence, substantiality, and satisfactoriness.

By cultivating the five intensifiers, we gradually remove the two 'veils' that hide the face of reality from the unenlightened eye. The first of these is said to be 'the veil of impurities', while the second is 'the veil of views'. The 'impurities' of the first veil are unskilful emotions – craving, hatred, and all their ugly offspring – while the 'views' of the second veil are our deluded misunderstandings of the nature of reality. The first four intensifiers strip away the veil of impurities. In other words, on the basis of emotional engagement, resolve, and attentiveness, we develop absorption, which finally blows away the obscuring clouds of craving and hatred. At this stage, however, the second veil – the veil of views – still remains. We only tear that aside by developing transcendental wisdom, which reveals reality at its deepest level.

In practice, of course, the Dharma life is not as neat as this may sound. Yet this broad overview of it can be very helpful, especially in meditation. We can use the intensifiers as a conceptual aid to going further in meditation, just as a map and compass might guide a traveller through a strange landscape. To begin with, we can systematically cultivate emotional engagement. When we've got emotional engagement going, we can check for doubts and overcome them with resolve. Then we can build up attentiveness, and on the basis of that start to experience absorption.

The fundamental intensifier is emotional engagement, and many of us probably need to put our main effort into cultivating that. But, in time, we will find all the intensifiers useful as working tools to build up the (ultimately insubstantial) edifice of meditation practice.

One of the most inspiring things about the system is the presence of penetration at the pinnacle of that edifice. This can come to bear if we include an element of reflection in every meditation session – especially reflection on the object of meditation, such as the breath. In other words, we can use the close engagement with an object that we have developed in the meditation as the basis for deeper reflection upon that object. At the end of each session of *śamatha* meditation, we can do at least a little work on penetration. We could do this regularly, even if we are relatively new to meditation or if we haven't succeeded in developing much absorption in any particular session.

Such reflection could consist in considering the object in the light of one or other of the three characteristics of conditioned existence: impermanence, insubstantiality, and imperfection. In any particular meditation session, we should always choose just *one* of these three characteristics for reflection; reflections are too diffuse to be effective if we are just ranging around the three characteristics. And we should always take care to reflect not only on the negative but also on the positive aspect of the characteristic that we have chosen. It is important to consider that each of them, whilst telling us about the contaminated and egoistic world, is also the opening of a door (*vimokṣa mukha*) through which the meditating mind can pass to liberation.

Chapter 7

....

The variables

From the ethical point of view, the constants and the intensifiers are indeterminate: they can be skilful, unskilful, or neutral, depending upon the context in which they arise. They take their ethical colour from the other mental events that co-arise with them, just like chameleons turning green among foliage or grey upon rock. For instance, emotional engagement is unskilful if it is a product of craving, but skilful if associated with faith (*śraddhā*).

This chameleon quality isn't confined to the constants and the intensifiers. There are four more mental events that are ethically 'variable'. For convenience, I will call them the four variables. The first two are a pair of opposites: sleepiness (*middha*) and disquiet (*kaukṛtya*).

Sleepiness

Sleepiness is mentioned in a list well known to anyone who has received any training in Buddhist meditation, namely the five 'hindrances' to meditation.[62] In English translations, one of those hindrances is usually translated as 'sloth and torpor'. The word translated as 'torpor' (*middha*) is what I am calling sleepiness.

While sloth is always an unskilful mental state, in this system of classification appearing as 'inertia', sleepiness is not intrinsically unwholesome (hence its inclusion in the variables). It is just the natural prelude to sleep, and isn't good or bad in itself. Although the scientific debate about the full biological reasons for sleep remains inconclusive, common sense suggests that sleep is necessary for the mind's refreshment. It is a morally innocent fact that you need sleep, and part of that fact is feeling sleepy before you actually drop off. (Very few people remain bright as a button up to the last moment and then go out like a light.)

Awareness is a cardinal virtue in Buddhism, so for Buddhists it doesn't make sense to live in a way that damages awareness – such

....

as habitually going short of sleep. We can't be fully wakeful if we are not getting enough sleep. Hence there is no merit in depriving oneself of sleep unnecessarily. Of course, there are people who overindulge in sleep, but I suspect that nowadays the opposite problem is more common: our way of life tends to makes us keyed up at work and hungry for distraction in our free time. Consequently, many people today live almost constantly in an overstimulated mental state, so they don't sleep well, and therefore rarely experience their full potential for alertness and clarity. That is not a good basis for the practice of meditation or for the spiritual life in general.

We need to ensure we get adequate sleep, especially when we are ill or have become exhausted. Those in the habit of burning the candle at both ends need to get into a healthy routine of sleeping properly. Most of us know people who don't sleep well. In some cases it is hard to see a reason, but I have come across quite a few people whose attitudes, lifestyle, or habits were obviously contributing something to the problem. For example, I notice that some people tend to keep intensely active in one way or another right up to the moment they lay their head on the pillow. With such an overstimulated mind, it isn't surprising that they often can't get to sleep, or wake up too early. We need to prepare for sleep.

But from time to time we all find ourselves in a situation where we can't avoid going short of sleep – times of crisis or unavoidable pressure at work. When that happens, we need to be particularly careful about our mental state – to be aware that our guard is down, perhaps leaving us more susceptible to negative moods, or more liable to say or do something rash.

How much do we actually *need* to sleep? The question is hard to answer in the abstract because individuals vary so much. If you are meditating a lot, you will probably need less sleep than the average person. On the other hand, if you are very busy, or carrying weighty responsibilities, you may well need to sleep more. You are also likely to need extra sleep when you are ill.

Sleepiness is usually ethically neutral – simply an aspect of our psycho-physical organism with no moral dimension. Can it ever be classed as 'skilful'? Perhaps only in the limited sense that a good night's sleep contributes to wakefulness the next day. As a depleted state, sleepiness does not have much direct potential for good. But it can sometimes become unskilful, or at least contribute to unskilful states. There seem to be two ways in which this can happen.

Firstly, sleepiness lowers our guard, making us easy prey for unwholesome moods. When we are tired, we don't have enough energy to be fully conscious. In some ways, tiredness is akin to depression, and when we are exhausted we are more likely to get irritable or despondent. We all know how it feels when pressing tasks prevent us from getting enough rest: we can easily become snappy or self-pitying, and we are much more prone to make bad judgements.

Secondly, sleepiness can be unskilful when it settles into habit. Some people get so accustomed to weariness that it becomes a part of their personality. This is when sleepiness becomes *sloth* – no longer a passing physiological state, but a settled habit of dullness and lassitude, which in its extreme form becomes a kind of depression. It often results from intense inner conflict, because any energy you have is locked in the conflict. It is unskilful not so much because it leads to unskilful actions – although it can – but because it means that you do not exert yourself skilfully, to mindfulness, and to the cultivation of the intensifiers, thereby to penetration of the true nature of things. Habitual sleepiness leads to a loss of a sense of moral agency, so that you are simply a prey to what comes, and it is usually accompanied by a tendency to see things through decidedly darkened spectacles.

This state can become very serious, and people become locked in it to such a degree that it becomes very hard to get out of it. It is self-fulfilling in so far as a certain amount of energy is needed in order to break free from it, and energy is precisely what one is lacking. One has developed a perspective in which it seems as though there is no point in engaging with anything, when in fact finding some way of engaging with something is what one needs to do. The chief antidotes are almost embarrassingly obvious and straightforward: fresh air and exercise, through which you can develop the physical vitality that counteracts the feeling of crushing weariness.

Sloth can also result from being involved in situations in which you have no real interest, so that you become habituated to not engaging with them. One finds this often in the case of people who have very little choice about what they do and are doing boring and repetitive tasks because that is the only way to earn a living. Because they have no interest in their work or investment in doing it well, they become habituated to being bored, frustrated, and irritable at the idea of having to do anything at all. If you are in such a position, the only thing you can do is to try to do the job well. If your work is so unskilful that you cannot identify with its purpose, you are in an almost impossible dilemma. But there are few jobs, even menial ones, that don't allow scope for getting some satisfaction out of doing them honestly, and with a sort of pride.

Disquiet

Disquiet is the opposite of sleepiness: it is an agitated or troubled state – the kind of mood that might keep you awake at night.

As a matter of fact, this is one of the most interesting of all the mental events listed in the Abhidharma. Like sleepiness, it appears in the canonical list of five 'hindrances' to meditation. In the context of the hindrances it is sometimes translated as 'anxiety' or 'worry', but these English words don't bring out its wider meaning. The Sanskrit is *kaukṛtya*, which means '[the sense of] having done something wrong'. Accordingly, some translators use 'remorse' instead of 'anxiety', but neither is exactly right, for *kaukṛtya* fuses the meaning of both. 'Disquiet' is not really strong enough, but because it expresses the troubled quality of the mental state, and can imply either 'anxiety' or 'remorse', it perhaps gets nearest to expressing the underlying idea.

As a variable, disquiet can be ethically neutral, but it can also be either wholesome or unwholesome. Let's start by looking at the ethically wholesome form. Imagine that you have had a heated exchange of words with somebody. Afterwards, you feel a nagging unease – something more than the unpleasant aftertaste of the other person's rudeness. Thinking it over, you admit to yourself that you spoke harshly, or not quite truthfully. You realize that *that* is what you really feel bad about.

We often push away such uncomfortable feelings, although they yield such valuable insights into our own behaviour, but, if we allow them to become fully conscious, we are bound to feel some responsibility for putting things right. You might think, 'Oh well, there were faults on both sides, but I'm going to apologize for my part, whatever he/she may choose to do.' This obliges you to swallow a bit of pride, but, if you can bring yourself to do so, you feel much better – cleaner and lighter – afterwards. The preceding sense of disquiet, which we might connect with the idea of conscience, counts as a skilful mental state because it was what provided the impetus for self-purification. (It is worth noting, in passing, that skilful states of mind are not always comfortable ones!)

If you are particularly sensitive and emotionally positive, your disquiet might make you go a bit further and start reflecting on the elements in your own character that made you speak harshly. That self-examination might produce some constructive ideas about how to prevent such a slip in future. You might, for example, see some ways to stop tense situations from reaching the 'critical mass' that triggers your aggression, or – given that one can't always forestall such situations – how you might keep your head when they do occur. More fundamentally, you might have some insights into the psychological sore spots that make you touchy and defensive, and think about ways to heal them. Discussing such matters with friends is the best way to nurture this healthy process of reflection and resolution. Of course, it may take us years to eliminate completely an unskilful tendency in ourselves, but we can start by taking these kinds of steps to get rid of it, and allowing ourselves fully to feel disquiet can be a key to doing so.

These wholesome fruits of disquiet constitute the four aspects of confession, namely remorse, confession proper, making amends (that is, remedying the harm you have done, as far as possible), and making resolutions (to prevent yourself from doing it again). The first item of the four, remorse – ethical disquiet or, as we often call it, the sting of conscience – is indispensable as the seed from which the other three grow.

The power of remorse is directly proportional to one's spiritual aspirations: the more you set high standards for your behaviour, the more you will feel remorse when you do wrong. We need to heighten our sensitivity to ethical disquiet, and the best practice by which to do so is confession to spiritual friends. Regular confession produces growing confidence: after confession we feel more at ease in ourselves because we have restored our moral dignity. This is a subject I will come back to in Chapter 8.

Because any form of disquiet is uncomfortable, we can't allow ourselves to feel it without doing something about it. If we are unwilling to do something about ethical disquiet – at least to confess it – we will feel driven to suppress it by one means or another. But, while it can be suppressed, it cannot be destroyed. It remains as a sort of background noise in consciousness, eating away at the mind, and producing a variety of unwholesome symptoms: cynicism, sloth, depression, self-hatred, and (perversely) the blaming of others. In such ways, suppressed disquiet simply displaces itself on to other things. It then becomes a major barrier to the development of the Dharma life in general and to meditative concentration in particular.

While its suppression is unskilful, ethical disquiet itself is highly skilful. But there are other forms of disquiet that can be either neutral or unskilful.

Firstly, there is what we might call 'false disquiet'. This is a feeling of guilt about actions that have no moral significance. It is really a fear of punishment, or the withdrawal of somebody's love, or rejection by the group. False disquiet has its roots in social conditioning, especially the fears that we acquire in childhood.

Conscience can be a complicated business, especially for those whose upbringing instilled in them belief in a wrathful God. For such people, a supernatural judge seems to loom behind the frowning figures of parents, teachers, and policemen. A revealing exploration of this mindset can be found in James Joyce's novel *Portrait of the Artist as a Young Man*, which contains a vivid description of a hellfire sermon on the evils of sex, and of the feelings that the sermon produces in the narrator. (It comes as no surprise that the upshot of all his terror is a visit to a brothel.)

It isn't always easy to distinguish false disquiet from the genuine article. The whole thing can get terribly complicated. For example, we may experience false disquiet in response to a genuine moral issue. This happens when we really have done something wrong, but our anxious feeling about it springs more from fear of being punished (or of losing other people's esteem or love) than from real empathic concern for those we have hurt.

Arguably, conventional morality relies in part on false disquiet. To the extent that people lack a mature, individual conscience (and how many of us are fully mature in this regard?), their 'good behaviour' must be founded on the dread of punishment or disgrace. But there is a price to be paid for this mechanism of social control, and many pay it in the form of neurosis and insecurity – or in acts of rebellion, covert or not.

Finally, there is what we might call 'functional disquiet'. This doesn't have any moral dimension at all, either real or imagined. It happens, for instance, when you have just left the house for the day, and suddenly get a nagging feeling that you have left a window open or the back door unlocked. Like the other forms of disquiet, this too is a sensation of 'wrong done', but not an ethical wrong – just a potentially harmful mistake or oversight in the practical business of living. If it has any moral significance at all it is as a symptom of lack of attentiveness.

Functional disquiet is a necessary protective mechanism, but it becomes debilitating if we are too prone to it and it becomes anxiety. Some people are always imagining that they have left the back door open when in fact they have double-locked and bolted it. Habitual anxiety can diffuse itself through the mind, and then attach itself to whatever objects are available. This happens for all sorts of reasons. Some people pick up the habit of anxiety in childhood from their parents. It seems it can even be acquired in the womb and during the earliest years of infancy. Others acquire it while living through great dangers or prolonged stress, such as war or persecution, where it may develop into what is now termed post-traumatic stress disorder. But, however we acquire it, this habitual anxiety – if never confronted and transformed – can have harmful consequences. It may ruin our health. Worse, we may try to palliate our anxiety by controlling other people. Someone who is tensely preoccupied with 'getting things right' as a way of dealing with habitual anxiety often ends up pushing others around.

If we suffer from such an excess of functional anxiety, we need to acknowledge it and take it into account. Even if we can't entirely eliminate it, we can at least keep it in check and not let it drive us into unethical or insensitive behaviour. Until we do that, we will constantly be struggling to take control of apparent 'problems' that are really phantoms of our imagination.

Such then are the three forms of disquiet – ethical, false, and functional. Ethical disquiet springs from a genuine moral and spiritual sensitivity. One can either acknowledge its promptings and act appropriately (leading to spiritual growth) or suppress them (leading to a variety of ethical and psychological problems). False disquiet springs from the desire to conform and be approved of or liked. It may play a useful social role in making people 'play by the rules', but it also produces a lot of irrational guilt and can lead to damaging reactions. And there is functional disquiet, which at best is a healthy instinct alerting us to our lack of attentiveness and at worst is a neurotic brooding upon the safety and welfare of oneself or those one loves.

This analysis of the forms of disquiet gives us a useful schema for sorting out what may be a large and murky area of our emotional life. It is not for nothing that the modern era has been called 'the age of anxiety'.[63] Many Westerners who take up meditation discover (if they didn't already know) that anxiety is the main hindrance that they have to contend with. Most of us need to do at least some work to sort out our personal 'disquiet zone' – the broad area of our emotional life that includes remorse, shame, embarrassment, irrational guilt, and so on.

The first thing to do is analyze our feelings of disquiet in terms of this schema. Do the feelings spring from a real problem, or are they just a manifestation of a habitual state? If they include misgivings about our actions, do those misgivings spring from a real moral lapse? Or is the disquiet false – a by-product, perhaps, of a childhood starved of love, or a repressive religious education?

If all three kinds of disquiet are entangled with one another in our minds – as is quite possible, and perhaps even likely – we need to disentangle them and form some estimate of their relative proportions. This may be quite a long job, and we may first have to get to know ourselves much better through meditation and honest communication with trusted spiritual friends.

Having cleared up the precise nature of our disquiet, we need to do something about it. For example, let's say that we find in ourselves elements of genuine ethical disquiet – a sense that we have done harm to somebody, or neglected a duty. It might be something we've done recently or something in the distant past that we have buried away and never faced up to. In either case, the remedy is the same: to acknowledge what we've done, confess it to our spiritual friends, and do whatever we can in practical terms to repair the damage.

By contrast, we may come to see that our disquiet is mostly a product of unhelpful social or religious conditioning. If so, we must start to detach ourselves from the old prejudices and wrong beliefs that make us suffer. For instance, if you've had a conventional, perhaps rather old-fashioned, Christian upbringing, you may have a certain amount of guilt connected with sexual feelings, especially if they do not run in socially acceptable channels – if, for example, you are attracted to people of the same sex as yourself. You need to resolve that, and recognize that the guilt you feel is not rational because sexual feelings themselves are not unskilful.

Alternatively, you might see that you are prone to neurotic functional disquiet. If so, you need to address that too. This might not be easy: the habit of anxiety often goes deep and even becomes embedded in our physiology, so we shouldn't expect to dispel it overnight. But we can start by learning to identify it when it shows its face, and soothe it with a wry smile of recognition. We can learn to feel it without giving way to it. We can also resist the compulsion to infect other people with our anxiety, or to alleviate it by controlling them.

In the longer term, we can dispel neurotic disquiet through our spiritual practice as a whole – through the calm and confidence that flow from the practice of kindness and generosity, from meditation, and from the sense of security that comes with deepening friendships.

Thinking-of and thinking-about

Now we come to the second pair of variables. These are two different aspects of thinking: thinking-*of* (something) and thinking-*about* (something). The second is a possible (but not inevitable) outcome of the first. Whereas sleepiness and disquiet are opposites, the transition from one to the other of this pair represents a qualitative shift in the mode of attention.

Thinking-of and thinking-about refer to that most characteristic of human functions, the one that arguably distinguishes us as humans: the ability to use concepts. Animals are able to form a sensory picture of the world but they are, so to speak, trapped in their immediate sensations, for the most part unable to step outside them to survey the past and future, even the moment itself beyond what is present now. Humans are liberated from the immediate by their capacity to translate what is experienced into concepts that can be transported into other circumstances, situations, and even times. We can then think about those concepts, connecting and contrasting them, finding new possibilities in new combinations of ideas.

This power of reflection is actually the basis for the Dharma life itself. First of all, it enables us to identify ourselves and to reflect on our situation. Then we can bring our experience from the past to bear upon our present and reflect on new possibilities for the future. We can think of being different from what we are now. We can even think of becoming a Buddha. We can study the Dharma, which means learning from the experience of others and applying it to ourselves. We can even read a book on Abhidharma and see what relevance it has to us!

Thinking-*of* means turning one's attention to a particular object and applying a concept to it: broadly, it means recognizing it as something in particular, distinguished from the otherwise undifferentiated flow of sensations around it. Thinking-*about* means allowing the mind to roam around the features of that object, reflecting on its particular internal parts and characteristics and its external connections and relationships – reasoning about it. For example, you might think *of* a friend (in the sense of calling that person to mind) and then start to think *about* his or her typical moods, mannerisms, and characteristics. Thinking-of is traditionally compared to one hand grasping a pot, and thinking-about to the action of scouring around inside the pot with the other hand, as if to clean or polish it.

Both kinds of thinking occur naturally all the time, and they are in themselves neutral functions that are often highly useful to our human lives, being the crucial element in the creation of our whole civilized environment. They are just tools and that is why they are considered to be variables, but, like any other tool, they can be put to good or bad use – sometimes very good or very bad indeed, as the history of humanity readily reveals. The key issue is the states of mind that they accompany and even serve: are they joined with the positives or with the afflictions, are they put to inspired and creative uses or do they serve unhelpful, even evil, ends?

Most of the time, of course, our thinking is neither good nor bad; it simply drifts along, stimulated to a brief life of rather vague rumination by our daily encounters or chance memories. Often we are only half-conscious of our thinking and have very little recognition of what thinking really means, for we are not able to clarify the difference between our words and our thoughts and the things they refer to. We are not sufficiently awake to the power of the tool we are so casually wielding, a bit like a drunkard wandering through the market place with a live chainsaw.

This vagueness very easily leads us into trouble, for our thinking is easily colonized by half-conscious moods and buried tendencies in the mind that carry us away. The mind begins to drift, connecting more and more things together, driven by those currents under the surface of our minds. This is known in Buddhist psychology as *prapañca*, which literally means something like 'spreading out' or 'diffusing', connecting more and more things together in a network of contaminated and egoistic ideas without clearly realizing what one is doing.

If this drift is not checked, it readily develops into theories and interpretations of the world around us, whether in general or in particular respects, which then start to shape our experience and actions. These are called *dṛṣṭi* or 'speculative views or opinions' in Buddhism, and they are a major blockage on the path, as we will see. For instance, from a single bad experience we can come to form theories about ourselves or even about a whole class of people and then live on the basis of those ideas. We may explain our own suffering, for instance, in racist terms or by reference to our being miserable sinners, justly punished by a vengeful God. Our own theorizing gets caught up with ready-made theories propounded, often vigorously, by others. Often our minds are tangled and choked with ideas swirling around us that we take for our own because they give expression to the point our minds have drifted to.

Gaining awareness of the thinking faculty, in both its identifying and its reasoning aspects, is thus crucial for a healthy and ethical life, and it is also of the greatest importance for the practice of the Dharma. We need to know what the limitations and the value of thinking are, when to think and when not to think. We need to recognize that, valuable as it is, knowledge gained through reason is not the same as knowledge gained through direct experience or insight; knowledge is not the same as wisdom.

But in so far as we do think, we should make sure that we think clearly, accurately, and responsibly. We even need to learn how to think, especially through engagement with clearly written books and people who think clearly. This is why Buddhism puts so much stress on study of the Dharma, notwithstanding the fact that all that study of the nature of reality must ultimately be transformed into seeing reality face to face through wisdom, unmediated by words and concepts.

Thinking-of and thinking-about are both highlighted in Buddhist texts because in the practice of meditation we need to be aware of them and make conscious use of them. Indeed, thinking in both forms plays an important part in all the intensifiers, because it helps us to navigate deeper and deeper into the truth. Again it should be stressed that the truth about reality itself is not to be discovered in a thought, but thinking plays a vital role in bringing us to that discovery.

Usually we think of many different things in the space of a minute: the mind hops from one thing to another. Very often, when we think *of* something, we scarcely think *about* it before moving on to something else. In meditation, we try to direct the two aspects of thinking more purposefully. For example, we deliberately and repeatedly think of the meditative object (e.g. the breath) until our thought starts to 'stick' to that object. Thinking-of is like striking a spark, while thinking-about is the point at which the spark ignites a steady fire. Or, to change the metaphor to a watery image, thinking-about is the stage of getting interested in the object, when the flow of our mental associations starts leading us around the object rather than away from it.

To use yet a different image, sometimes the mind is like a grasshopper jumping from one stem of grass to another, and sometimes it is like a snail wrapping itself around a single stem. Thinking-about is the mind in its snail-like mode. We are all familiar with this, but the trouble is that we have little control over it. It happens much more easily with sense-objects (which stimulate our emotions strongly) than with the subtle objects of meditation (which offer nothing immediate to please our appetites or ego). This has always been the case, but perhaps more so today than ever before. We live in an age of grasshopper mind. Every day our culture offers us more and more fascinating sense-objects to excite our desire or feed our anxiety. I have met schoolteachers who complain that their students' attention span is getting shorter each year. But whether this is true or not (and perhaps schoolteachers are occupationally prone to consider the quality of their students to be deteriorating), it is certainly the case that many would-be practitioners of meditation find it hard to generate thinking-about in connection with meditation objects, such as the breath. Consequently, they find it hard to develop absorption in dhyāna.

The secret is to harness thinking-of and thinking-about to the meditation. As we direct thought to the meditative object, we become more and more absorbed in it, and, as that absorption gets deeper and deeper, we eventually enter the first dhyāna. Both kinds of thinking are still present in the first dhyāna, but they are very strongly directed to the ends of the meditation itself. They die away in the second dhyāna, in which there is still a very subtle thought, but none of the inner 'verbalizing' or 'conceptualizing' that characterize ordinary discursive thought.

Having gained some understanding of all the ethically undetermined events – the constants, the intensifiers, and the variables – we are now in a position to explore the thirty-seven ethically determined mental events. This is the central part of our task, because it will equip us for mind watching – the psycho-ethical 'sorting out' that is vital to our spiritual progress.

Part 4

Transforming the mind

Chapter 8

···

Faith and shame

We now begin the task of dividing our mental states into two kinds, as the Buddha put it in *The Discourse on the Two Kinds of Thought*: the skilful mental events on one side and the unskilful on the other. In traditional accounts of this particular Abhidharma analysis of mental events these two kinds are expounded first by listing the eleven positives, then the six fundamental afflictions, and lastly the twenty subsidiary afflictions, which are really aspects of the main six – followed by the variables that we have just visited. This is what you will find, for instance, in Urgyen Sangharakshita's *Know Your Mind*. I am, however, giving them a different ordering, exploring them in terms of pairings of contrasting wholesome and unwholesome mental events.

I have done this because in presenting this material during retreats I have found that this best brings out the nature of the ethical work that we need to do, by emphasizing the strong connection between each positive and one or more afflictions and subafflictions. If we recognize that an affliction is simply the denial of a positive, we have already made a connection with what we must do. There is another reason, in terms of the 'narrative' of this book. If we were to go through it in the traditional sequence we would have to wade through twenty-six afflictions and subafflictions almost to the end of the book, the positives left far behind, which could leave us feeling a little despondent!

Before we set out on the first such pairing, however, there is a little bit more to say about the positives, which may help us to understand better what we are dealing with. There are eleven skilful mental events, as we have seen, which for convenience I am calling the eleven 'positives'. They seem to enjoy one another's company – as befits 'positives' – because they tend to come not alone but in a happy band. According to the Abhidharma, no less than ten of the eleven are present in every skilful mind-moment. Admittedly, in some cases this 'presence' seems to be more potential than actual. In a skilful state, for example, you would not consciously experience shame if you had nothing on your conscience. Yet if in that skilful state an unwholesome impulse did try to slip into your mind somehow, shame would immediately spring forward to resist it, as if it had been waiting in the wings for its cue. By contrast, someone in an unskilful state – someone in a drunken frenzy, for example – may do appalling things with little or no shame.

The eleventh positive, serenity, is usually said to arise only in dhyāna. However, one or two of the traditional authorities take a different line and say that serenity too occurs in all skilful mental states. But even if serenity is only to be found in dhyāna, the news as a whole seems very heartening. Skilful states are not remote from us; we are already pretty familiar with most of them, if only in dilute form. All we need to do is strengthen them.

But I am not going to plunge into an account of all eleven positives together. I am going to look at them in terms of five groupings, each consisting in a number of pairings that have some connection with each other. In this chapter, then, we will explore the first three positives – faith and the two kinds of shame – together with the afflictions that are their opposites.

Faith

First and foremost among the positives is faith. This is the mind's natural responsiveness to higher values, to what is good and admirable. It is not something constructed or added on to us but is intrinsic to human consciousness, or at least latent in it. It comes to us all naturally, at least from time to time, without having to be 'worked up' artificially, because it is a capacity of the mind itself. Of course, we can nurture it, draw it out – and indeed we must, if we want to progress spiritually. But whether we are nurturing it or not, faith comes spontaneously, even if it comes but rarely, or only to be turned away by habitual cynicism. It is actually (not just potentially) present in all wholesome mind-moments.

Faith is of central importance to the Dharma life, so it is vital that we understand it clearly. The Sanskrit word is śraddhā, and it is sometimes translated into English as 'confidence', no doubt to avoid the connotations that the word 'faith' carries for many of us. This translation brings out aspects of what śraddhā means, but it is too vague and weak, and also ethically ambiguous (after all, rogues can be 'confident' in their roguery). 'Faith' is better, so long as we are not misled by its connotations of blind religious belief.

Faith isn't an exclusively religious emotion at all. It turns up in many areas of our life, not just the formally religious sphere. It arises whenever we feel an appreciative response to goodness in other people, when we see them performing generous or noble acts or being generally of a loving and helpful disposition. For example, it is one of the foundations of friendship between decent people: we respond to the good qualities in each other. Faith is also present in our response to the truth when we hear it spoken, especially perhaps when the speaking requires courage. The truth concerned might not be a deep religious or philosophical truth; it might just be the truth in the mundane sense – saying what is really the case. Seeing people who have the courage to point out the truth about an oppressive regime, for instance, even at the cost of their personal safety, is very inspiring, and one's response of admiration is a form of faith in this Buddhist sense.

We feel faith all the more when we hear a higher kind of truth, the kind that reveals to us the deeper patterns of our existence. In particular, we feel faith when we hear the truth of the Dharma, especially when it is communicated with deep feeling and understanding. In this, its most specific and developed form, faith is the response not just to ethical goodness but also to the Dharmic values that underlie ethics.

Such Dharmic values are not just abstractions: we find them first and foremost embodied in people. Nevertheless, we can also meet them vividly, if indirectly, in words on a page, or in works of art. Alternatively, faith might come to us not from any outward stimulus at all, but from an inner source – perhaps in the form of a dream, a spontaneous vision, or an existential insight. In the context of Buddhism, faith might arise when we read a sutra, or see an image of the Buddha, or when we hear somebody teaching the Dharma, or meet somebody whose way of life is deeply rooted in it. In traditional accounts, perhaps legendary, of the life of the Buddha, his first moment of faith was when – shortly after witnessing sickness, old age, and death for the first time – he saw a wandering religious ascetic.

For a more analytical definition of faith, we can turn to Xuanzang, the great Chinese Buddhist traveller and scholar of the Yogācāra, who lived in the seventh century AD. Xuanzang said that there are three kinds of faith – faith in realities, in qualities, and in capacities.[64] By 'realities' he meant fundamental existential truths. He mentions in particular the truths of dependent arising and karma. These teachings reveal in conceptual terms important aspects of the fundamental nature of things – respectively, that everything that arises does so in dependence on conditions, in the absence of which it ceases, and that all our actions have an effect on the future unfolding of our experience. Rationally or intuitively (or perhaps in both ways) a sensitive mind must respond to these truths as true and precious when what they mean is really recognized. The response is not merely one of calm agreement, but a wholehearted assent on every level of one's being, one that brings great satisfaction and even perhaps relief.

Secondly, according to Xuanzang, faith can be awoken by *qualities* – the beauty of goodness as we sometimes witness it in certain people. We may sense this beauty, for example, when we hear about the qualities of the Buddha, as evoked perhaps by the scriptures, or when we see the serene form of a Buddha image. Living individuals may also inspire us, as when we encounter the ethical and spiritual radiance of members of the sangha.

Thirdly and finally, Xuanzang says that faith arises in response to the *capacities* that we intuit, however dimly, in ourselves. Sooner or later it hits us that the Dharma is not something remote from us, but the reality within which we have our being. We therefore see that Enlightenment is not just something to be attained by 'special' people whom we cannot hope to emulate, but a living possibility *for us* – a seed dormant in our own hearts. The sources of faith are not entirely outside and 'above' us; we also find them in our inmost nature.

Although Xuanzang wrote particularly eloquently about these three forms of faith, the analysis was not of his own invention; he was drawing on a long tradition. The three dimensions of faith had already been enumerated earlier, termed 'deep', 'lucid', and 'longing' faith.[65] Nor was Xuanzang the last to write about them. Centuries later, the same threefold analysis was taken up and given a distinctive application by the great Japanese teacher Shinran (AD 1173–1263) – perhaps the greatest advocate in Buddhist history of the central importance of faith.[66]

Each of the three aspects of faith can be understood as a highly skilful form of one of the constants. Deep faith in realities obviously has to do with seeing things in a certain way, and is therefore essentially a quality of interpretation. Lucid faith in qualities is a kind of joyous responsiveness: a pleasant mental feeling. Longing faith in capacities is a movement of will. Indeed, all five of the constants – contact, feeling, interpretation, will, and attention – must participate in faith to some degree. Faith therefore involves one's whole being. Let us look at this idea more closely.

'Deep faith' is the reorganization of interpretation brought about by the Dharma. It is not a narrowly intellectual understanding of Buddhist teachings, but an intuitive comprehension of them and a conviction that those teachings are true, because they articulate and clarify our intuition of the nature of reality. In other words, we experience deep faith when we 'see', at least to some degree, that reality is as described in the Dharma, and that the appropriate response to that reality is to emulate the Buddha and participate in the sangha.

This idea is worth pondering. We are already familiar with the idea that the spiritual life *ends* in seeing the truth of the Dharma for oneself. But in a sense it not only ends but also *begins* there, or at least with an intimation of it, tentative as it may be. This is precisely what distinguishes faith from 'blind faith'. It involves a kind of 'knowing'; it already discerns, if only faintly, the outlines of reality. For example, faith sees, to some extent, the truth of the three characteristics of conditioned existence. It distinguishes, at least in a rough and ready way, between wholesome and unwholesome attitudes and actions. It is drawn, with gratitude and delight, to the ideas and the people that can feed its own faint and flickering flame. Faith is the seedling that will eventually become the tree of wisdom.

The sense of reality brought by faith is at first intuitive: the mind can touch it, but not firmly grasp it. It must be tested by reasoned analysis and experience. The Buddha explicitly encouraged this critical and even sceptical approach to his teaching.[67] Nevertheless, right from the start, faith is a kind of 'knowing', not just a willed optimism, or a bet on an outsider. It involves not just a conviction, but a conviction rooted – if a little shallowly at first – in the way things really are.

Lucid faith is a matter of feeling, akin to aesthetic responsiveness. As our understanding deepens, we start to take delight in the qualities of the Three Jewels. The feeling is called 'lucid' because it flows from a growing sense of clarity: the scattered pieces of the jigsaw puzzle of existence have begun to assemble into a coherent picture. This clarity naturally brings with it a sense of confidence and equilibrium, rather as daylight frees us from the uncertainties and anxieties of night, revealing to us clearly the world and our place in it. In this metaphor, the rising sun corresponds to the Buddha, whose function is to reveal the world as it has been all along, and to dispel the cloak of darkness that shrouded its true nature.

Lucid faith brings a growing relaxation and happiness. This is not a smug pride in knowing a secret that others don't possess, but a humble confidence that we know the real purpose of life – know where we want to go, and how to get there.

Longing faith is the skilful form of will par excellence. The 'longing' involved is the desire to fulfil the possibilities that faith sets before us, an urge to realize the spiritual potential now revealed within us. Self-confidence is part and parcel of this; you can only feel such a longing if you are convinced that attainment of the spiritual goal is a real possibility *for you*. Without this longing-with-confidence, faith is mere devotion – admiring something from a distance, but seeing it as essentially beyond you. Central to faith is the sense that you can realize fully the highest ideal, however far off it may be at the moment.

Each of these three aspects – depth, lucidity, and longing – adds something vital to the totality of faith. We need to give due weight to the cognitive and volitional aspects, and not think of faith – as some people mistakenly do – exclusively in terms of pleasant feeling. I have occasionally heard Buddhist friends asking themselves, in a mood of despondent self-scrutiny, 'Am I really a Buddhist? I'm not sure. I don't feel inspired!' When this happens, I try to persuade them to look at themselves and see that, although they may not *feel* inspired, nevertheless they are trying to practise the moral precepts, they are meditating every day, or at least quite often. They have been doing these things for many years and clearly intend to go on doing them – almost despite themselves. Faith is often like this – a subterranean power, not necessarily ecstatic, and perhaps barely manifesting in conscious feelings at all, but nevertheless a real force, a feeling deeper than we can feel.

Of course, faith does sometimes manifest in strong feelings of devotion, but it would be a mistake to equate the two things. In India, I have seen lots of devotion – bhakti – among the followers of all religions, but, even among Buddhists, devotion isn't always accompanied by faith. Devotion, though it can be very beautiful and pleasurable, is not necessarily linked with insight into reality, or with the desire to change oneself in accordance with that insight. This is not to deny its value. When it is connected with deep and longing faith, the expression of devotion – in worship, chanting, singing, making offerings, and many other ways – can help to strengthen and channel faith. But we should not make devotional moods the sole measure of faith.

Faith purifies the mind in the sense that it drives out the afflictions. Firstly, it drives them out by making them painfully obvious. In the light of faith, the ugly and painful nature of unskilful mental states is exposed. But faith also purifies the mind by bringing order and clarity into it. When faith is present, we know 'which way is up'.

Finally, it should be said that faith *tends to action*. Because it is not just a passive admiring-from-a-distance, faith impels you towards its objects. It is this active dimension of faith that leads us, sooner or later, to go for refuge to the Three Jewels.

Faith is a very beautiful, profound, and far-reaching quality. Though we experience it most fully in our response to the Three Jewels, it finds expression in many ways. As we have seen, faith is present in all skilful mental states, and this should restrain us from identifying faith with formal religion. People who are not committed to any spiritual ideal can still respond to something higher, at least to some extent and from time to time. Any selfless action implies the presence of an ideal – however vague and inarticulate – in the mind of the person who performs it.

The logical corollary of this is that no spiritual tradition can claim a monopoly on faith. Of course, Buddhists consider that the Three Jewels constitute the highest objects of faith, and that view plays an important part in nurturing their faith, and channelling it effectively. However, merely professing allegiance to the Three Jewels is not the same as faith. By the same token, faith manifests in every decent human action, whether performed by Buddhists or anyone else. Reflecting on this, Buddhists should rest in mindfulness of their affinity with all good people.

It is worth concluding this discussion of faith by dwelling for a moment again on its inherent character as a natural capacity of the mind. One might even think of it as the faculty of responsiveness that allows us access to those higher values and truths that the ordinary mind, based in the senses, instincts, and intellect, cannot know, or can know only indirectly. It is vitally important for us to recognize that we have such a capacity, to identify and value it, and, more significantly, to 'educate' it, bring it more and more into play in our lives as the principal guiding factor.

It might be argued that there has been a gradual undervaluing of this faculty of responsiveness in the modern West, especially since the European Enlightenment of the eighteenth century and the dawning of the 'age of reason', and with the needful rejection of so much false hierarchy and dead religious belief. It has largely been artists and poets who have kept alive a recognition of its value and importance, for instance in the notion of 'imagination', and who have often embodied that in their work. Because of this larger cultural background, many of us probably have quite a bit of work to do to value this faculty in ourselves. We need to find it and feed it in ourselves, giving it as much significance as we do our eyes or our brain – or perhaps even more.

Lack of faith

The absence of faith is not an innocently neutral state. If a mind has no sense of the good at all, that is because something else has driven it out, leaving not just the absence of faith, but the presence of its opposite – lack of faith, literally 'non-faith' (*āśraddhya*).

The characteristics of lack of faith are, point for point, the opposite of those of faith. Firstly, interpretation lacks any sense of spiritual realities, and this vacuum is inevitably filled by the view that ethical principles and spiritual ideals are merely polite fictions draping self-interest. Secondly, as a result of this lack of conviction, the happy clarity of lucid faith is clouded, and the mind finds itself inhabiting an ever-darkening world, where 'strength' means the accumulation of power and wealth, and 'happiness' means the attempt to douse a fundamental unhappiness in pleasure and comfort. Thirdly, in the absence of conviction and lucidity, the heart's intrinsic longing for spiritual development is buried deep underground, covered by mean and ignoble drives for merely selfish ends.

A mild form of lack of faith is part of the currency of everyday life. I remember an incident in the late 1970s, when I was supervising the building of the London Buddhist Centre. We used to buy second-hand materials from local traders, and I discovered one day that one of them was getting his building materials from dubious sources. I warned him, 'We can't use anything that is stolen.' He smiled and said, 'This stuff isn't hot – just a bit warm!' I insisted, 'Well, everything has to be perfectly cool.' He threw me a look of mingled pity and derision, and explained, 'Now look, mate ... *you just can't live like that!*' The words stuck in my mind as a neat informal summa of the world view that sees crime as too risky but honesty as too expensive.

People who are involved or interested in Buddhism – the likely readers of this book – are likely to be free of this kind of lack of faith. Nevertheless, many people who find the Dharma plausible and attractive still find it hard to believe that they themselves can 'live it out' to the full. This is an awkward situation: to hold simultaneously a love of an ideal and a conviction that it is beyond one's capacities is painful. If the love and the negative conviction are both strong, they can lead one to despair. The problem of despair has been discussed quite a lot in the Buddhist tradition, especially in Mahāyāna writings – probably because the Mahāyāna ideal (the leading to Enlightenment of all sentient beings) is so dizzyingly high that it can easily start to look unattainable. In one scripture, the Buddha speaks of the ideal Bodhisattva as one who does not tremble when he hears 'the mother's deep tenets' – the 'mother' being the Perfection of Wisdom itself.[68] In other words, when he hears the ultimate truth proclaimed, he doesn't think, 'Oh no! That is way beyond me.' But if this is the 'ideal Bodhisattva', a less-than-ideal one may be susceptible to just such a thought. And indeed, for many of us, a lack of confidence in our own abilities is the form that lack of faith takes.

Unfortunately, it may not stop there: lack of confidence in oneself can start to corrode deep and lucid faith. Lack of faith, if persisted in, produces a mind that is dull and lazy. Not knowing 'which way up' everything is, one has no way to evaluate ideas or actions, and as a result one's mind becomes slow and dull. You don't feel like making much effort, because you have no response to value.

At its worse, lack of faith can become cynicism – a definite *aversion* to value, a nihilistic denial of it. Hard-line cynics laugh at any ideal, and at those who try to live by it. They are also likely to espouse false values, often with very destructive consequences – for example, the notion that 'greed is good', which is often found among proponents of neo-liberal economics.

In milder forms, lack of faith can be a sort of muddle between faith and the afflictions: it is possible to have a genuine response to the ideal, but express it in the wrong way. People may have some genuine faith in their responses, but it gets distorted by sentimentality, or they try to make out that it is more than it really is in order to make themselves look good.

In cultivating faith, we need to make sure we are cultivating the real thing, and not just something that looks like it. Faith easily gets mixed up with 'near enemies' – states of mind that bear a superficial resemblance to it. After all, we human beings tend to want something to believe in. Sometimes, too, we want a substitute 'parent' – somebody to look after us, someone upon whom to shrug off the burden of responsibility. What appears to be faith may in reality be a kind of foolish trust – something not really thought through or tested. At least in a mild form, this is very common among religious people, and Buddhists are by no means immune to it. In fact, it may be impossible to avoid it altogether, because when we become Buddhists we open ourselves up to ideals that we haven't personally realized. It takes time to sort out genuine faith from the other needs and desires that we bring to the spiritual life.

Faith and lack of faith are not just individual experiences. Each has a social aspect. In an environment pervaded by faith, where you know that others share your faith, you can share *yourself* more fully. But many people who feel faith can't share that aspect of themselves beyond a certain basic level because they do not live among their spiritual brothers and sisters.

Time spent in an environment where lack of faith predominates tends to undermine one's own faith. Lack of faith is only too common in our culture (although of course there are many features of faith at least in the broadest sense). You only have to walk around a shopping mall or watch an evening's television to realize how little interest most people have in a higher dimension to life.

The two kinds of shame

To have faith is to have a sense of the good, a sense of how a human being should live and act. In short, it is to have values. If you have a measure of faith in your heart, you will, when you fall short of those values – as you sometimes must – feel ethical disquiet. In everyday language, you will feel *shame*. To feel shame is to feel uncomfortable. This may be a definite physical sensation: you may blush and feel hot. You may want to avoid meeting other people's eyes.

If you experience such uncomfortable feeling in connection with shame, it is worth prizing because it is a guardian. It will prevent you from acting unskilfully, because you won't want to experience that discomfort. As a result of cultivating that painful consciousness, you are thus protected from acting unskilfully, and, when you do so, you are impelled to put it right, to make amends for what you have done.

There are two different ways in which ethical disquiet can be triggered, two different varieties of shame that are considered as positives. These may be called scrupulousness (*hrī*) and reverential shame (*apatrāpya*). Which of the two kinds of shame you feel depends on whether the feeling flows from your private conscience or from a vivid sense of the values held by others whom you revere as wiser and kinder than yourself.

Scrupulousness is the product of one's personal conscience. That conscience is not something artificial, a kind of superego conditioned into us by parents and teachers. Like faith, of which it is perhaps an

Mind in Harmony

aspect, it is a natural responsiveness to the sufferings and joys of others, and indeed of our own selves. Empathy is natural to us; the life in us responds to the life in all, and we are directly affected when that life is harmed. As a result, if we are at all sensitive, we feel disquiet when we have acted unskilfully, harming others or ourselves, or even when we just feel tempted to do so. That disquiet is triggered by our own immediate sensitivity to life.

Scrupulousness also has another dimension. Even if you do not immediately feel that something you have done is wrong, you may come to think of it as wrong because you have a general understanding and respect for the Dharma. When you discover that the Dharma teaches – through the moral precepts, for example – that such and such an action is unskilful, scrupulousness starts to arise, though suppressed until that point. So scrupulousness can be triggered either by your innate moral sense, or by your love and devotion to the Dharma. Obviously, the most significant part of the Dharma in this respect would be the precepts, which are guidelines for moral behaviour. The precepts come in various lists, the best known containing five that enjoin non-harm to living things, not taking what is not given, not misusing sex, not lying, and not clouding the mind with drink and drugs. These and other such lists of precepts give us objective criteria against which to measure our own behaviour, so that our shame can be triggered if we see that we have fallen short of them.

Scrupulousness therefore emerges from an inward sense of the Dharmic ideal. In contrast, reverential shame springs from the sense of that ideal triggered into life by our relationship with another person or persons – not people in general, but those whom we see as strongly imbued with that ideal. While such people may not necessarily be perfect, they have enough of the spirit of wisdom and kindness to inspire our trust, admiration, and love. In other words, we feel a significant measure of faith 'through' them. To the extent that we have such feelings, we will naturally tend to feel shame when we do something they would regard as unskilful. It doesn't matter whether they actually know what we have done or not; the point is that, when we have acted or spoken unskilfully, the recollection of such good friends makes us feel disquiet, where perhaps self-generated scrupulousness was not enough to do so.

The Sanskrit word (*apatrāpya*) that I am translating as 'reverential shame' is usually rendered as 'fear of blame by the wise'. No doubt this translation is linguistically more correct, but it may be spiritually misleading in the present context. I doubt whether the cultivation of fear can be helpful in the task of mind training, especially in a culture where many people still suffer psychological damage from religious guilt and fear instilled in early life. We would do better to found our ethical sense on positive emotions like gratitude, and to distinguish reverential shame from anxious forebodings of punishment.

As we saw when we examined disquiet among the variables, it is easy for us to get moral feelings mixed up with pseudo-moral feelings based on our religious training, our early childhood experiences, and so forth. Often, neurotic guilt masquerades as a moral sense. We need to understand this. But we must also be very careful not to throw out the baby with the bath water. Many people recognize a need to free themselves of neurotic guilt and become more authentic, but they sometimes go too far, and don't allow themselves to be influenced by a proper regard for others. There is a great danger that the quest for 'authenticity' may end by neutralizing the skilful emotion of reverential shame, and that would be a spiritual disaster.

Reverential shame is probably a more important moral force than scrupulousness, much as we may like to think of ourselves as relying only on ourselves. While we all experience scrupulousness, it isn't usually a very finely tuned instrument, and we all have blind spots and well-developed ways of rationalizing ourselves into doing what we want against our better instincts. Reverential shame is more likely to raise our standards, and conscience is more difficult to dodge or silence when it is embodied in a being independent of ourselves. We are social creatures to a greater extent than we realize, and we are very strongly influenced by what other people do and think.

I don't have to say this sort of thing in India, because people there don't mind being influenced by others. It is what they expect. In fact, the trouble in India is that people regard morality too much in terms of social conventions. But in the West people don't want to be influenced by others. Our theme song is 'I did it my way.' But I suspect we go too far. I know for myself that reverential shame is a very powerful tool. It has been very important in my spiritual development, and is something that I still need to exercise even more fully.

Scrupulousness and reverential shame are treated as positives, skilful mental events, yet oddly they are painful experiences. This may seem strange if, as is often the case, we too closely identify the ethically positive with the pleasant, and the painful with the negative. But ethically positive experiences can be painful, and negative experiences of course can be pleasurable. Scrupulousness and reverential shame are positive mental events even though they involve a painful feeling. Eventually they become an extreme ethical sensitivity, so that you only have to think fleetingly of the mere possibility of acting unskilfully, and they come into play and defend you. That is why in Buddhist tradition they are called 'the two guardians of the world'.

In one of the oldest works of European literature, Hesiod's *Works and Days*, is a remarkable passage describing the age of iron, which – according to Hesiod's mythical history – was the rusty successor to the nobler ages of gold, silver, and bronze. For Hesiod, the age of iron is the smoky candle-end of time, a period of violence and lies that he ruefully identifies with his own era.

> *Last, to Olympus from the broad-pathed Earth*
> *Hiding their loveliness in robes of white,*
> *To join the gods, abandoning mankind,*
> *Will go the spirits righteousness and shame.*
> *And only grievous troubles will be left*
> *For men, and no defence against our wrongs.*[69]

By 'the spirits righteousness and shame' Hesiod may well have been thinking of something like what I am calling scrupulousness and reverential shame. (According to the translator, 'shame' here includes 'the fear of what other people would think'.) Likewise, Asanga speaks of the two forms of shame as the essence of ethics.

The two forms of shame guard the world in that they prompt human beings to acting morally. We therefore need to cultivate them, especially through confession. Confession is the way in which we make our consciences tender. By expressing remorse, we enable ourselves to feel it more fully and delicately. Conversely, if we don't express remorse, a sort of carapace grows over it, and we become less and less able even to feel it. In the context of an effective sangha, an arena is usually provided or established where confession can take place. In traditional Buddhism the bhikkhu and bhikkhunī sanghas would meet in chapters for this purpose;[70] and in the Triratna Buddhist Order we have an equivalent in our regular chapter meetings of Order members, principally for the purpose of confession. A chapter of this kind is an ideal arena for the fostering and application of reverential shame. Our peer friends in the spiritual life may not be perfect moral exemplars, but collectively they represent a weight and depth of commitment that we can respect – a suitable basis for reverential shame.

Unscrupulousness and shamelessness

The opposite of scrupulousness is unscrupulousness (*āhrīkya*), and the opposite of reverential shame is shamelessness (*anapatrāpya*).

Unscrupulousness is the lack of a personal conscience. We all act badly from time to time, but those who have no aspiration or ideal have no basis on which to feel that they have let themselves down. If any feelings of disquiet or remorse do arise, they ignore and even suppress them – until they cease to arise any more. Such people have no respect for the Dharma and so they don't feel remorse when they break the precepts. In its place, they may even have an anti-moral sense, like that articulated by Milton's Satan: 'Evil, be thou my good.'[71]

We may get into this mood when we are in a phase of moral rebellion, trying to get rid of false remorse. In such a mood, we may go to the opposite extreme and start doing things that are morally reprehensible, justifying them with a sophisticated rationalization. We may tell ourselves (and perhaps others), 'This is good for my development' – like Raskolnikov, the hero of Dostoevsky's *Crime and Punishment*, who murders a female pawnbroker in the belief that transgressing conventional moral boundaries is necessary for his progress towards greatness. (Less extreme versions of this were quite common for a period in the Triratna Buddhist Community; for example, people used to get drunk and rationalize that they were thus overcoming irrational guilt.)

A quantum of unscrupulousness is said to be present in every unskilful action. If you could listen to your thoughts attentively at a moment of secret wrongdoing, you might notice a voice whispering words of self-congratulation. At such times, something in us cocks a snook at our moral sense. Consciously or unconsciously, we often feel a sneaking pride in breaking the rules.

Shamelessness is the same, but in this case the psychological foundation is one's attitude to other people. Having nobody that you really respect or look up to, you don't care what anyone thinks. Even if you do know some good people who 'deserve' respect, you don't care. In fact, you may feel a desire to shock or upset them.

At least in mild forms, the attitude is very common. Once, at a gathering of some of my relations, a young man laughingly remarked, 'God! Last night I was drunk as a skunk!' and glanced around to invite admiration of his audacious, playful spirit. I didn't know how to respond, having long forgotten the rules of this kind of game, so he scornfully added, 'That's the trouble with you religious people: you are so po-faced!'

Like unscrupulousness, shamelessness is present in all unskilful action. What is more, evil born of unscrupulousness involves a rejection of good per se, not merely in oneself but in others too, at least tacitly but perhaps quite openly and publicly – shamelessly indeed.

The mind is a moral battleground between the impetus to act skilfully (or at least, not to act unskilfully) and the impulse to do what gives immediate gratification, which is often unskilful. We need all the help we can get to strengthen our conscience. Often, scrupulousness is not enough. One can too easily rationalize a way around it, and, of course, there will be moments when unscrupulousness is stronger than shame.

I think this is particularly true when we are alone and nobody can see what we are up to. Here we enter what I have already referred to as 'the morality of the private moment'. We might, for example, venture onto a pornographic website. Nobody else knows that we are doing it, and it is not part of our public presentation of ourselves. This activity in particular is all too common these days, particularly amongst men, and it is better to admit it and try to deal with it than to hide it away. Indeed, the task of deepening one's spiritual life necessarily involves opening up such private moments to other people. Only by communicating them can we objectify them and start to transform them by the power of reverential shame. This is why it is important to develop a confessional element within spiritual friendship. In the Triratna Buddhist Order, chapters are the ideal context for this.

The practice of confession is the key to getting more closely to grips with one's own habits and mental states. Surprisingly, it is often the *petty* weaknesses that are hardest to transform. Confession starts with a feeling of remorse, which leads you to disclose unskilful actions, words, or emotions. Where necessary, confession should 'follow through' into making amends for any harm you may have done, and taking steps to ensure you don't do it again. All this is only possible with the benefit of a clear understanding of the mental processes that led to the unskilful action, and this is why the Abhidharma can play a very helpful part in the task. The method only really works in a context of regular practice and intimate, trusting communication, so confession is best understood as an aspect of spiritual friendship.

Faith, scrupulousness, and reverential shame are the most important of the positives, because together they are the basis of spiritual and moral life. All the others, in that sense, flow from them and could even be described as forms of them. Nāgārjuna, the great founder of the Wisdom school, even said that faith is more important than wisdom (*prajñā*), for the simple reason that without faith there could be no wisdom. Faith has to come first because it is what motivates the spiritual life, the skilful desire that impels us forward on the path. Scrupulousness and reverential shame are the two guardians that keep us on that path, and warn us when we are straying from it.

Chapter 9

....

Contentment, goodwill, and compassion

In this chapter, we are going to deal with three more positives – contentment, goodwill, and compassion – together with the afflictions that are their opposites: respectively, craving, hatred, and malice.

Sometimes the simplest and clearest way to explain the sense in which we are using a word is by indicating its opposite. Something like this seems to be true of the positives: it is sometimes easier to understand them in relation to the unwholesome states that they oppose. The best way to explain the nature of the positive mental event called contentment is thus by identifying it as the opposite of craving. Craving is found in the Sanskrit list of afflictions as *rāga*, but an exact equivalent more commonly found is *lobha*, and what I am here calling 'contentment' is listed as *alobha*, which simply means 'non-craving'. Non-craving or contentment is the opposite of craving in the sense that it is the state of mind that is free from craving, so, to begin with, we need to understand what craving is.

Craving is the tendency of the unenlightened mind to long for or cling to objects. 'Object' here means 'something experienced by a subject' (i.e. by a mind) and covers a wide range of possibilities. I am using the word 'craving' to signify two closely related emotions that can be distinguished as 'longing' and 'clinging'. 'Longing' is the desire for a pleasant object you don't yet have, while 'clinging' is the desire to keep hold of a pleasant object that you have at present (or ignorantly imagine yourself to 'have').

The object may be a thing – a house, perhaps, or a car – or it may be a person who is dear to you; often other people are the objects of our deepest and most powerful longings. It could be an event, experience, or feeling, whether past, present, or future – a memory or a fantasy. It may even be a *mental* object like an idea or set of ideas. We do commonly cling to certain ideas – to our political or religious convictions, for example, or certain notions about ourselves – because they make us feel secure

....

in some way. Indeed, we may suffer just as badly when our ideas are threatened as when we are in danger of losing an important possession or a loved one. People are willing to kill, even to die, for an idea – and not necessarily a very good one.

The distinction between sense-objects and mental objects is not at all clear-cut. After all, as the Yogācāra distinctively insisted, what we experience as sense-objects are themselves mental objects: images that our sense-organs and brain serve up to us as representations (*vijñapti*) of an object 'out there'. But the afflictions add a layer of distortion onto that representation. By its very nature, craving entails a false interpretation of its object. In the case of a sense-object, this false interpretation amounts to the creation of an imaginary and distorted mental object, which we superimpose on the initial representation of the sense-object. Although we think we are craving the sense-object, we are always really craving an illusory mental one that we have projected onto our representation of it.

This is an important point, worthy of deep and frequent reflection. Craving always involves a distortion in our interpretation of the craved object, and this distortion always has essentially the same form: we tell ourselves a flattering tale about the object, and we swallow that tale – hook, line, and sinker. To put it in more technical language, we exaggerate the object's pleasant aspects, and overrate its power to give us pleasure or happiness. By the same token, we conceal from ourselves, or at least minimize, the object's painful aspects. Consequently, the craved object always appears to us to be far more pleasurable, far more necessary for happiness, and hence far more important to us, than it really is – or ever could be.

Let's take a simple example, such as alcohol. We see a bottle of wine or whisky, and in our mind arises the idea of happy forgetfulness, that pleasant mood of easy relaxation in which we don't worry about what we say or do and all our cares have evaporated. At the same time, we choose to ignore the fact that we are going to wake up the next morning with a splitting headache, and realize with a groan that we have made fools of ourselves, at the very least. In this way, we exaggerate the pleasure-power of the alcohol, and deny its pain-power. And this in fact is what we always do in relation to anyone or anything that we crave or cling to.

Something else happens too. We imagine that 'having' that object will secure or enhance 'me' – the 'ego', our sense of our own identity, that fragile construction that is the chief focus of unenlightened insecurity because we dimly feel its hollowness and insufficiency. Mixed up in our craving is a belief that having that object – whether a thing, an experience, an idea, or a person – will give solidity to our sense of ourselves, making that feeling of existential inadequacy go away. And, in a limited sense, we are right: if we get what we want, we do generally feel more solid and secure. We feel effective, ahead of the game, and pleased with ourselves. Our ego swells. But, of course, this is rather brittle: our sense of identity has been boosted by success, but this is dependent on our contact with the object and that can, in the nature of things, only be temporary.

An important distinction needs to be made at this point. All desires are not craving. We can recognize a difference between craving and natural desires such as hunger, thirst, sex, and even things like well-being and social acceptance. These are simply the needs of the organism and arise quite naturally in a healthy body. Of course, it is very easy for these natural desires to get caught up in the vain effort to solidify ego-identity – indeed it is very unusual to keep them clear of it, especially in matters like sex that involve the combination of our relations with other people and strong urges and powerful pleasures. Whilst it is quite normal to feel hunger, that hunger can very easily become greed. Food can be imagined as satisfying not merely our natural need for sustenance but our craving for affection, for instance. In other words, natural desire is not the problem, but craving, which all too easily appropriates those natural desires.

Craving is thus not just a straightforward matter of the appetites and emotions. It is always bound up to some extent with a fundamental need to secure one's identity. Everyone who is unenlightened is insecure, whether grossly or subtly, about his or her identity. Some people are more psychologically insecure because, for example, they didn't get enough affection when they were children. But there is a more fundamental level of insecurity that is not just a quirk of individual psychology, but a dim perception of a disturbing truth. The fact is, by their very nature our identities *are* insecure, for any identity that we cling to is challenged by impermanence, and ultimately by death. All the time, the ego is under threat. Consequently, we try to secure it by grasping pleasurable objects, or objects that we associate with pleasure, because pleasure gives us the illusion that we are winning the race against destruction and decay. For a few moments we believe that we are secure, released briefly from our sense of existential dread. We give unwise attention to such objects, distorting their true nature, seeing them as more pleasurable than they really are, as less painful than they really are, and as having a real substantial existence.

In this way, we are always distorting the bare data of contact, turning its object into a contaminated and unreal object. We pay scant attention to the bare sensuous impressions of the object, and instead focus upon its pleasurable aspects. (In the case of hatred, as we will see shortly, we do the opposite, and overfocus on its painful aspects.) What we see is an image projected by our mind, not the object itself. Here we have the very essence of the unenlightened mind. All the other afflictions are simply variations of this process.

Our clinging to particular objects (whether things, people, or views) tends to spread out into a sort of generalized clinging to the matrix in which we experience those objects. In the case of humans, that matrix is the sense-world (*kāmaloka*), but the same tendency exists at every level of the 'triple world'. The angelic inhabitants of the archetypal world are addicted to the rapture and bliss of *rūpa dhyāna*. Likewise, the dwellers in the formless world are attached to the exalted happiness – inconceivable to us, as transcending ordinary pleasure and pain – of *arūpa dhyāna*.[72] They identify themselves through the refined pleasant experience that they continually experience in those worlds. Although their experience undoubtedly is very pleasant compared to ours, it can still be overvalued, for it is not permanent, and attachment to it constitutes a subtle but powerful obstacle to the final liberation of Enlightenment. However sweet the apple, the worm of impermanence gnaws from within.

This attachment to the matrix of our experience is called craving for existence. But running alongside it, like a shadow, is craving for non-existence – the death wish, the nihilistic desire not to be. This is the underside of craving. For most people, and for most of the time, it is hidden, or is only a potentiality, but when life gives us more pain than pleasure and we see no prospect of escape, we may long to step across the boundary between existence and non-existence. We must say, however, that craving for non-existence is not a rejection of existence itself but rejection of it on the terms on which we now experience it: world-weariness of this kind is just frustrated worldliness.

Perhaps the most powerful form of craving for sense-objects is the craving for other people – people we see as a potential source of pleasure, happiness, or security. Most of what the world calls 'love' is really craving, in which the lover identifies the beloved as the solution to his or her inner emptiness and insecurity. Here, as in all forms of craving, we do not understand the real nature of the object: we disregard its painful aspects and its impermanence. In a sense the other person does not exist for us as a real person, but as an object that we believe

Mind in Harmony

will remove the pain of our own longing and the insecurity that gnaws at the root of our identity. Of course, all our human relationships are not of this kind, and it is possible to have loving relationships that are not simply disguised craving, as we will see when we come to discuss goodwill. But frequently, if we are honest, there is quite a bit of selfish interest in our relationships that shows itself in our upsets and reactions when the objects of our affection do not behave as we want them to.

Finally, it is important to reiterate that we cling not only to material things, not only to people, and not only to a particular 'world'. We also cling to ideas – what Buddhism calls views. This seems to be one of the distinctive insights of Buddhism: that we all cherish and cling to certain notions about who we are, and what the world is like. As much as sense-objects, views give us a sense of satisfaction and make us feel secure. The Buddha himself explores this process in a very important scripture that is the very first in the Pali canon, the *Brahmajāla Sutta*.[73] He shows the chain by which feeling gives rise to craving, which in turn leads to grasping, including grasping onto views that appear to substantiate pleasurable feeling and justify our rejection of painful feeling. I will explore this point more fully when we deal with ignorance and views.

Evidently then, craving includes a vast range of possibilities. Everything that can be an object of the mind can be an object of craving, and thus a contaminated and unreal object – one that is mixed up with our insecurities and distorted thinking.

Craving is the most fundamental of the afflictions in terms of our experience. Ignorance is arguably more fundamental objectively, but we don't experience it so directly because it is the ground we stand on, so to speak. But we experience craving because it is what drives us, and we feel it very directly.

Contentment

Contentment is the positive that drives out craving, as can be seen from the Sanskrit *alobha*, which literally translates as 'non-craving'. We may experience the early stirrings of contentment simply as revulsion from craving, for a sensitive mind eventually starts to feel humiliated by its own craving. One experiences a loss of dignity, a feeling that one is demeaning oneself, a recognition that craving is a kind of voluntary slavery, and, as a result, one may begin to feel the impulse to give up that ignoble, distorted mode of being, and to experience something purer and truer. So begins renunciation.

As we obey that impulse – as we let go of the objects of craving – we start to experience not just revulsion from craving, but also a positive state of peace and satisfaction. The more that grows, the less we have to struggle to push the objects of craving away: we simply are not interested in them any more. We feel complete, so we don't require external things to bolster our ego. Our sense of identity is deeply rooted in the real nature of things. This is the fullness of contentment.

We started by seeing contentment and craving as opposites, and so they are, but now we can see that the opposition between them – unlike, say, that between left and right – is not symmetrical. Craving is like going deeper into a cave as it narrows and darkens. Contentment is like moving towards an entrance, where the cave gets wider, lighter, and airier. The opposition between each positive and the affliction that corresponds to it is always asymmetrical in the same way. We can talk about the positive as the absence of the affliction, and this is a very practical way of talking – like explaining, 'Move to where there is less rock and more open space.' However, the absence of the affliction is the presence of something that is more, and moreover *augmenting*. It is not an opposition between two balanced things: the positive is not only higher, but also offers the possibility of endless progression.

Possessing this degree of contentment, one is increasingly able to give things up – not just material goods and neurotic attachment to people, but also views. Instead of craving things, we use them wisely and disinterestedly, or just appreciate them aesthetically. Instead of craving or hating people, or turning away from them in indifference, we delight in them for what they are in themselves. No longer exaggerating their pleasure-power or pain-power, we can see them more as they are, and rejoice in their diversity. Instead of clinging to our existing views, we feel free to give up ideas when they become irrelevant or inadequate, or when we see for ourselves how they constrain or harm us. Indeed, we enjoy the process of going beyond ideas in order to develop deeper and more adequate ideas – or to go beyond ideas altogether. Contentment thus includes a kind of mental flexibility; whatever situation one finds oneself in, one can respond to it with a fresh, open mind. The opposite state – rigidity of mind – comes from insecurity: the attempt to deal with life in terms of a set of relatively fixed ideas, because those ideas protect you against the loss of self.

Our contentment spreads as we also relinquish craving for existence or non-existence. Contentment ripens into detachment from the three worlds. Whichever of the three worlds we dwell in – the sense-world, the archetypal world, or the formless world – we still experience it, with all its pleasures and joys (and, in the case of the sense-world, its pains and sorrows), but we don't crave the pleasurable aspects, because we don't exaggerate them. Similarly, we don't hate the painful aspects. Instead, we see that pleasure and pain come and go, and we tranquilly accept their coming and going.

Contentment and 'the three times'

It is also said that contentment is detachment from the three times – the past, present, and future. Firstly, we don't crave the past: we feel no nostalgia. Many people live in the past to some extent, especially the elderly, but not only them by any means. Nostalgia takes many forms, and it takes a distinctive shape within the spiritual community. People who have followed a path of renunciation may start to miss the things they have given up. This can happen particularly when life gets difficult, or when we feel disappointed – perhaps because the sangha hasn't lived up to our hopes, and our fellows aren't treating us as we think they should. We may then begin to suspect that our renunciation was foolish. Perhaps our first wave of inspiration has spent itself, and we find ourselves in a trough. In that state it is easy to revert to cravings for the past.

That is attachment to the past. Perhaps attachment to the present doesn't need much comment, but the sources do mention a form of it that is peculiar to the spiritual community: craving for the mundane benefits that accrue from spiritual life. The authors of the Abhidharma probably had in mind things that admiring lay people typically gave to monks – fine robes or choice food. Perhaps they were also thinking of authority and respect within the sangha, and so on. These things may not seem particularly dangerous to us, in the present faint dawn of Buddhism in the West, where so few devote themselves full-time to a Dharma life, and Buddhism as yet has very limited public prestige and support. But that may change and even now, within a small world such as our own Buddhist movement, there are still peaks of status or influence to be attained, petty as they may seem by comparison with worldly achievement. Even these may become objects of longing and attachment.

Craving for the future, in a spiritual context, is said to be the calculating renunciation of material things now, in the expectation that you will get them back with interest later on: practising in the hope that you will gain prestige or wealth, or in order to achieve psychic powers or charisma through which you can manipulate the world to your advantage, or – looking beyond this life – hoping to go to heaven or attain a happy rebirth.

To reiterate the point, craving is the opposite of contentment. Contentment drives out craving, and brings a very positive state of detachment. Actually, it is better to call this state non-attachment rather than detachment, because we don't even feel attracted. It is not that we counteract attraction: we just feel free. Contentment is a feeling of happiness that comes from freedom, dignity, and self-confidence. It is a very important aspect of spiritual life, and one that we should expect to experience more and more over the years, as our spiritual practice progresses.

One cultivates contentment initially through deliberately checking craving and schooling oneself to sit with the experience of restlessness and boredom. It is very important to give regular time to doing nothing, so that you learn to sit beyond what is comfortable and wait until something fresh and spontaneog us arises. An important aid to this process is the cultivation of sensuous experience that is not associated with craving, which is where nature, art, and deep communication are helpful. Wholesome, fulfilling experiences of this kind help you to overcome discontent and experience the flowering of contentment itself.

Secondary afflictions arising from craving

But there is more to be said about craving, which has many secondary forms. Before we look at these, I should speak a little more about the Abhidharma's classificatory system, which I am treating rather freely in this book, to save you from getting confused if you look at other works on the subject, such as my teacher's *Know Your Mind*.

The eleven positives are usually presented as a single list without further classification, each being given equal weighting, but the afflictions come in two lists: the six afflictions proper (*kleśas*) and then twenty subsidiary or secondary afflictions (*upakleśa*), which are considered to be categories or further ramifications of the major ones. We have already encountered three of these secondary afflictions: lack of faith, unscrupulousness, and lack of reverential shame, which I have expounded in relation to their respective positives as contraries. Craving is therefore the first major affliction we have examined. The fact that craving is a major and lack of faith a secondary affliction seems to me a little arbitrary. Perhaps craving is in some way more fundamental than lack of faith, although contentment and faith are presented as equal positives, but, if so, the reasons are not clear to me. I suspect that this version of the Abhidharma, no doubt like others, draws together different traditions and sources and does not always reconcile them into a single coherent system. No doubt this reminds us that the mind is not a machine and that it always eludes the Procrustean beds of all classificatory systems, however useful they may be.

Some of the afflictions, however, are very clearly secondary forms of the major ones, which are usually each the direct contrary of one of the positives. The secondary afflictions are, so to speak, branches from the main trunk. Four important secondary afflictions are picked out in the Abhidharma as emerging from craving. The first is avarice, and the remaining three belong together in a family group: concealment, pretence, and deceit.

Avarice (*mātsarya*) means identifying happiness with *having* things, rather than using or enjoying them, as, for example, someone who prefers having a lot of money in the bank to spending it. Avarice is having fifteen suits hanging in your wardrobe but never wearing any of them because you don't want to get them dirty. Not so long ago, I read a newspaper account of a classic case: an old man, thought by his neighbours to be virtually down and out, was discovered dead in a very squalid house in complete disrepair, and under his bed were found suitcases full of banknotes and share certificates worth a very large amount of money indeed.

Avarice doesn't really produce any happiness, because it always brings anxiety about losing the goods, money, and so forth that one has accumulated. And, of course, it can never be satisfied. No matter how much you've got squirrelled away under the bed, it will never be enough. It is a perverse mental state, but easier to fall into than we imagine. It is a kind of congealed craving, in which the desire becomes its own object, and it is a very cold state emotionally: misers are notoriously hard-hearted, since they see other human beings as potential squanderers of what they have hoarded. Dickens' Scrooge is, of course, the archetype of the avaricious miser.[74]

According to our sources, there is apparently a form of avarice that fastens on the Dharma: some people keenly accumulate knowledge of Buddhism, but are not inclined to share it. And, of course, they don't think of actually practising what they know, but only of piling up more.

The antidote to avarice is generosity, an attitude of giving in which one lets go of the tendency to solidify one's sense of self through clinging to things.

The remaining three secondary afflictions – concealment, deceit, and pretence – belong together. They are three progressive stages of the impulse to disguise one's true nature and intentions, and in particular to hide one's faults from other people. They are reckoned as aspects of craving because they flow from the fear that honest self-disclosure is a hindrance to obtaining one's desires.

Why did the Abhidharma texts elaborate its discussion of this one fault into a group of four subsidiary afflictions? Why did it seem so important? Perhaps because those who are practising the Dharma in the context of a sangha are prone to some very specific faults. In the sangha certain activities or behaviours are highly valued and respected: meditating regularly, studying the Dharma, renouncing things. To an extent this is very healthy and valuable, especially when it is connected with reverential shame. But we may easily see it from the point of view of craving. We may crave the acceptance and esteem of our fellow Buddhists. We may crave their respectful attention and interest when we talk. We may even crave a 'position' in our Buddhist subculture – tiny though that is as yet. We therefore begin to disguise what is really happening in various ways and put on a show of being a 'good Buddhist'. This is rather more common than one might like to think. The desire to *appear* good can easily eclipse the desire to *be* good.

The first of these three afflictions of craving is concealment (*mrakṣa*). This means concealing one's faults with the aim of making others think one is better than one is. But, at this stage, the deception is limited. The sly person doesn't actually tell lies, or actively pretend to be other than he is: he just makes sure that people don't find out the truth. When certain questions arise, he changes the subject or answers off the point, or somehow contrives to imply, without actually lying, that he is innocent of the fault in question.

A common feature of concealment is the tendency to conceal what one has been up to, and where one has been. In a Buddhist communal household, you sometimes encounter a certain kind of person whose whereabouts are always a mystery. They walk into the dining room with a deliberately mindful air, as though they have just come from the shrine room, but actually nobody is quite sure where they have been. They are adept at spreading a fog around themselves and their movements. They are adroit with ambiguities and half-truths. They don't actually

Mind in Harmony

say, 'Oh, I have just been meditating in my room', but somehow or other they give you that impression. And if, on finding out the truth, you suggest they have misled you, they indignantly insist, 'But I never said that I was meditating!'

The aspects of one's inner being that one conceals in this way may not be grossly unskilful. Nevertheless they are usually things that one does need to change. By concealment, we avoid being challenged, and so avoid being transformed. Often the things that we conceal are much less spiritually damaging than the concealment we employ to hide them. Not only do we avoid being challenged and therefore transformed, but we cut ourselves off from full and deep communication, because we are always avoiding opening up certain areas of our life or mind. Moreover, concealment requires a considerable effort and consumes a certain amount of energy unnecessarily, because we have to keep our story straight and to be watchful for anything that might give us away: 'Oh what a tangled web we weave, when first we practise to deceive.'[75] The general outcome of this obfuscation is that we are, in effect, only half involved in the Dharma life.

Pretence (*māyā*) goes a little further than concealment, by actively creating a false appearance. We don't exactly lie, but our outward behaviour contrives a false image for the sake of reputation and advantage. For example, we might sit there in the meditation room, with thoughts as scattered as leaves in a gale, but wearing a beaming smile and sitting very still, as if to tell the world, 'Ah, what bliss!' Or when Stream Entry – the stage of insight into the Dharma at which one becomes irreversible on the path – is mentioned, you start speaking in a casually knowledgeable way. Of course, you don't actually claim, 'I am a Stream Entrant', but you artfully induce others to think of you as such. Where there is pretence, there is almost bound to be concealment too, because the pretender is usually privately doing things that don't fit his public image, and which therefore have to be concealed.

The last and worst of the three is deceit. This means telling outright lies for the sake of advantage and reputation: speaking falsely to create the impression that you are better than you are, or that you don't have faults that, in fact, you do have.

The antidote to concealment, pretence, and deceit is the same: to open up and reveal one's private moments to one's spiritual friends. We need to observe ourselves and notice which of our actions or thoughts we feel reluctant to disclose to our spiritual friends. Usually, those things will be the very ones we most need to tell them about.

In my case, I have tried to make that a chief criterion for what I talk about in my chapter meeting. Often, at the meetings, as we sit there together, I remember certain things and I think to myself, 'Hmm ... I won't say that. It would bother them, and anyway I have talked about it before...' At that moment, I usually realize, 'Oh no! Actually, that is precisely what I need to talk about!'

It is only when we conceal and deceive that we fear exposure. If we stop defending ourselves we have nothing to fear. If we let other people whom we trust look at those areas that we have been trying to conceal, to our surprise we hardly ever find that anybody gets censorious, feels shocked, or despises us for what we've revealed.

Concealment, pretence, and deceit are social evils. Prompted by craving for material advantage or regard, they distance us from others, and in particular from the very people we should be closest to – the members of our spiritual community. This is perhaps the deeper reason why they feature prominently in the Abhidharma. It would have been easy to list other unpleasant outgrowths of craving, but these three were picked out because they are destructive of the sangha or spiritual community itself, and are especially dangerous for that reason. An intrinsic part of life within the spiritual community is the vital but very difficult process of becoming ever more transparent to our spiritual friends. We need to recognize concealment, pretence, and deceit as major obstacles to that task.

Contentment is, among other things, the complete opposite of concealment, pretence, and deceit. Perhaps it begins with a kind of revulsion from these things – a distaste for the falseness and pettiness involved in them. As it deepens, contentment ceases to cling to high reputation and the benefits it may bring. Contentment therefore includes complete candour about oneself – the attitude of having nothing to hide, of being quite open. We still feel ashamed of our faults, but we do not mind people knowing about them. The person who truly possesses contentment is also characterized by being fully open, having absolutely nothing to hide.

Goodwill and hatred

Goodwill is the opposite of hatred (the Sanskrit word for goodwill is *adveṣa* – literally 'non-hatred'). Once again, the easiest way to understand the positive is by understanding the affliction. We therefore need to examine – unpalatable though the task is – the nature of hatred.

The first thing to understand is that hatred (*dveṣa* or *pratigha*) is a reaction to suffering. It extends beyond the experience of suffering to the perceived causes of suffering (and even to the inanimate objects that are instrumental in it). In particular, hatred focuses on the people who are (or seem to be) the causes of our harm. At best, we wish to push them away. At worst, we wish to harm them in return, even to destroy them, so that they no longer threaten us. Of course, if we act on that impulse, we create negative karma that will bring further suffering down on our head.

The impulse to retaliate stems not just from the desire to protect oneself from further harm, but also from the desire to restore one's sense of self – one's ego. Somehow, we feel that suffering diminishes our selfhood, and we want to replenish it by striking back at those who have hurt us. If they are not to be found, or are beyond our reach, we may feel driven to strike out at something or someone else as a substitute.

We saw how craving falsifies its object – exaggerates the pleasant features of the object, and minimizes its unpleasant or neutral features. Hatred falsifies its objects in the opposite way: it focuses intently on the painful and offensive features of its object, and denies or ignores anything that may redeem it, any features that are admirable or pleasing. It thus 'legitimizes' the idea that eliminating that object will make us happier and more secure. Hatred always produces a contaminated and unreal object.

Hatred is more than a conceptual misconstruction, however. It affects the whole psycho-physical organism, disturbing both body and mind, and is painful in itself. The same can be said of craving, of course, but there the pain and damage is mitigated or masked by the thought of pleasure. For this reason, those who by nature incline more to craving than to hatred – sometimes called 'greed types' in Buddhist texts – are usually more likeable than their opposite numbers, the 'hate types' (though greed types are not necessarily morally better overall).[76] Those who are disposed to hatred are often unattractive personalities, partly because they are prone to lashing out, and partly because – being in a state of suffering – they lack joy and may be preoccupied with their own woes and the wrongs done them.

Secondary outgrowths of hatred

Like craving, the basic affliction of hatred has a variety of unpleasant outgrowths. The Abhidharma names four such secondary afflictions: rage, resentment, spite, and envy.

Rage (*krodha*) is the most direct manifestation of hatred. It is an overwhelming desire, in the presence of the hated object, to attack it. Rage sweeps the mind away in a wave of emotion that loses all sense of proportion. It is a kind of possession. The Abhidharma, in a picturesque phrase, characterizes rage as 'picking up the stick'.[77] The violence that results from rage isn't always physical – it may be verbal – but it is not necessarily any the less rage-filled for that. The consequences of harsh words may be just as serious as physical violence, and the subsequent sense of remorse just as deep.

Rage is very disruptive of human society in general, and especially of sangha, in which one is trying to cultivate loving communication. Even if someone who is subject to fits of rage always apologizes and tries to make amends, it still becomes a barrier to deep and honest communication because people don't know when the fuse is going to blow, and they become fearful of provoking rage, so unpleasant is it when it comes.

Less overwhelming than rage, but more insidious, is resentment (*upanāha*). This is the tendency to nurse hatred while keeping it hidden and waiting for an opportunity to vent it. The resentful person bears a grudge, and waits for the moment when the enemy is off guard. This cherished and concealed form of hatred is very dangerous. Rage at least has a sort of honesty and spends itself quickly, but resentment can become poisonous and long-lasting. Indeed, it can be kept up indefinitely. I have known people to hold grudges for as long as thirty years – even on account of some wrong that was entirely imagined!

Resentment may have as its object not a single person but a whole class of people, perhaps a whole race or nation, and, in the case of nations, grudges may be cherished not just for decades but for centuries – a poisonous legacy handed down over generations. Sometimes there are historical reasons that make this understandable to a degree, but sometimes the whole thing is rooted in myth. Resentment is clearly a spiritually very dangerous emotion. If one has any predisposition towards it, one should work hard to eliminate it – and especially not to carry it into the spiritual community.

Thirdly, there is spite (*pradāśa*). Whereas rage and resentment dedicate themselves to specific objects, spite is more in the nature of a general disposition. The Abhidharma, in another picturesque phrase, describes it as the tendency to bite. We usually 'bite' with words. The spiteful person is prone to snap, or to make barbed or cynical comments. In English, this sort of temperament used to be called 'splenetic' (in the sense defined by the *Oxford English Dictionary* as 'having an irritable and peevish temper'). Nowadays we might call it 'spikiness'.

But perhaps the most unpleasant of all these afflictions is envy (*īrṣyā*). Envy is the form of hatred that springs from one's displeasure at the success, achievement, honour, or goodness of others. You don't have to know someone personally to envy them, but, if you do, the envy is likely to be much nastier. If we inwardly accuse ourselves of lacking achievement, worth, or popularity, especially if the accusation is not fully conscious, we may feel hurt by the success of others in any of these departments. To get rid of that hurt, we may want to take the envied person down a peg or two – to close that painful gap a bit.

I suspect that we greatly underestimate the power of envy as a force in personal relationships and society as a whole. It is a destructive but often invisible emotion, because by its very nature it cannot be frankly avowed. We cannot reveal our envy, except in the spiritual act of renouncing it, because we intuitively know that nobody will honour it. In this respect it differs from hatred proper. Other people may accept and even respect our hatred if they think that we 'have a right' to it (that is, if they agree with us that we have been treated unjustly); but to reveal envy is to expose an inner meanness that nobody can admire, except those who share it. Consequently, many people never admit their envy – even to themselves – and so remain in its grip. Yet envy is a very common experience, and probably very few escape it entirely. The only way to express it skilfully is to confess it and so purge oneself of it.

The antidote to envy is sympathetic joy (*muditā*), and the way to cultivate that is the practice of rejoicing in merits, openly expressing one's admiration and even gratitude for the good qualities that people have, the positive actions they perform, and their skilful achievements. This is very important in spiritual life. As human beings, we inevitably have weaknesses, and consequently we have feelings of inadequacy. It is easy to feel diminished by the achievements of others. We therefore need to go out of our way to try to cultivate genuine pleasure in the talents, qualities, and achievements of others, especially our friends. The more we do that, the more we develop qualities that fill up the sense of inner poverty that breeds envy.

Hatred and its secondary afflictions are an unpleasant collection of mental states. Unlike some of the afflictions, it isn't easy to find an amusing, forgivable side to them. Nevertheless, we all experience them to some degree, so we have to face them as the first step towards going beyond them. But for all the evil that they can produce, underneath them is a kind of neutral, primal energy – something that is part of human nature, that becomes hatred when it is checked or frustrated. This energy is not itself something to be extirpated or denied, but something to be acknowledged and transformed. The secret of dealing with aggressive energy is to find a positive outlet for it, to channel it before it becomes hatred. This no doubt is one of the major issues of life and especially of a life devoted to the Dharma.

Goodwill

But let us come back to goodwill and end on that most pleasing and inspiring note. We have seen that 'goodwill' is my rendering of the Sanskrit word used in the traditional classifications, *advesa*, which literally means 'non-hatred'. We have explored what hatred means and so we know what goodwill or non-hatred is not. It is not that desire to exclude, expunge, destroy whatever is perceived to threaten our sense of ourselves, and it has nothing to do with those bitter emotions of rage, resentment, spite, and envy, so painful even to think about. But what actually is it?

The key to understanding the roots of goodwill lies in the question of our sense of identity. Hatred and craving both emerge from our fundamental feeling of insecurity about our very existence as a separate self, a feeling that is so deeply imbued in the structure of our ordinary minds that we usually don't know it is there. Hatred is our attempt to resolve that anxiety by removing anything that seems to threaten us, while through craving we seek to secure ourselves by including in our identity anything we think will protect us and solidify our being. Goodwill then is not based in that insecurity. It emerges from a happy weakening of our sense of being separate, a sense of connection and expansion to include in our concern the being of others. We sense that the life in them is the same as the life in us. We feel empathy for them and reach out to them as if they are, to a greater or lesser extent, parts of ourselves or we parts of them.

The word 'goodwill' may suggest a quite ordinary and unremarkable quality, though highly laudable, that most people would acknowledge feeling themselves and experiencing from others – the basic fellow-feeling that emerges in a friendly and helpful mood or disposition. However, that is but the bottom rung of a golden ladder ascending to the highest selflessness that identifies spontaneously with all that lives and is embodied for us in the figure of the Buddha himself as the supremely compassionate one (*Mahākāruṇika*).

One can discern a number of rungs on that ladder. The first is found in a growing sense that we cannot harm other people, even other living creatures, because we begin to recognize our fundamental identity with them. As we are alive, they are alive; as they like pleasure and dislike pain, so do we. We feel that common life more and more immediately, and we are increasingly as little able to harm other beings as we are to harm ourselves. We therefore become increasingly sensitive to the pain that others feel and actively desire to avoid being the cause of it. One could call this the negative ethical phase of the ladder of goodwill, corresponding almost exactly to the term 'non-hatred'.

Based on a deepening sensitivity to the life in others around us, there emerges the positive ethical phase – indeed, probably the two phases usually more or less coincide. We don't merely seek to refrain from harming others; we actively wish them well and we are prepared to contribute to their well-being, at least to some extent – that extent perhaps determined by how much we ourselves are inconvenienced in helping them. At this stage, we are still fundamentally concerned with ourselves and the preservation and enhancement of our own identity, but we are willing to reach out to others, to the extent that that does not affect our own interests, because we can identify with them to some extent. This is perhaps what we usually mean by goodwill.

However, gradually our sense of our own separate identity is dissolved in a larger identification with life itself as it manifests all around us. We are more and more prepared to lay aside our own interests in order to serve others, and we do it joyfully and spontaneously because we feel for that life in them as much as we do for our own life. Here perhaps we find that we must use the word 'love', understood in the sense of a disinterested going out of ourselves in feeling for others. (Of course, what we commonly call love is actually highly selfish, as is seen by the speed with which it can turn to hatred when we are rebuffed.) We might dare to quote Saint Paul on *agape* or love from his famous First Epistle to the Corinthians 13:4–8, which can hardly be bettered as an expression of *maitrī*, this most Buddhist of virtues, despite its being so frequently quoted at weddings!

> Love is patient, love is kind. It does not envy, it does not boast, it
> is not proud. It does not dishonour others, it is not self-seeking,
> it is not easily angered, it keeps no record of wrongs. Love does
> not delight in evil but rejoices with the truth. It always protects,
> always trusts, always hopes, always perseveres. Love never fails.

Eventually, love or *maitrī* leads to the complete transcendence of our self-attachment. Through the swelling of that love we recognize that there is no fixed separate identity, that we have nothing to defend or secure, whether through hatred or craving. We are open to and identify with all life and so we think, feel, and act only for the benefit of all beings, not excluding ourselves. We are even willing to give up our own life in the interest of others, if that seems best to serve life. At this, the top of the ladder of goodwill, are to be found the Buddhas and Bodhisattvas who are, from this point of view, simply the living embodiments of love or *maitrī*.[78]

Malice and compassion

Goodwill and hatred, with its secondary ramifications, seem adequately to cover this fundamental ethical spectrum. However, the Abhidharma adds a further polarity that brings out another dimension of it: that between compassion (*avihiṃsā*) and malice (*vihiṃsā*). Both these words, in Sanskrit, are built around the element *hiṃsā*, which simply means 'harm'. The particle *vi-* is an intensifier, so that *vihiṃsā* means something more like 'cruelty' or 'malice'. In other words, it is not just inflicting harm but enjoying doing so.

Whereas hatred and its associated secondary afflictions certainly involve causing harm to other beings, they do not do so for the pleasure that is gained from others' suffering. If you feel driven by hatred to cause harm, you feel a pleasurable satisfaction when you have done so, but not because you specifically enjoy the fact that pain has been caused. Hatred seeks to make one's identity secure by discouraging, repelling, or destroying the hated object. One's aim is to get rid of the threat, and we feel pleasure to the extent that we achieve that objective.

But malice goes way beyond this. The aim is to cause pain, and pleasure is gained when that happens. It does not necessarily have anything to do with a perceived threat. A bully, for instance, enjoys watching his victim squirm in fear and pain, even though the poor victim offers no threat and has often been chosen for that very reason. For some, watching an animal writhe in agony can be a source of pleasure, even though that animal does not endanger them at all.

The extreme of such malice is enjoying the infliction of actual bodily pain, even unto death, but the tongue can be just as effective a means of torturing others; verbal bullying can cause intense suffering and can ultimately destroy someone. A common form of malice is gossiping and backbiting, spreading malicious rumours and the like, manipulating social feeling so that the mood of the group turns against someone, whilst watching with delight the effects of one's actions. The great surge in the use of social media has unhappily revealed a great deal of this kind of cruelty; it seems to be more common than we might have imagined.

This mental state seems to have two major elements. Firstly, the ability to inflict harm demonstrates one's own power and that gives one a stronger sense of identity; the infliction of one's will upon others may seem to secure one against the sense of powerlessness and insignificance that one must inevitably suffer in the face of impermanence and death. Perhaps it is also connected with early-life experience. Of course, such a means of satisfaction must be short-lived, only lasting as long as the pain inflicted. To regain that sense of power, further suffering must be inflicted, and thus an addictive cycle commences. A second factor may be a deep inner sense of being wronged, a kind of burning pain within from which one is momentarily relieved only when others suffer, even though they are not usually connected with whatever caused the sense of wrong.

Malice is the extreme of isolation, even alienation, from life. The malicious person does not have any sense of identity with his victims. They are simply objects to him, for which he feels nothing except the pleasure of seeing them in agony. It is not merely that there is no empathy; there is a kind of negative of empathy, a 'dispathy', completely cut off from the living world around.

Non-harm is exactly the opposite of that. It is not just not harming others; it is not even desiring to harm. You don't even feel like it. When somebody hurts you, you don't feel like hurting them back; you don't feel like retaliating so that they suffer. Indeed, you feel a revulsion against any such action. As non-harm gets stronger, you feel more and more repelled by the idea of causing suffering to others. At its most fully developed, this becomes compassion, the desire to help others overcome their suffering on the deepest level. Compassion, at its highest, is the complete overcoming of all self-attachment and an identification with all life.

Of course, compassion is closely related to goodwill, and indeed in some traditions is considered as almost a secondary positive to goodwill. The Abhidharma does not assign secondary positives, but one might well do so here, from this point of view. Goodwill is a general responsiveness to life beyond ourselves, in whatever state we happen to find it. When confronted with suffering, that goodwill becomes compassion (*karuṇā*), and we desire to do whatever we can to remove that pain. The higher up the ladder of goodwill we have climbed, the more we are willing to do to remove pain – even to the point of sacrificing ourselves – and the more we recognize the underlying causes of that pain in attachment and ignorance. The remedies we then apply strike increasingly to the heart of the problem, especially in terms of helping people to use the Dharma to resolve their suffering in the deepest and most complete way possible.

When goodwill encounters happiness and joy in others, it does not turn to envy, as we have seen that hatred does. We share in the joy of others and rejoice with them. This aspect of goodwill is sympathetic joy (*muditā*), as we have already seen. But what of goodwill when it suffers the ill-will of others, or is the victim of their insensitivity and self-interest? Equanimity (*upekṣā*) is the response, a mood of calm non-reactivity in which the deep sense of solidarity with others is not disturbed by their hostility or lack of feeling. Such deep imperturbability of *maitrī* is suggested by the image of Mara's arrows falling harmlessly as flowers at the feet of the Buddha under the bodhi tree.[79] This degree of love is remarkable and rare indeed.

While goodwill is clearly the fundamental mental state, it forms with compassion, sympathetic joy, and equanimity an important set, known as the four sublime dwelling-places or brahma viharas, which constitute with faith the emotional attitudes that we try to cultivate as Buddhists. This is why one of the two most basic meditation practices commonly taught in Buddhism is the Development of Goodwill (*maitrī bhāvanā*, commonly known by the Pali term: *mettā bhāvanā*),[80] and we are all enjoined to cultivate some experience of the other three sublime dwelling-places.[81]

Hatred is clearly the opposite of goodwill, being called its 'far enemy'. But there is a near enemy too, one that is goodwill's counterfeit and can easily be mistaken for it – indeed very commonly is. That is selfish affection (*prema*), here indicating that attachment to other people that appears as concern for them – until they cease to do or be what we want. This of course is a common feature of sexual, romantic, and family relationships, being really an aspect of craving. The other sublime dwelling-places similarly have far and near enemies – their direct opposites and their selfish simulacra. Compassion is directly opposed by malice, as we have seen, and has sentimental pity for a near enemy; envy is the far enemy of sympathetic joy, while its near enemy might best be called sycophancy or hypocrisy; and reactivity directly opposes equanimity, with indifference as its negative simulacrum.

Even though compassion is considered as a form of goodwill in some traditions, it is such a significant mental state that it has rightly been awarded a separate status in this Abhidharma list. Loving others, caring for them, to the point that one is willing to sacrifice oneself for their well-being, cannot but be the highest manifestation of the human spirit, and in compassion at its fullest this sacrifice is made completely spontaneously and naturally, not as a duty or a practice. One has transcended self-attachment and identified with all life to such an extent that it is as natural for one to try to relieve the suffering of others as it is to try to relieve one's own suffering. Such compassion only comes about on the basis of complete clarity that has decisively defeated ignorance. This is embodied in the figure of the Bodhisattva, the being who pursues the path of the Dharma no longer from a narrowly personal point of view, but for the greater good of all life, because no separate self is any longer recognized.[82]

Chapter 10

....

Clarity and ignorance

The most fundamental of all the afflictions is ignorance (*avidyā*). In the Buddhist scriptures, there is a range of words that are synonyms for ignorance, and they carry various nuances, but they all boil down to the same basic idea: that we fail to be aware to our fullest capacity and so do not see things as they really are. In our ignorance of the true nature of our experience, we act in ways that cannot but bring us suffering. In the terms that I introduced in Chapter 6, ignorance is the tendency to perceive 'unreal' objects. And, of course, unreal objects easily become contaminated objects – that is, objects to which we respond with craving or hatred.

Ignorance permeates the three worlds. Whether you inhabit the sense-world, the archetypal world, or the formless world, you are – to some extent at least – in the grip of ignorance. The darkest ignorance is found in very evil minds – the minds of torturers and mass murderers – but some quantum of ignorance is present even in advanced Bodhisattvas, right up to the brink of full and perfect Enlightenment. Until then, at least a small trace of ignorance clouds one's vision: there remains some particle of resistance to seeing the way things really are.

Ignorance is like the root of a poisonous plant, growing deep within the soil of our minds, which again and again brings forth blooms of ever-various delusion and pain in ever-new realms of experience, cut off in one moment only to grow again in the next. The root of ignorance grows in four successive stages. Firstly, a shoot pushes up from the root below the surface of the soil: this is self-view (*satkāyadṛṣṭi*). From that shoot, the stem, branches, and leaves of craving, hatred, and conceit uncurl as the second stage. At the third, the sickly and ill-favoured flowers of views begin to blow. And fourthly, the poisonous stench of 'vagueness', put forth by these ugly blossoms, drugs the mind and deadens the soul, so one cannot choose but wander, lost and suffering, through the terrifying dangers of existence.

Ignorance is the basic affliction that conditions this malign growth, and it is implicit in each of these four stages. As we have seen, it is the

....

tendency to misconceive reality, to misunderstand, misinterpret what we are experiencing. In terms of the constants then, ignorance is a fault – perhaps a 'design fault' – in interpretation. Consequently, each of the stages of outgrowth is also to be understood as a defect of interpretation. This sets ignorance and its four offshoots apart from the other afflictions, which are unwholesome desires or volitions – unskilful modes of will.

From the Buddhist viewpoint, the elimination of afflictions of will is vital, but not enough to set us free. Unless interpretation is also purified by the destruction of ignorance, the afflictions may eventually return, even after a long absence. Unless uprooted by clarity, ignorance remains present even in minds that are free of afflictions and that are therefore ethically very positive and aware to a high degree. One's state of mind in dhyāna, for instance, is unequivocally skilful, but ignorance is very likely still to be present. Thus, ignorance is itself neither skilful nor unskilful, but the potential for both skilfulness and unskilfulness is inherent in the ignorant mind.

This brings us to an important issue. We have spoken of ignorance as being like a root below the surface of the mind, and as permeating all the worlds. We could even speak of it as a habit, the sort that one is bound to repeat unconsciously, like drumming one's fingers on the table, fiddling with one's beard, or saying, 'Umm!' This habit is so deep and so formative that it is not so much that we *have* that habit but that that is what we *are*. We are the habit of misinterpreting our world by attributing to it a permanence, substantiality, and potential for satisfaction that it cannot have – and, of course, by imputing a real and permanent self as the owner of experience. That habit is ignorance.

Where did this habit come from? When did it begin? In terms of this life, it is said that it was born with us – indeed, it could be said that it is ignorance that caused us to be born. Buddhist tradition teaches that we are born into this life in dependence on a previous life and that we inherit some of the effects of that life as an influence on this one. That influence, the Yogācāra says, is of two kinds. Firstly, there is an influence coming from the actions performed in that previous life that is the primary force forming this one. This shaping force is the accumulation of the results (*vipāka*) or fruits of that previous undischarged karma, and it determines the basics of our new birth, including the fact that we are born as humans at all.

But there is another kind of influence accompanying that of our previous actions: that generated by our previous interpretation of reality, more or less imbued with ignorance. That leads us to seek a new embodiment in the first place and is inherited as an unquestioned distortion at the roots of our experience. Ignorance gives rise to our birth, is born with us, and born into us. And that habit is repeated moment by moment and will be handed on to some new life, if we do not shine the light of clarity upon it, finally chasing it from our minds.

There is another way of looking at the aetiology of ignorance, connected with our biological evolution, while not necessarily at odds with the previous interpretation. The capacity to know the world through concepts emerged in human beings and was selected as a means of enhancing the species' survival and prospering. Perhaps the chief among these concepts was 'I', which then became the focus of each organism's endeavours and was the basis of the rich complexity of human life and enterprise, in all its heights and depths of good and evil. But that concept 'I' is simply a construct, referring to no identifiable reality, merely a useful tool for survival. While we fail to recognize it for what it is, we live in servitude to it and therefore suffer. And that is ignorance.

However we seek to explain its origins, this fundamental error in understanding is inborn. Until clarity is brought to bear upon it, it will bring us suffering – and cause us to inflict suffering on others, too, if we do not cease to be subservient to it. It is this inborn ignorance that elaborates itself again and again in each new life, indeed in each new moment, as the shoot of self-view; the stem, branches, and leaves of craving, hatred, and conceit; the poisoned flowers of views; and the stench of vagueness.

We will now trace the articulation of ignorance through each stage.

Inborn self-view

The first step is the formation of self-view. Here we must make some distinctions, because, it will be observed, the notion of 'views' arises twice in this flowering of ignorance, once here at the first stage and again at the third. There is a major difference of kind underlying these two appearances of views.

The Abhidharma makes a distinction between afflictions (including views) that are inborn and those that are acquired in the present life. Inborn views are attitudes carried over from our previous existences. As such they are part of the deeper fabric of our mind, lying below the level of words, and we may or may not articulate them clearly. Acquired views, in contrast, are the ones we learn from our parents, teachers, and friends, or – in modern culture – from books, newspapers, television, and the Internet. These include political stances and attitudes towards religion, whether of belief or of non-belief, and towards certain behaviours. For instance, fifty years ago we might have been taught that homosexuality was bad, but now it is generally seen as acceptable. Cultural attitudes – what art to like or dislike, as well as views such as the idea that all aesthetic judgements have only relative validity and semi-articulated assumptions about the sources of happiness – are subtly (or not so subtly) communicated all the time by the commercial world that surrounds us. All these are acquired views, which must be relearned each lifetime, though presumably they may be influenced by views acquired in previous lifetimes.

Inborn views are attitudes of which we are usually only dimly conscious, and they can all be lumped under the one heading of self-view: the belief that existence is divided into self and other – 'me' and 'the world'. This view has accompanied us not just since the last life, or the one before that, but from beginningless time. It seems that each human mind cherishes the notion that it is (or perhaps has 'inside' it somewhere) a *self*: the mysterious, invisible entity that each of us imagines to be the subject of 'my' experience – the thing that thinks my thoughts, feels my feelings, wills my desires, and so on. Although we may never put the idea into words, or reflect on it, we all believe in such a self – the core of our personal identity, the bedrock that somehow abides underneath the body's growth and decay, and throughout all life's comings and goings. We also think of our self as something set apart from other selves, though within hailing distance – like an island in an archipelago.

We are usually not at all clear what that self is – it seems so obvious as to require no analysis – though deeper investigation shows that we identify it in various ways: with the body, or our feelings or thoughts, or with our acts of will, with other people, possessions, nation or culture, and so forth. But in the first place, at this inborn level, self-view is not at all articulate. It is simply a deep, unthinking habit of seeking an identity and then working tirelessly to preserve it and enhance its power and happiness.

The immediate consequence of self-view, of this absolutely root attitude that one has a 'self' (separate from the world and other selves), is the arising of the three other basic afflictions – craving, hatred, and conceit. As we saw in the last chapter, craving arises from self-view because we believe that we can secure our self by experiencing or possessing certain pleasant things. Likewise, hatred is the belief that we can secure it by harming or destroying what seem to be sources of pain. Conceit arises because the notion that one is or has a self inevitably leads to comparison with other selves. We now need to examine conceit a little more deeply.

Conceit

Once you start distinguishing and classifying things, the impulse to compare them with one another is logically (and psychologically) inevitable. Comparison is the essence of conceit (*māna*, sometimes alternatively translated as 'pride' or 'arrogance'). Our belief that we are or have a self inevitably leads us to believe that our own self is unique and special, and to compare that self with other selves.

Such comparison has three possible outcomes: you may conclude that you are superior to other people, or 'equal' to them, or inferior. Each of these represents a possible form of conceit. The affliction of conceit therefore has a rather wider reference than the 'puffed up' everyday usage of the term. Of course, it's true that the impulse to compare oneself with others always contains a desire to be better than them. (Even when you think that you are worse, you *want* to be better, and feel bad because you think you are not.) From the viewpoint of the Dharma, all three notions are different forms of the same affliction, because they all spring from and reinforce the deluded notion of being or having a separate self. Each of the three variants is therefore unskilful in itself and liable to produce harmful consequences. A sense of one's own inferiority, for example, can lead to hatred for oneself and envy of the 'superior' person.

Conceit is not the same as recognizing, in a calm, non-attached way, that some people possess certain skills or qualities to a lower or higher degree than you do – or that you excel in ways they do not. In fact, to do so betokens the *opposite* of conceit, which is humility. It is only in the absence of conceit that one's comparison is healthy and objective, turning readily to respect and reverence for those who are better than you in some sense and sympathy and helpfulness for those who are not. We need to be able to assess our own skills and capacities, to recognize that we are good at some things and not good at others. Whilst if necessary we must simply do what needs to be done, if there is a choice, we need to see who is objectively the best person to do it. Sometimes that might be someone who is not so good at it, because they would benefit from the opportunity to stretch themselves. Comparison is inevitable. The problem is that it becomes mixed up with our self-cherishing.

There is a danger that a critique of conceit as an affliction can be used to dismiss difference and excellence, which taken to an extreme undermines the notion of spiritual growth. I once heard it argued that the Buddha wasn't more developed than anybody else but only *differently* developed, which would be laughable if it wasn't so sad. If you don't acknowledge somebody else's superiority, you can't revere, and you are thrust back upon your limited selfhood, which is painful. Also, it is sometimes important to recognize that somebody *doesn't* have your powers and capacities, which might enable you to help them. This need not be done in a patronizing way or in order to emphasize your own superiority. If you compare without pride, you are not attached to others seeing you in any particular way; if you are not needed, you are happy not to be made use of.

As an affliction, conceit is something we need to eliminate, but a word of caution is needed here. A certain amount of pride is 'normal' – indeed healthy. Ultimately, it has to be relinquished, but in the meantime it is important to come to terms with it. If you refuse to accept that you are important to yourself, it will be difficult for you to have a healthy self-love, and a healthy self-love is the necessary starting point for developing yourself and then for cultivating love of others and ultimately transcending the difference between self and other.

To begin with, you have to recognize that you do, in fact, love yourself quite naturally and spontaneously. Even if you hate yourself, that hatred is just a perverse form of love: you wouldn't bother to hate anyone you weren't keenly interested in. We all think of ourselves as a bit special in some way. One doesn't have to destroy that attitude – one must just get it into proportion, and make it healthy and positive through goodwill. You can move the feeling in a positive direction by reminding yourself, 'Well, I am not the only one. Other people love themselves in the same way.' Strange as it may seem, you will then be more able to identify and sympathize with others.

On this score, as on others, Buddhism is pragmatic and psychologically realistic. It doesn't say, 'What? You love *yourself*? Oh no! That's a terrible sin!' It says, 'So you love yourself. Fair enough. Actually, we all do. It's necessary. So let's try to focus on what we've got in common.' That sets you off on the right track. Later – probably much later – you can go beyond that, and realize that actually there is no distinct 'I' and 'you'. There is only love.

One lesson we should draw from this is that we'd better be a little cautious with the idea that pride is an affliction. It is, of course, at least as conceit, but that should not lead us into a morbid self-negation, which is, in any case, only another form of conceit – and a less healthy one than normal, 'pagan' self-love.

One of the secondary afflictions that flow from conceit is inflation. The Sanskrit word here is *mada*, which can mean 'madness' or 'intoxication'. Inflation includes any form of getting carried away with yourself, particularly with your real qualities, skills, and achievements: for example, having a few blissful meditations and then claiming to be the next Buddha.

Any kind of success can produce inflation. However, there is at least one common form of inflation that needs no special achievement to inspire it – the intoxication of youth. When we are young and have good health and abundant energy, we take it for granted. We have not yet been humbled by disappointments or entangled in life's snares. We tend to think of our strength and confidence as somehow our own achievement, and inseparable from us. We cannot see that they depend upon a temporary state of the body, and therefore cannot last. Similarly, we can be intoxicated with health, even with life itself. And of course, when we are inflated, we do not make a real spiritual effort.

Craving, hatred, and conceit together lead to the proliferation of views, specifically in the acquired sense, which we must now look at more closely. These acquired views are the working-out of these three afflictions in terms of one's personal attitudes and opinions.

Acquired views

The Abhidharma enumerates five kinds of views. We have already examined self-view in its inborn aspect as the basic view. As such, self-view is a sort of false intuition common to every unenlightened human mind, and it may or may not be formulated in conceptual terms. However, the acquired views, which we will now examine as a separate category, always take shape in terms of some particular expressed structure of interpretation. Sometimes, in fact, they are elaborated into philosophies and ideologies. Mostly though, they find expression in much less 'worked out' forms – perhaps as prejudices, or just assumptions embedded in the kind of language that we use. Many people would be astonished to realize there is a sort of inarticulate philosophy embedded in their routine way of talking about things, but there always is, however irrational it may be when examined closely or however much the different attitudes we hold may contradict each other.

While inborn self-view has essentially the same form in everyone, the acquired views – although the tendency to have them is universal – take multifarious forms, according to culture, individual temperament, history, and conditioning. The five categories of acquired views are their main types.

Acquired self-view

The first is the acquired aspect of self-view, the articulation, however inarticulately expressed, of inborn self-view in terms of ideas, attitudes, and opinions. This can take the form of any notion or theory about what a 'self' is. The tradition lists various typical possibilities. For example, there is the attempt to understand the self in terms of the body and its sense-organs. And there is the opposite view – that the self is something quite other than the body. Refinements and variations are possible. For example, there's the idea that the self is something that is somehow 'in' the body, or that it is 'outside' the body, and so on: one might assert that there is a soul that is quite different from the body, as many theistic religions do, or argue that the self is just made up of electrical impulses in the brain, as do many naïve materialists. Alternatively, one can attempt to define the self in terms of aspects of human experience other than the physical body – feelings, thinking, 'consciousness', or whatever. In the Buddhist perspective, all such notions are a kind of wild goose chase because in the end no self can be found.

Acquired self-view in articulate form centres on two principal positions, as we shall shortly see in more detail: the eternalist belief that one has as one's true being an immortal soul (or *ātman*) and the nihilistic belief that one's conscious experience is simply a by-product of one's body that ceases to exist when one dies. Of course, these are seldom expressed so baldly, and they exist in many shades and varieties, but these are the essential alternatives. Buddhism teaches that neither of them is true, pointing instead to the processes of conditioned arising in the course of which, under the influence of ignorance, the sense of a self is constructed again and again, to be relinquished only when we attain Enlightenment, at which point we pass beyond both being and non-being.

One-sidedness

The second type of view is what I will call one-sidedness. It is the spiritual equivalent of trying to push a wheelbarrow while holding only one handle: it is bound to lead to problems. This is a very important aspect of views, and indeed of the whole phenomenon of ignorance, and we have already briefly encountered it in connection with acquired self-view. To understand it we need to go a little into Buddhist philosophy.

What does it really mean to 'be'? The word 'being' implies something that endures, at least for a while, but when we look at things carefully, we see that nothing has 'being' in this sense. Nothing is solidly 'there'. Everything grows, decays, and dies, without finding a single moment in which it simply abides unchanged. Everything that we experience, inside us or outside, is like a cloud, never the same from one instant to the next. Of course, most things change more slowly than clouds: mountains, trees, and houses, for example, seem solid to touch, and appear persistent from the viewpoint of our human time frame. But, in fact, they are ultimately no more substantial than clouds.

Of course, the specifically human form of 'being' differs from the being possessed by clouds, trees, or any merely physical entity. As conscious (and self-conscious) entities, we know ourselves to be somehow different from things. Nevertheless, having no other models at hand, we tend to misunderstand the mystery of our being in terms of the thing-world. We imagine something in us that corresponds to the apparently solid thing-ness of external objects. In particular, we are prone to imagine that there lurks in us a 'soul-thing' and to hope that it may somehow prove to exist outside the flow of change that destroys external things.

The Buddha's most astonishing and fearless insight was to shine a bright light on the inner world, to find out where this soul-thing was hiding: to show that in fact it was nowhere to be seen. He saw that there was only the ceaseless coming and going of the five constants, and that they themselves were not things, but terms to indicate processes that were even more fleeting and insubstantial than clouds.

Being always shows itself to us in two main aspects: on the one hand, coming-into-being; on the other, going-out-of-being. Here we see arising; there we see cessation. Houses and cities are built, then crumble, or are demolished. Seeds sprout and grow into plants and trees, which later wither and die. Clouds and continents emerge, mutate, and vanish. In fact, the two threads of arising and cessation are so finely intertwined that they cannot really be separated: to be is not to be. But, from our human viewpoint, these two opposed perspectives of arising and cessation are so vivid that our eye must always be caught by one of them. When that happens, we may become mesmerized by that one, and feel reluctant to look steadily at the other. Some people fix their eye on being, and try to ignore or circumvent non-being. Others do the reverse. Buddhism regards both of these tendencies as extreme and one-sided views, and labels them 'eternalism' and 'nihilism' respectively.

Eternalists think in terms of absolute existence. They prefer to minimize or deny change, and are therefore obliged to develop strategies to deal with the awkward fact that, in the world we actually inhabit, things clearly don't last. They therefore reimagine the world, claiming to discern a 'real world' of unchanging entities or essences, beyond the turmoil of the visible world. Change, they say, is illusory, and reality is unchanging. Or perhaps – if it must be granted that things are changing now – we *will* find an unchanging world in the end, perhaps after a final showdown between good and evil. Eternalists tend to believe in a heaven, in which they envisage themselves arriving and remaining permanently. This belief gives them their characteristic angle on ethics and behaviour: we must sacrifice things now for the sake of this unchanging happy future. Logically enough, eternalists often distrust or despise the body and its pleasures.

For nihilists, in contrast, what seems most real is non-being. They see change and decay in everything around, with nothing and nobody that abides. When we die, say the nihilists, the lights go out, and the rest is silence. Admittedly, this thought has some consolations. ('No hell below us; above us only sky', as John Lennon poignantly sang.)[83] But, in the end, such a world view makes it difficult to escape the feeling that nothing matters greatly, or means very much. Nihilism leaves us with no bearings beyond the imperatives of pleasure, comfort, and whatever limited, precarious security we can piece together by force, cunning, or patient effort. In terms of ethics, nihilism has a built-in tendency – becoming ever more visible in contemporary culture – to drift towards hedonism, albeit mitigated by the diluted influence of the ethical culture of the past and a desire on most people's part to avoid unneccessary trouble for oneself while life still lasts.

Such are the two poles of eternalism and nihilism, and, until we are Enlightened, we will tend to drift back and forth between them. As we try to puzzle out the paradoxical opposition between arising and cessation, we vacillate between the two, at one moment seeing arising as more 'real', at the next, cessation. We can be optimists or pessimists.

As we strive for a more balanced position, we may become pessimistic optimists (hoping for heaven but trembling in terror of damnation), or optimistic pessimists (perhaps hoping for 'a better world for our children').

Elements of nihilism and eternalism are present in everyone's mental make-up, but most people tend to lean more towards one or the other. Which side we choose – eternalism or nihilism – is often a fundamental part of our character, one of our inborn views. But, to some extent, it is the consequence of experience in one's present lifetime. Some people grow up with a strong feeling that the world is a bad place ('You can't win'; 'Everything always goes wrong') because that is the lesson that life seems to teach them. If they are thoughtful types, they may work up those lessons into a philosophy, or adopt a ready-made one that reflects their attitude. Conversely, some people tend to tell themselves, 'OK, I admit there are some problems, but, on the whole, it is all getting better. Personally, I feel that the world is moving towards some wonderful moment when everything will flower, and then it will just stay there. It will be eternal spring.'

One-sidedness arises from our false interpretation of our experience, our failure to see things as they are. Reality is neither being nor non-being, but the middle way between the two – the process of arising–cessation in dependence on conditions.

Wrong views about morality

The third variation of the affliction of views can simply be called 'wrong views' (*mithyā dṛṣṭi*), although it is really more specific than that, because the two kinds we have just looked at – self-view and one-sidedness – are also 'wrong' in the sense that they are a misperception of reality. Those two are so fundamental to the ordinary human mind that we can't avoid them altogether, or at least not until we become Enlightened. However, 'wrong views about morality' are definitely optional, and we don't have to wait until we are Enlightened to clear them up. In fact, we can – indeed, we must – get rid of them before we can make any real headway towards Enlightenment, because wrong views about morality are misconceptions that stop us from following the Buddhist path. In fact, they undermine not just the practice of Buddhism but any form of ethical human life.

The sources usually list four forms of wrong views about morality, four beliefs, or rather disbeliefs, that cut away the very basis of an ethical and spiritual life by denying what one might call the universal mechanisms or laws of nature on which that life is based.[84] I will not use the traditional formulae, whose interpretation can be a little obscure, but spell out what they really mean, as I see it.

The Dharma life is based on the recognition of oneself as an ethical agent, responsible for one's choices and capable of altering the moral direction of one's life. If one had no such agency, there could be no Dharma life, because there would be no one able to undertake it. It is therefore a fundamental wrong view to deny that one has that capacity – and that responsibility.

Furthermore, there could be no Dharma life if one's moral choices did not have a consistent outcome, skilful choices broadly leading to a beneficial result and unskilful ones bringing unpleasant consequences sooner or later. In other words, the Dharma life depends upon the principle of karma. If there were no law of karma, one's efforts to develop love in the Mettā Bhāvanā meditation would not produce any effect – or an effect would follow at random. However much one strove to cultivate more positive mental states, one could not be sure of achieving them. The denial of the principle of karma as a natural law governing the relationship between our willed efforts and their experienced effects is therefore a serious wrong view that completely negates even the idea of effort.

The Dharma life is a process of growth and augmentation. As we make our efforts, we find that our minds become more sensitive to the world around us, see things more and more truly, and have a stronger sense of wholeness and fulfilment. At a certain stage, this process of creative unfoldment becomes spontaneous, carrying us upward on a current that is not of our willing, as if we are blown along by the wind of the Dharma.[85] This spiral process, as opposed to the worldly, cyclic one that simply acts and reacts between opposites, carries us beyond self-clinging towards Buddhahood. A further principle of conditionality underlies this process of growth, which could be called the law of Dharma, and it takes over increasingly from karma as skilful action becomes dominant. This is the natural law that governs the arising of high Dharmic attainment, even of Buddhahood itself.[86] The denial of this spiral-like Dharma law as a naturally occurring potentiality in reality is a wrong view that removes all possibility of a Dharma life.

This Dharma process carries us beyond ourselves, we might say. We cease to be identified with the artificial self that has been the source of so much trouble. But this ending does not result in a mere negation.

Something new works through us, that is neither self nor other and that can only be understood in terms of the Bodhisattva, ultimately of the Buddha. To deny the possibility of such an outcome or to conceive of it in merely negative terms is a wrong view that destroys the Dharma life.

One could sum all this up by saying that wrong views about morality involve the denial of *pratītya samutpāda* itself (that is, the denial of the truth that whatever arises does so in dependence on conditions); the denial that conditionality functions at the level of the self-conscious individual according to the law of karma; the denial that the Dharma processes arise once we have weakened self-clinging through karma; and the denial that those Dharma processes then carry us beyond self-identity to the ultimate transcendence of Buddhahood.

Wrong views of this kind take two common forms nowadays. There is first the belief that some kind of divine power governs the universe, though this is perhaps not so common in Europe as it once was. This at least has the benefit of supporting some sort of moral life, albeit on what Buddhists would consider a false basis, in so far as it stems not from a genuine natural moral responsiveness but from fear of divine retribution. Much more common, even amongst those who superficially espouse theistic beliefs, is materialism, in the philosophical sense, albeit not usually consciously held or articulated as such. From this point of view, matter is paramount, consciousness is but a by-product of the organism and life is confined to the interval between birth and death. In Buddhist terms *ucchedavāda*, usually translated as 'nihilism', results in the attitude that the only purpose of our existence is to enjoy ourselves. This attitude is increasingly common, even amongst good Buddhists.

Consumerism, which is an outgrowth of philosophical materialism and the chief religion of our times, comes from the half-formed belief that there are always better consumer goods to be had – better in the sense that they will give you greater happiness. This belief is quite consciously manipulated, especially in the field of consumer technology, by making sure there's always a new, somewhat better, product on the horizon. Envy of those who have the latest product is deliberately stimulated so that you will do whatever you can to get it yourself. Philosophical materialism is thus quite consciously manipulated by the marketing industry and is, in a sense, the basis of our economy.

Very few people would admit to, or even be aware of, holding these four wrong views about morality, but they are widely held, for all that, and those who hold them with any degree of conviction are scarcely human, because they interpret the world in a way that does not lead them to treat others in a considerate and sensitive way or to develop their own human potentialities. How could they act skilfully, when they don't believe it is possible, let alone necessary?

Precisely the opposite views are essential to a truly human life, and in particular to a spiritual life. One must recognize that human action has a moral dimension; that unskilful actions will tend to produce suffering for the person who does them, and skilful actions will produce happiness. One must also see that each of us can freely choose to act either skilfully or unskilfully; and that skilful effort can lead not only to a more fulfilled human existence, but also to a state higher than the ordinary human state. Without these views, one could believe that it was possible to live virtuously and end up in hell, or to rob and murder one's way through life and still get to heaven (or at least to a serene, remorse-free old age). It is important to recognize that many people who are not Buddhists – nor yet follow any other religion – have some perspective on this, even if it is not necessarily articulated or fully developed. After all, the Buddha simply gave particularly clear expression to natural laws that are always there, waiting to be discovered. It is fortunate indeed that this is the case, for the world would be doomed otherwise. Yet we must make this view fully conscious in ourselves, purify ourselves of its opposite wrong views, and follow through its implications to the end.

One of the consequences of having right views about morality is that one will not guide one's life on the basis of merely seeking happiness and avoiding unhappiness. One will think more in terms of fulfilment or a deeper satisfaction. Most people's idea of a happy life is one in which they have a steady supply of pleasure and are kept reasonably free from pain; and it is obvious that living consistently by moral principles may very well lead one to experience pain, at least in the short term. If I sacrifice my life for others, or for a noble ideal, I am not going to find that pleasurable, but I may find it deeply fulfilling. Conversely, in certain circumstances it may be possible for a selfish person to arrange his life so that he is kept fairly happy, at least in worldly terms; but it will not be a *fulfilled* life.

It is worth examining oneself very carefully in the light of these wrong and right views about morality. Having read this book as far as this page, you may well now be thinking, 'Of course I accept these principles!' That's all well and good, but how deeply are you convinced? How far do these principles actually guide your own actions? That is the acid test that reveals the views we really hold. What matters is not so much the principles that people say 'yes' to, but the ones that shape their choices, which often don't match what they say or think (or think they think). And if we find that our lives are still in fact shaped by wrong views about morality, we need to cultivate a deep understanding and appreciation of the principle of dependent arising, especially in its two special forms of the laws of karma and of Dharma. Then we will know that it is possible for us to guide our lives so that we find real satisfaction and fulfilment.

Dogmatism

The fourth form of the affliction of views is dogmatism (*dṛṣṭi parāmarśa*). This is an attachment to some view that one sees as of central importance in life. It often takes the form of insistence upon an ideology that claims to offer a complete explanation of human existence or society. The dogmatist seizes upon such systems with the thought, 'This is special; this is it, and everything else is wrong.' For some vivid examples, we need look no further than the history of the twentieth century. Fascism and communism are just two of the more prominent examples of dogmas that people believed in so vehemently that they were prepared to slaughter for them on a massive scale. In earlier centuries in the West, Christianity was the main source of dogmatism.

But dogmatism is not the prerogative of any one time, part of the world, or belief system. As Buddhists, we must be very careful not to cling to Buddhism, or use it as a kind of stick to beat people with. Dogmatism is an attachment for selfish, personal reasons to a set of ideas, and even ideas that are 'correct', from a Buddhist point of view, may be used for this ignoble end. It is possible to be convinced by ideas – even strongly convinced, to the point of being willing to die for them – without being attached to them. The indicator of your level of attachment is how you feel when the views in which you believe are denied or even ridiculed. There are two extremes of response: at one extreme, you feel ashamed of those views, and at the other, you feel upset and insulted. Neither of these has any place in Buddhism. In the *Brahmajāla Sutta*, the Buddha warns against becoming angry on hearing any disparagement of him, the Dharma, or the Sangha, or becoming elated on hearing them praised. Instead, one should try to be objective, correcting what is false and acknowledging what is true.[87] One could add that it is natural to feel sad and disappointed if you hear someone traducing the Dharma, because you know its value, and you may even have a sense of what their denial of it may mean for that person. Likewise, when you see the Dharma prevail in some situation, it is natural to feel pleased because you know that people will benefit. But to get upset and angry, especially to the point of wanting to commit violence, to oneself or others, whether that means blowing oneself up in a marketplace or setting fire to oneself, is to go to a dreadful extreme. Thankfully, that sort of fanaticism is very rare.

Religious formalism

Fifthly and finally, there is religious formalism. The Sanskrit words (*śīlavrata parāmarśa*) mean 'treating rules and rituals as supreme'. This is the belief that merely conforming to some prescribed pattern of behaviour is enough to lead you to the ultimate spiritual goal: for example, thinking that meditation means sitting for a long time with your legs crossed and your eyes closed, rather than making the effort to transform the mind. As practitioners of the Dharma, we need constantly to ask ourselves whether we are really practising or just going through the motions.

Such are the five kinds of views. In practice, they often overlap. For example, many religions – at least as understood by their average, unreflecting adherent – offer personal immortality to those who follow certain rules. By succumbing to the advertising and 'buying' such a spiritual package, one falls simultaneously into one kind of acquired self-view, one-sidedness (of the eternalist variety), religious formalism, and possibly dogmatism as well. Buddhism itself, if shallowly understood and 'practised' in mere conformity to the social norms of a Buddhist culture, is just as vulnerable as any other religion to being reduced to a set of views in this way. It is quite possible to cling to the forms of Buddhism for personal benefit, without any real understanding of what those forms signify, or any personal commitment to transforming oneself in accordance with them. For instance, in some forms of Buddhism it is common for people to give dāna to support monks because that is believed to be especially meritorious and therefore to ensure benefits in this life and a better rebirth. The basis of this belief is that monks who are genuinely practising the Dharma are especially worthy people, living a life of real virtue, so that supporting them is an expression of the values they uphold. However, giving dāna to monks is often not done in that spirit, but as a kind of magical exchange regardless of the actual worth of the individual monk, thereby negating the essential value of giving to him.

A lot of Buddhism, we must admit, is of that formalistic, conventional kind, and perhaps this is inevitable and largely leads to benign results, in the sense of producing a culture in which people are at least doing worthy things, even if for shallow reasons. But dogmatism can also be seen in the Buddhist tradition, especially when Buddhism is mixed up with national, ethnic, or cultural identity – a phenomenon Sangharakshita has called 'religio-nationalism'.[88]

Each kind of acquired view can be subdivided into gross and subtle. The gross ones can be eliminated by a clear presentation of the Dharma, which, as we will see later in this chapter, is the first level of penetration: penetration through hearing. The subtle acquired views can be got rid of by the second level: penetration through reflection. But the inborn views can only be destroyed by the third level: penetration through cultivation – leading to transcendental wisdom itself. Cultivation means entering into a deep state of concentration, usually in meditation, and in that state reflecting on the nature of things. One can thereby destroy the roots of ignorance in the mind's very structure. Only in this way can ignorance finally be removed, letting clarity shine finally through.

Vagueness

Because ignorance has flowered as views, the next stage unfolds: the sickly stench of vagueness (*vicikitsā*) pervades our lives. This is a sort of ineffectual vacillation between different views – a reluctance to make the effort to think clearly, and sort the wheat from the chaff in our ideas and attitudes. While vagueness can manifest in any area of life, its significance in Buddhist discourse is as a major obstacle on the spiritual path. Vagueness is passivity or indecision in the face of one's existential situation, a failure to decide whether to live the spiritual life, or *how* to live it. In terms of the five intensifiers, it is a refusal to take the step from interest to resolve.

Vagueness is consequent upon views. Wavering between views, you can fail to come to any conclusion. In particular, you can waver in your conviction as to whether there really is such a thing as the spiritual life, or – if there is – whether you yourself are capable of living it. Or you can vacillate in choosing the most appropriate way to live it.

This affliction is often translated as 'doubt', but this doesn't bring out its full flavour. In any case, doubt can often be reasonable, appropriate, and wise. It is right to doubt something that doesn't yet add up logically or experientially. The doubt you experience in the process of honestly trying to sort out your opinions is not an affliction, but a valuable function of the mind, so long as it is relatively free from craving, hatred, and conceit.

Indeed, one could go further. Honest doubt is not just something that one resolves at the preliminary stage of a spiritual path, thereafter to progress in rock-solid certainty. It is a vitally important part of that life from start to finish. Doubt can become an attitude of deep questioning that sits loose in relation to all supposed certainties, a fresh and constantly open state of mind that eventually ripens into wisdom itself. Doubt, in this sense, is an aspect of transcendental wisdom – a profound awareness of the relativity of all our knowledge and a recognition that words and concepts are not the same as reality.

If we choose to understand doubt in this way, we need to distinguish it from the affliction that I am calling vagueness. The latter is a neurotic doubt that tries to evade resolution. The Sanskrit word *vicikitsā* literally means 'two-pointedness' of mind. Far from leading us to wisdom, vagueness keeps us at a distance from it, and makes us fall into deeper confusion by dithering between those two points. Vagueness is essentially a wavering indecisiveness, an inability to make up your mind and put your energies into the spiritual life.

Some people seem to be constructed in such a way that they find it hard to make decisions quickly, and even agonize about things like whether to put jam or peanut butter on their toast at breakfast. Hesitancy in making decisions can just be an aspect of a particular kind of temperament, and to that extent it is ethically neutral; in fact, sometimes it is sensible not to make decisions quickly. But when this hesitancy gets too pronounced, it can become a barrier to the spiritual path, for that path requires wholehearted commitment and vigorous practice. If you never make up your mind about what you believe, or how to practise, or if you repeatedly change your mind about these things, you will make little or no spiritual progress.

For some people, this kind of vagueness is so habitual that they do not even notice it. It can be like a grub, hidden under the earth but gnawing away at the roots of resolve. When you sense that sort of doubt in yourself, you need first to define it. What exactly is it that you doubt? According to the tradition, doubt commonly fastens onto six things: each of the Three Jewels (i.e. the Buddha, Dharma, and Sangha), the practice you are doing, the context in which you are doing it, or the teacher under whom you are training.[89] If we are vague about any of these things it will undermine our Dharmic efforts, and we won't be able to commit ourselves.

You might find yourself thinking, 'I don't know if the Buddha did actually gain Enlightenment, or even if there is such a thing.' You might hear the notion, which is current in some quarters, that a fully Enlightened being doesn't transcend the afflictions, so you start thinking of a rather reduced Buddha in more narrowly human terms or as weak and fallible – which will limit your horizons drastically. This is not very inspiring; indeed, it completely alters the nature of the Dharma life. Or you might think that Enlightenment is possible but still doubt whether Śākyamuni achieved it, in which case you will not be confident in the Dharma, in so far as the teaching came to us from him.

Examples of doubts about the Dharma are legion. Some people, for instance, are drawn to Buddhism, but worry that it may be nihilistic because it talks so much about 'emptiness'. Others are troubled by the thought that it is essentially Asian, and therefore unsuitable for Westerners, or that its asceticism is 'life-denying', or that its philosophy is too introspectively preoccupied with the mind. Some might accept the truth of the Dharma in the abstract, but find themselves thinking, 'That's all very well, but does it really apply to *me*, 2,500 years after the Buddha?'

Thirdly, you might doubt that there can be an Āryasangha, a Sangha as refuge, because you doubt that the Dharma has been effectively transmitted through the ages, or doubt that it is possible for a real Sangha to arise, in which everybody has transcended self-clinging to some degree.

For some readers, such doubts about the Buddha, Dharma, or Sangha may prompt nothing more than a derisive snort. For others, they might bear an uneasy resemblance to thoughts they once had, or still have. Any one of these thoughts could easily be enough to hold somebody back from embarking upon the Dharma life, or even cause them to jump ship when many miles out at sea.

Besides showing itself in the form of doubts about the Buddha, Dharma, and Sangha, vagueness affects our attitudes to our own Dharma teacher, the practice we are doing, and the community in which we do it. These can be seen, respectively, as mundane correlates of the Buddha, the Dharma and the Sangha.

It might well be difficult to know whether your teacher is a refuge in the sense of having unshakeable transcendental realization, but, whether or not you feel you can determine that, your teacher is your gateway to the Buddha, because through him or her you know the Buddha and his Dharma, so you need to have confidence that he or she is able to show you the path and the goal. If you don't have confidence in your teacher in this way, you won't be able to commit yourself to practising under his or her guidance, and it would be only sensible for you to find another teacher, rather than trying to adjust the teachings you have received so that they are comfortable for you, because you may simply refashion them to suit your own wrong views. The whole point of having a teacher is that they are outside the bubble of your own egoistic perspective and can help you to burst free. If you don't have sufficient confidence in them as being able to do that, they are unlikely to be able to perform that function for you.

Doubting your teacher may lead you to doubt the practices that you are doing. For example, my teacher, Sangharakshita, asserts that practising the Mettā Bhāvanā fully and effectively will lead you to transcend self-clinging and therefore potentially can take you all the way to full Enlightenment.[90] This seems to be in accordance with what the Buddha himself says, but quite a few modern Buddhist teachers assert that the Mettā Bhāvanā is only a preliminary or *samatha* practice.[91] Unless you are clear on this issue and have resolved any doubts you may have about it, you won't find it easy to put yourself into the practice wholeheartedly, which means that it certainly won't have the effect that Sangharakshita claims is possible.

Instead of trying to resolve the difficulty, it is tempting to follow some other teaching or practice coming from elsewhere, which you think may give you what you are looking for. This is easy to do these days because so much is available. Not all of what is available is by any means bad and wrong, but it may be superficially presented or ill-digested, which could produce a confusing and undermining effect. The key point is that one is recommended to commit oneself fully and wholeheartedly to the discipline one is engaged with. If you decide that that discipline is not for you, find another one, but mixing and matching your own Dharma discipline without definite guidance is not likely to be effective. What you need in order to make significant progress is very little, but you do need to have confidence in it, and to practise it very wholeheartedly.

You also need to be able to engage with a particular Dharma community, a particular sangha, without naïve expectations of it, but also with sufficient conviction that it is an effective Dharma community, which is, at least sometimes and in some places, moving in the direction of becoming an ideal Dharma community. It is possible to see so many faults and failings in one's Dharma community that one loses sight of what is truly effective about it. You might hope that there is a better one elsewhere, but it doesn't take much looking to discover that all Dharma communities have their difficulties and disharmonies. That leads many people to become disillusioned with even the possibility of true sangha. But if you don't believe that true sangha is possible, your involvement with a Dharma community will be as a kind of club or social group, and you will yourself be part of what prevents it from becoming true sangha. In the end, if you can't resolve these kinds of doubts, you need to get out, for your own sake as much as everyone else's.

If you are prone to a doubting frame of mind in relation to your Dharma community, it is important to spend time with people at their best. When people start to lose confidence in the sangha, they tend to withdraw – they stop going to events, and look for different contexts for their retreats – so they don't see other sangha members at their best, sincerely trying to practise the Dharma in good conditions, and they forget what is possible. Unfortunately, when one begins to waver, one tends not to do the very things that would help to stop that wavering.

Because it's not an Āryasangha, a Dharma community will inevitably have an amphibious nature: it functions partly on the dry land of real aspiration and partly in the muddy waters of mundanity, and we need to know that. We need to go for refuge to the Āryasangha, not to the mundane sangha that we've joined, and it's the same with our teachers. You need to go for refuge to the Buddha, not to your teacher; but your teacher is your gateway to the Buddha, just as the sangha is your gateway to the Āryasangha. You need to be able to recognize that, although the sangha is not a full expression of the ideal, it is a valid and developing attempt at the ideal in which you can practise the Dharma effectively.

Vagueness has to be resolved if one is to make any progress, and the first step to resolving it is to make it conscious. All too often, we do not even recognize that we are being affected by vagueness: it can envelop us invisibly, like a gas, only manifesting itself indirectly, perhaps as a lack of zest in practice, or tensions with our spiritual friends. You have to make it conscious by honestly examining your thoughts and feelings, clarifying the issues about which you are vague, and thinking them through honestly. This may require you to do some study. It will certainly require reflection and discussion with more mature spiritual friends. Doubts, once you have them, can't just be put aside.

Where vagueness about one's teacher, practice, or Dharma community are concerned, there are likely to be specific issues about which you need to get clear. One important caveat here is that you should be really sure of your facts, not go on rumour, and be willing to give the benefit of the doubt where the facts are not clear. Where it is the refuges that you are doubting, it is important to make a careful distinction between them and their mundane correlates: your teacher, his or her system of teaching, and the Dharma community with which you are practising.

Once you are clear that you are suffering from vagueness in this or that area, you need to confess fully and freely to your spiritual friends, acknowledging it to be an affliction and therefore unskilful and resolving unambiguously to overcome it. With the help of your friends you then need to form a clear strategy to deal with it.

The main antidotes to vagueness are study of the Dharma and association with those who have faith, especially those who are more experienced in the practice of the Dharma than oneself. The trouble is that, when one is in a doubting frame of mind, one is more inclined to associate with people who share and reinforce those doubts rather than with people who are likely to challenge them sympathetically.

Everyone in the spiritual community is likely to experience both vagueness and doubt to some extent or another, and at one time or another. It is therefore important to deal with manifestations of doubt in your friends and acquaintances sensitively, and in a way that genuinely conduces to clarity, by encouraging clear, honest, and independent thought. Sometimes doubt erupts forcefully in somebody who has previously seemed an exemplar of inspiration – a 'good girl' or 'good boy' who suddenly, shockingly, says, 'I am not sure if I am a Buddhist.' In this situation, it isn't helpful to insist, 'Of course you are!' It would be better to say, 'Good! So, given this is what you think, now you've got an opportunity to find out whether you are or not!' You can then encourage them to identify the questions they have, then think them through in solitary reflection and in discussion with others. You can also make sure you are available to help in that discussion, in a genuinely open way that is only concerned about the integrity of the process, and is willing to accept whatever conclusions your friend reaches.

When we make an effort to clear up the intellectual side of doubt through this process, what is usually revealed 'at the bottom' is something more emotional – a fear, or an unacknowledged desire, perhaps. But very often that discovery can only be reached through an honest attempt to resolve the doubt at the level of ideas.

We shouldn't be frightened by other people's doubts, and, if we are, we should recognize in our fear a clue to an unexamined doubt of our own. Phases of doubt – our own or other people's – are inevitable. They can also be spiritually very valuable in the long run, provided the doubt is not of the destructive kind that is driven by a sense of personal injury and resentment. But, even in its destructive form (and even if it draws one away from the spiritual life), doubt may be part of a longer process that will ultimately lead the doubter closer to truth.

So we need not fear doubt. In fact, we can save ourselves a lot of time, trouble, and turmoil by making an effort to identify and address doubts, and resolving those that really boil down to vagueness. To put it another way, we should be open to doubt, but not let ourselves remain passively locked in indecision for too long. Some people indulge in unresolved doubt for many years. It is a pity to waste so much time.

Clarity

Clarity is the positive that drives out ignorance, just as light drives out darkness. That is why the Sanskrit name for it most commonly used in the Abhidharma lists is *amoha* – literally 'non-ignorance', *moha* being one of the principal synonyms for *avidyā*, which we saw was the term for ignorance in those lists. And ignorance, of course, means 'non-clarity', *vidyā* itself being a synonym for 'clarity'. No doubt, the point is now sufficiently well made: clarity is the direct opposite of ignorance!

But clarity, of course, has a positive character of its own. In brief, it is seeing things as they really are. Complete clarity is Enlightenment itself.

Clarity is a kind of knowledge, but, strange to say, not the kind that can be acquired or learned. It has to be revealed or released *within* consciousness, rather than added to it from outside. The Buddha himself says, in a famous passage in the Pali canon,

> This mind is luminous, but it is afflicted with adventitious afflictions.[92]

To use a common simile, the mind is like a mirror that happens to be obscured by a thick coat of dirt. If we can only clean the mirror, it will accurately reflect the world without distortion. By cleaning the mirror, we don't add anything to it, or improve its intrinsic quality: we just allow it to display the quality that it had all along, hidden under the dirt. In this metaphor, the dirt corresponds to the afflictions, of course, and especially to ignorance, while the action of cleaning the mirror represents Dharma practice.

Clarity is therefore the hidden potentiality, the unclaimed birthright, of every mind. As a potentiality it is deeper than any ignorance, for, if ignorance was fundamental, it could not be removed. We could say that clarity is intrinsic to the mind, while ignorance is merely inborn. We have to remove that ignorance so that clarity is revealed. Of course, we could not consciously undertake that task if we did not already possess some clarity. To some extent, however slight, clarity is therefore not just a potentiality but also an actuality. None of us is completely devoid of clarity. At the same time though, no one (except a Buddha) is entirely free of ignorance. Each of us is located somewhere on a spectrum ranging from very dark but not absolute ignorance to the threshold of perfect clarity.

In even the grubbiest mirror then, a faint and partial image of reality is discernible. This thought should reassure and encourage us. If things were otherwise, our condition would be dark indeed: we would be like people stumbling around inside a large cave, deep underground. Without even a glimmer of light, how would we ever find our way out? Worse, without eyes, how would we even glimpse a glimmer, were there one to see? We would be condemned to grope around at random, and so perhaps wander even deeper into the cave. Fortunately, things are not that bad. Even at our most ignorant, we retain some affinity with reality, some sight to see some light.

How are we to understand this in practice? Here we need to look again at our ideas about ourselves: our self-view in the acquired sense. We all interpret or understand ourselves in a certain way – usually a rather rigid way. Our self-view, by its nature, tends to make us fix ourselves as being 'such and such' a person. This very fixity tends to give self-view an oddly self-fulfilling character, and to consign us to replaying the same walk-on part in life's drama. Suppose, for example, that early in life you acquire the notion that 'I am too stupid to understand x.' With such an attitude, you are unlikely even to try to understand x; you will never risk the humiliating potential for failure that lurks within any attempt to understand x. And so of course you will remain largely ignorant of x throughout your life (and so into your next life).

But suppose your interpretation is better informed. Suppose you take the attitude (or have been taught to think) that nothing is fixed, that everything can change, and – if you make the necessary exertion

– can change for the better. Suppose, furthermore, that you apply this idea to yourself. In that case, your self-view, while far from extinct (or even fatally wounded, as yet), will nevertheless be significantly weaker, allowing other ways of seeing yourself to emerge.

Each of us therefore has at least some potential for softening the rigidity of self-view. If we only look, life is always showing us that things aren't as fixed as we think. At any moment, some experience – something as slight as a train of thought or mood – may tip the balance, and persuade the worst criminal to go straight, or the meanest Scrooge to do his Christmas shopping. And this potential for change reveals the intrinsic character of clarity.

Sometimes clarity reveals itself more or less spontaneously, as it seems, simply through the lessons of that harsh instructor, life. But we can also, and more surely, embark on its systematic cultivation through Dharma practice. The royal road to clarity is the development of penetration – the fifth of the intensifiers. Penetration, as we saw in Chapter 6, in its general meaning is the application of analytical intelligence to one's experience. However, the kind of penetration that is the basis for clarity is not the general kind (which can be ethically neutral or unskilful). It is penetration as applied not to the practical problems that arise within experience, but to the fundamental nature of experience itself. We could call this 'penetration of reality' or 'transcendental wisdom', transcending, that is, our self-view.

Of course, the necessary prelude to such transcendental wisdom is the whole spiritual path. In the classical model of Buddhist meditation, transcendental wisdom can only be developed by a mind established in meditative absorption, and the development of such absorption depends in turn upon the skilful development of the other intensifiers. There is no shortcut. Nevertheless, penetration is decisive as the final stage in that path. Without it, we will always fall short of final liberation, of complete clarity. It is transcendental wisdom that cleans away the dirt on the mirror of the mind, allowing reality to become visible.

This kind of penetration has to be developed progressively in three ascending stages, which are usually designated as listening, reflection, and cultivation. Penetration through listening refers to the effort to understand reality through hearing (or reading) what the Buddhist tradition says about the nature of things (for example, the three characteristics of conditioned existence). It consists simply in making sure you've heard it correctly, getting clear about what is being said, perhaps learning the key elements by heart.

Penetration through reflection means thinking over these ideas, digesting them, and applying them to one's own experience. It may consist in a certain amount of questioning, which is why it is so important not to confuse doubt in the intellectual sense with vagueness, as we saw above. Here one is becoming more deeply and personally absorbed in what one has learned, mixing the concepts with one's own experience. It could be said that this is the point where the Dharma really begins to strike home, directing one to what one feels to be the deepest issues of one's life. Sooner or later, if one engages in reflection on some aspect of the Dharma with sufficient intensity and wholeheartedness, there arises a sense of *conviction* that this is the truth – a sense that is no longer mediated by words and concepts but is immediate and integral.

Thirdly and finally, there is penetration through cultivation, in which you align your whole being behind that conviction and allow it to penetrate all the way through you, transforming you at a level deeper than the intellect can reach. This most classically happens in the course of meditation practice, but it need not. If one is sufficiently engaged with the Dharma and feels strongly enough the painful and humiliating nature of ignorance, one can be engaging with cultivation all the time and in all situations.

When we are doing *vipaśyanā* meditation, however, we need to be looking especially for the point of transition between reflection and cultivation, at which our reflection on the teachings has generated sufficient conviction to allow us to dwell in a direct experience of their truth, not mediated by words and concepts. If you become aware of that beginning to fade, you go back and reflect some more. And if that reflection is muddied you go back and clarify what the Buddha taught through listening or reading. In this way you continuously refine and refine your penetration into the Dharma.

These three progressive levels of penetration could be summed up as knowledge, understanding, and wisdom. Knowledge is undigested information – it doesn't get us very far, but it is an indispensable step towards understanding. By means of understanding, the grosser forms of confusion and delusion are held at bay. And, with wisdom, the truth itself finally dawns. This is the classical Buddhist route to clarity. It is as if at each of these three stages we clear a larger space within our mind so that the truth can take up residence in it. Or – reverting to my earlier metaphor – we clean away a bit more of the dirt that has accumulated on the mirror of the mind.

Penetration cleans away ignorance, but it doesn't do so in an abstract or generalized way. In practice, penetration has to deal with what we might call 'crystallized ignorance', that is, with views. As we have seen, ignorance becomes formulated and embodied in views, and especially in self-view, the first and most fundamental of all views. In terms of the metaphor of the weed of ignorance, we can't immediately just pull up the root, because we can't get to it through the noxious smell and poisonous sting of the developed plant. We have to stop the weed from spreading and then gradually clear away its growth.

This means that we must first overcome vagueness. Next, we need to gradually loosen our hold on views. Then we can make real headway to weaken craving, hatred, and conceit. If we can do that, we are in a good position to make an assault on self-view. And once inborn self-view is penetrated, clarity will shine forth more and more brilliantly, transforming our lives and those of all with whom we come into contact.

Chapter 11

....

Ardour, serenity, and equanimity

Each of the last three chapters has dealt with a set of mental events that are quite closely related to one another. In this chapter we will be looking at a rather more miscellaneous collection of mental events: three positives – spiritual ardour, serenity, and equanimity – each of which is the antidote to a specific affliction (or, in the case of equanimity, not just one affliction but two).

Ardour and inertia

Let's start with spiritual ardour (*vīrya*), which for the sake of simplicity I'll usually abbreviate to 'ardour'.

Ardour begins to appear when longing faith is strong enough to produce effective spiritual practice. The strength of ardour therefore depends upon the strength of faith. However, ardour isn't just a question of having very strong feelings of faith, but also of having the kind of mature self-governance that can nurture and channel faith effectively, and steer clear of the conditions that dissipate it.

The natural activity of ardour is to turn the mind towards wholesome states. An example may make clear what I mean by this. Suppose that you are trying to meditate, but your mind is drifting into a fantasy of sensuous longing. However, suppose too that you notice what is happening and get back in touch with faith. Through doing so, you summon up the energy that you need to steer your mind away from the contaminated, unreal objects of the fantasy (that is, contaminated by greed or hatred), and back towards the object of the meditation. That surge of energy is ardour – the action of turning your mind from the unskilful to the skilful.

But – and this is very important – ardour is not as black and white as this example suggests. It is not just the action of turning from the unskilful to the skilful. It is also the action of turning from the skilful to the more skilful, and from that to the very skilful. Ardour is thus a continuum that leads us over our current spiritual horizon. That continuum ends only – if it ends at all – in Enlightenment. Until we grasp this progressive dimension of ardour, we haven't fully understood what it means. Ardour is never satisfied.

Vīrya, which I am translating as 'ardour', has sometimes been translated as 'energy in pursuit of the good',[93] which is a big improvement on the usual energy or vigour, but I have come to feel that it is better to avoid the word energy altogether (even with the rider 'in pursuit of the good'). The trouble with energy is that it is such a general and neutral term. Breakfast cereals promise us energy; exercise improves it, and physicists tell us that matter is the condensation of it. Everything seems to boil down to energy in the end. But ardour is something much more specific: the mental force that seeks out the skilful or the more skilful, and abandons the unskilful or the less skilful.

As with some of the other positives, we will understand ardour better by examining its opposite. The affliction that is the enemy of ardour is inertia (*kausīdya*). This isn't primarily physical inertia (though that may be part of it), but moral and spiritual inertia. It is yielding to the inclination to turn from the skilful to the unskilful or the less skilful, or to persist in the unskilful, knowing it to be unskilful.

In some translations, this affliction is called 'laziness', but that suggests simply the absence of energy, whereas this mental event includes something more than that. The opposite of ardour is not (or not only) the absence of energy, but an active preference for the less skilful. 'Inertia' seems a more adequate translation, because in one sense inertia means no energy at all (like laziness), but in another sense it means energy rolling blindly down the line of least resistance. As an affliction, inertia is thus energy in pursuit of the bad (or perhaps just the mediocre). This is why many apparently energetic human activities – the quest for pleasure, wealth, or power, for example – are really forms of inertia, from the Buddhist point of view.

To be more precise, there are said to be three kinds of inertia. The first is traditionally described as 'the pleasure of lying down and not getting up'.[94] This could fairly be termed laziness, so let's call it 'lazy inertia'. Lazy inertia is the frame of mind in which you wake up, aware that it is time to meditate, but choose to stay in bed. You can see daylight through the curtains and hear people moving around, but you think, 'Mmm, this is so nice!' And you roll over and drift back to sleep. This is probably the most innocent form of inertia. Unfortunately, however, persistent indulgence in it leaves you less and less able to get up for meditation – or even for breakfast.

The second kind of inertia consists in passively allowing yourself to be swept along by the afflictions. In this case, you actually have a quantum of faith, and even some sense of the positives, but when the afflictions arise you tend to let go of the reins. After all, it is much easier to go along with afflictions such as craving, conceit, or resentment than to turn them into contentment, clarity, and goodwill. The people who suffer from this kind of inertia may be very active in worldly terms, very industrious in pursuing their less-than-skilful desires. The great Tibetan teacher Gampopa was thinking of this variety when he defined inertia as 'destroying enemies, accumulating wealth, and so forth'.[95] We could call it 'busy inertia'.

Shakespeare offers us a sharply observed portrait of busy inertia in *Troilus and Cressida*, his great drama on the Trojan War. The classical view of that war – as in Homer, for example – is of an outpouring of noble energy in the valiant exploits of Greek and Trojan heroes. Shakespeare ironically subverts this image, presenting Achilles as a monster of selfish vanity and Troilus as a brave, but rather silly, infatuated boy. Watching the intrigues and posturing of the heroes, Shakespeare's comic rogue Thersites sourly (but accurately) derides their doings as nothing but 'war and lechery'.[96] War and lechery can be energetic, but they are inertia: a headlong rush down the trench cut by conceit and craving, with no attempt to lift oneself out of it, or even to glance up at the sky.

But it is the third form of inertia that is the most interesting and revelatory: this is the 'inertia of self-excuse'. It can manifest in various degrees of intensity. Its extreme form is despair. More commonly, though, it is just the tendency to let oneself off the hook. It is the voice that whispers, 'Come off it. Who are you to live the "spiritual life"? *You* can't get Enlightened. No doubt the ideal is very noble, but somebody like you – what can you do?'

The inertia of self-excuse is, in other words, the victim mentality. It arises whenever we seize on our difficulties – our past traumas or present troubles – in order to absolve ourselves from moral or spiritual effort. This kind of inertia is particularly difficult to uproot because it is so adept at 'justifying' itself: it constructs a pseudo-moral rationale for limiting moral responsibility, and thus inoculates itself against the moral critique that might expose it. In effect, the inertia of self-excuse is the suppression of the third form of faith – longing faith, with its intrinsic belief in one's own capacity to develop.

There is another traditional analysis of inertia that is also worth exploring. In this perspective, inertia is understood as a negative stance towards the spiritual ideal. There are three varieties. The first is the 'inertia of cynicism'. This is cynicism, lack of faith, in the sense discussed in Chapter 8 – the affliction that stands opposite to faith. The inertia of cynicism sees moral principles as nothing but scarecrows erected to tame the foolish, and spiritual ideals as confectionery to console the weak. It is likely to be linked with one or more of the wrong views discussed in Chapter 10 – various forms of the belief that there is no moral order in the universe, or, if there is, that a pleasant existence can be had while ignoring it.

The second stance is 'procrastinating inertia'. In this case, you accept that the spiritual life is possible and perhaps necessary. You even feel some desire to live it. But you say to yourself, 'Not just now. I've got too much on. Maybe next year, or when I retire.'

Perhaps one of the weaknesses of Buddhism is that the doctrine of rebirth makes procrastinating inertia more tempting. Certainly, many 'born Buddhists' in Eastern countries tend to think, 'In my present life, I will just do enough to get a good rebirth. Perhaps in a future life I will make a spiritual effort.' Sangharakshita was thinking of procrastinating inertia when he claimed that 'the besetting sin of Buddhism is laziness.'[97] As a besetting sin, inertia may be preferable to fanaticism or morbid guilt, but a sin it is nonetheless.

The third negative stance towards the spiritual ideal is 'destructive inertia'. Here again you acknowledge spiritual effort to be necessary, but you find indulging the afflictions much more attractive. This is exemplified by Claudius, Hamlet's wicked uncle and stepfather, who guiltily struggles to pray to God while remaining unwilling to renounce his ill-gotten crown and queen (and determined to rid himself, by whatever means, of the troublesome Prince Hamlet).[98] Claudius' case is clearly an extreme form of destructive inertia. Dharma practitioners may encounter milder, but still significant, forms. For example, they may still frequently yield to a strong craving for alcohol or drugs, or to an urge to pursue an adulterous affair. Or they may be unable (even while knowing their emotions to be unskilful) to let go of bitter resentment towards another practitioner – perhaps so bitter that it drives them away from the spiritual community. At the mildest level of destructive inertia, one may sit down to meditate, sincerely intending to concentrate the mind, but then yield to the temptation to fantasize.

There are two major lessons that we need to absorb from the idea of inertia. One is that, whenever we are not trying to develop and maintain the positives, we are in a sense being lazy. The absence of ardour is necessarily the presence of inertia. Admittedly this is an uncomfortable idea, but we shouldn't react against it, or accuse the Abhidharma of trying to make us feel guilty. The purpose of the teaching is simply to challenge us to summon up a more heroic approach to the spiritual life. This is an objective necessity, for, if we lack all trace of that spirit, we stand little chance of making any progress.

Having accepted the challenge, we can start learning to identify our characteristic forms of inertia: to pinpoint our tendency towards, for example, lazy inertia, the inertia of self-excuse, procrastinating inertia, or whatever it might be. Once we have acknowledged and identified the inertia that possesses us, we have taken a significant step towards ardour.

But what can be said about ardour itself, the positive that drives out inertia? In the noble eightfold path, ardour is defined in terms of the four right efforts: the effort to eradicate unskilful states that have already arisen, to prevent fresh unskilful states invading the mind, to cultivate unarisen skilful states, and to maintain those skilful states already present. However, as we have already looked at the four right efforts in Chapter 1, we can take this opportunity to look at a rather different traditional account of ardour. In this scheme, there are five kinds.

Firstly, there is protective ardour: the 'ardour that arrays one in armour'. This is what protects you against your own unskilful tendencies – the effort you make to stop your mind drifting into unskilful states. It is interesting to note the military metaphor in the traditional explanation. In certain obvious respects, military and spiritual life are very remote from each other, yet both ways of life require toughness, determination, and the ability to be on guard at all times. A war can't be won by someone who isn't willing to fight after five in the afternoon, or on weekends, and it is interesting that the Buddha sometimes stressed that he came from the warrior caste, not out of caste pride, but to stress the heroic, ardent nature of Dharma practice.

The 'ardour that arrays one in armour' corresponds to the efforts of eliminating and preventing among the four right efforts. In effect it is also the same thing as vigilance (apramāda), which I will discuss in Chapter 12, so I needn't go into it further here.

The second form is the 'ardour of applied effort'. This corresponds to the efforts of cultivating and maintaining. It consists in systematically developing the positives, not only in meditation, but also amidst the ordinary activities of work and social life.

The important point to grasp here is that in general we all tend to put up with a lower state of consciousness than is possible for us.

With a relatively modest effort, we could dwell in a much more skilful mental state. Sangharakshita once went so far as to suggest that, for those committed to the spiritual life, it is possible to live in a 'dilute' form of dhyāna – to carry into one's everyday activities something of the purified and concentrated mental state found in a good session of meditation.[99] Obviously, while dealing with people and objects in the material world, we cannot remain as fully withdrawn from the senses as we can in meditation and we cannot dispense with conceptual thought. Nevertheless, it does seem to be possible to stay sufficiently focused on the positives to be able to carry out all the normal functions of life while maintaining a mood perfumed by the bliss of the first dhyāna. In such a state, one naturally floats up into dhyāna at moments when no outward task occupies one's attention, and the mind is left free to detach itself from the senses. Many of us glimpse this state from time to time, but we fail to realize that it could become our normal waking state.

The third form is undaunted ardour: the 'ardour that does not despair'. As its name suggests, this is the direct opposite of the inertia of self-excuse. It is the kind of attitude in which you say to yourself, 'Yes, I have some weaknesses and obstacles to deal with; I am not perfectly equipped for the spiritual life. But then, nobody is, at the outset. The point is that I can make an effort.'

In this frame of mind, one is undaunted by the loftiness of the spiritual ideal, even when it is presented in the most sublime terms. There is no doubt that the Dharma – particularly in the context of Mahayana Buddhism – can be very challenging. For example, as the doctrine of emptiness (śūnyatā) begins to sink into your mind, even at just the intellectual level, it may make you feel like a sleepwalker who suddenly awakes on the edge of a cliff. Likewise, as you digest the full import of the Bodhisattva ideal, with its uncompromising commitment to living for the benefit of all living beings, you may think, 'I could never even dream of that!' But with the 'ardour that does not despair', you delight in the immeasurable height and breadth of such ideals, while genuinely feeling that you can move towards them.

The fourth form is confident ardour: the 'ardour that does not turn back'. When we first set foot on the spiritual path, and especially when we are driven onto it by disillusion and difficulty in worldly life, we often assume that everything is going to get progressively easier from now on. With regard to the spiritual community, for example, we may have some naïve notions about the people alongside whom we are practising the Dharma. We may assume that everybody within the community is going to be mature and kind, and will understand us better than anyone outside it ever has. But even in the spiritual community there is conflict, misunderstanding, and ill-will. Facing such indifference or hostility, it is easy to think, 'It's too difficult for me!'

There are other possible setbacks, too. For example, after practising for some years, some people feel frustrated at the meagreness of the change that they have been able to produce in themselves.

What such experiences show is simply that, at the beginning, our faith is usually mixed with naïve optimism. When time and experience start to knock the edges off that naïvety, we need the courage and the fortitude to keep going under difficulties.

It seems that this 'ardour that does not turn back' doesn't come very naturally to us nowadays. Our hi-tech consumer society excels at giving us quickly and easily the comforts and pleasures we want. That is pleasant, but as a result we may not develop much robustness in the face of difficulties. Here we see another aspect of the warrior-like quality of ardour. I read some years ago that a major European nation had decided to abolish military service because so many conscripts were proving completely unsuited to army life. They couldn't sleep in tents. They couldn't march very far. Their arms got tired if they were asked to hold a rifle up for too long. Apparently, they were just not tough enough, and didn't have it in them to toughen up. Whilst of course the ability to do military service is not at all a qualification for practising the Dharma, this fact does suggest a general softening. Nowadays, in the face of discomfort and inconvenience, we tend to get indignant and look around for someone to blame: we feel sure somebody must have made a mistake, or failed to do their job properly.

This at least is how many Westerners respond to difficulties in the spiritual life. I risk asserting this because my personal experience allows me to compare and contrast attitudes in India and the West. I notice that my Indian Buddhist friends have a much greater capacity to put up with hardship and ignore discomfort and inconvenience when they are working for what they believe in. So perhaps we in the West need to make a special effort to cultivate the 'ardour that does not turn back' when the going gets tough. We can cultivate an awareness that there are greater issues at stake than our hedonistic desire for comfort.

Fifthly, and usually last, there is idealistic ardour: the 'ardour that is never satisfied'. As I said at the start, the refusal to rest content with any level of spiritual attainment is the hallmark of true ardour. Many people make a modest spiritual effort, achieve a modest result, and then think,

'I've done it! Time for a holiday!' It is a cliché, but often true, that the good is the enemy of the best. One of the curious unexpected by-products of spiritual practice is that it often makes us much more effective at getting what we want in worldly terms. Through ethics, meditation, and the cultivation of the positives we become more effective, more confident, more attractive and more popular. When this happens, it is easy to drift into just enjoying the fruits we have already produced: losing ourselves in a career, for example, or a romance – worldly goods whose elusiveness may have been what pushed us into spiritual life in the first place. But, if you have developed genuine ardour, you are sufficiently in touch with the ideal not to forget the ephemeral nature of such early dividends.

Some traditional analyses of ardour add a final and vital category that the other systems don't bother to mention: compassionate ardour, the 'ardour that consists in benefiting other beings'. This firmly puts ardour in a bigger context – that of the Bodhisattva ideal.[100] Without this framework, the concept of ardour as personal striving for attainment could easily become individualistic, not to say egoistic. We should never forget that the positives are positives precisely because they lead us away from the unreality of self-view, away from the contaminated states of craving, hatred, and conceit that are linked to self-view, and so towards an unwavering awareness of our fundamental solidarity with all living beings.

Serenity and stagnation

The affliction of stagnation (*styāna*) is the direct opposite of the positive of serenity (*praśrabdhi*), so once again we will discover the meaning of the positive best by seeing what it is not. What I am calling stagnation appears in the classical list of five mental hindrances to meditation, where it is usually called 'sloth' in English translations. In that context, it is paired with sleepiness (or 'torpor'). However, whereas sleepiness is a variable (and thus not necessarily unskilful), as we have seen, stagnation is definitely an affliction.

The name 'stagnation' may suggest something similar to inertia, and it may indeed contribute to lazy inertia in some cases. Nevertheless, stagnation is a much more specific affliction than inertia. It is a kind of emotional stiffness or even depression. It has three typical symptoms. One of these is a lack of physical energy, a feeling of heaviness that makes it seem wearisome to move. Secondly, there is a lack of ardour: one feels spiritually stuck, unable to find any genuine enthusiasm for the ideal.

Mind in Harmony

The third aspect – which is perhaps the defining one – is a lack of mental pliancy: the mind is so dull and rigid that it is unable to respond to what faces it. Stagnation is inattentive, and also inefficient. At the level of sense-perception you don't fully take in what you see or hear. Inwardly, you can't marshal your thoughts effectively, can't make decisions. It may superficially resemble sleepiness, but it is really a kind of congealing of the emotions, an inability to respond. It is that stolid unresponsiveness one finds in people who have received a sudden shock, but here it becomes a habitual state of mind.

A factor in stagnation can be as simple as prolonged lack of physical exercise. If you don't use your body much, and especially if you eat too much, your mind will eventually grow sluggish too. These mental effects of habitual physical inactivity are common among those whose avocation or position in society discourages bodily exertion, for instance those from upper classes or castes in some cultures. Unfortunately, the fact that in South East Asia it is often considered improper for Buddhist monks to work means that many young men in robes become quite dull – and overweight. In this respect, perhaps we should take our inspiration from Far Eastern Buddhism: in Zen it has even been said that 'A day without working is a day without eating.'[101] Such physical dullness can often be associated with a state of depression, and the antidote is simple: do some physical work, get some exercise.

But the real roots of stagnation lie deeper than lack of exercise, which may be as much a symptom as a cause. Stagnation is essentially the product of inner mental conflict. Even when you try to do things, somehow you just can't put much energy into them, because your energies are divided. Your feelings, if you could bear to listen to them carefully, would tell you that you don't want to do what you are doing. Or at least they would tell you that there are other things that you want to do much more – things that you are ignoring.

Such mental conflicts are the ultimate source of stagnation. Of course, everyone experiences inner conflicts to some extent, but stagnation becomes a palpable affliction at the stage when a lot of your energy becomes locked up in these conflicts. There develops a sort of trench warfare within the mind – the opposing powers are dug in against one another, and nothing can move. The special danger of this affliction is that it easily becomes self-perpetuating: it just digs a deeper and deeper ditch for itself. The more you suffer from it, the less you feel like doing anything.

The positive that drives out stagnation is serenity (*praśrabdhi*). In its pure form, serenity is a rather lofty mental event. It appears only in a mind that is immersed in a high meditative state – the third dhyāna. The three main characteristics of serenity are therefore closely associated with this dhyāna, and they reverse those of stagnation point for point.

Firstly, at the physical level, serenity is a feeling of lightness and ease. Your bodily experience has become very subtle and elastic, without any sense of tension anywhere. Rather than being fixed in the hard musculature and stiff skeletal frame, one is experiencing the body's subtle energy, its *prāṇa* in the sense in which that term is used in Indian yoga systems or its *qi*, as it is described in Chinese physical disciplines. When you develop it to a high degree, you feel almost as if your body is floating – like thistledown on the wind.

Secondly, at the mental level, serenity is a state of calmness and composure that begins to predominate once one enters the third dhyāna, representing the culmination of one phase in a definite process of integration and refinement. We could say that this process starts from stagnation, although fortunately most of us seldom experience the extreme of mental blockage that stagnation implies. Nonetheless, most of us will experience inner tensions and oppositions that hold back the free flowing of our energies. We start off unintegrated and therefore feel inner stresses and strains as our contrary desires and attractions pull us now this way, now that, cancelling each other out and blocking the mind's full resources.

Meditation begins to work on this right from the start. Its effect, when it is successful, is to gradually integrate those forces of the mind so that they increasingly flow into a single current, deep and full, and satisfyingly purposeful. Once, through this process, the grosser conflicts are quieted, one enters a state of inner focus, known as dhyāna, in which the senses fade to the background of attention and previously pent-up energies steadily release themselves from their conflicts and blockages, blending together in an increasingly harmonious whole. That release is experienced as ripples of intense pleasure running through both body and mind. This rapture (*prīti*) is one of the defining characteristics of the first two dhyānas. Once that release completes itself, one enters the third dhyāna. One no longer experiences that rapture because all conflict has been resolved for the time being and there is no more blocked energy to be released. The result is not any lessening of positive experience, but a passing to a far more refined state: a lightness and calm replace the more ebullient, even in a sense disturbing, rapture – and this is serenity.

The third characteristic of serenity is mental pliancy and adaptability, lacking altogether any of the stiffness that comes from fixed attitudes and opinions or the dullness that comes from inner conflict. The mind is elastic and ready, easily flowing wherever it is bidden by the meditator. Its openness and flexibility means that it can readily mould itself to new understandings and can freely expand to previously unknown horizons of awareness. This kind of pliancy of mind is clearly essential if one is to destroy ignorance, breaking through the mind's fundamental delusions about the way things are and seeing them with clarity as impermanent, insubstantial, and ultimately incapable of granting fulfilment. In other words, it is the indispensable foundation for transcendental wisdom.

Although serenity is most fully experienced in the third dhyāna, we shouldn't think of it as lying beyond the average practitioner's range of experience. The pure form I have just described – 'dhyānic serenity', to coin a phrase – is just the final distillation of something we can all taste, even in states below dhyāna. Stagnation and serenity are the extreme ends of a spectrum that encompasses all possible modes of energy, from the most immobile to the freest (from earth, through water, fire, and air, to space, in terms of the symbolism of the elements). Everyone is familiar with a certain range within that spectrum, and very few dwell at the extremes. Most of us are somewhere between: sometimes our energy is rather dull and sluggish, sometimes it is somewhat lighter, freer, and more pliable. Our strategy should be to be aware of where we stand on the spectrum and to widen our personal 'bandwidth' on the serenity side – cultivating more and more serenity, especially through meditation.

Equanimity, restlessness, and distraction

Equanimity (*upekṣā*), a positive, is opposed by two afflictions: distraction (*vikṣepa*) and restlessness (*auddhatya*). These last two are all too familiar and we will therefore look at them first, especially for what they reveal about what equanimity is definitely not.

Distraction is a sort of wavering between a range of different objects, the mind hopping or drifting from one thing to another, never fully attending to anything in particular. It is typical of a mind that has not developed the intensifiers to any degree. Some emotional engagement does connect us to an object, but there is insufficient resolve or mindfulness to hold it steady, let alone absorption or penetration to see into it at all deeply. The process of intensification beyond that initial emotional engagement repeatedly breaks down, allowing the mind to flit chaotically across a wide range of objects, according to association or what immediately calls for our attention.

It is an interesting and sobering fact that the Abhidharma presents distraction not just as a deficit of the intensifiers, but as an active process in the mind. Indeed, this is true of all the mental events, including especially the afflictions: each of them is a 'presence' or a 'something' – whether benign or malign – not just an 'absence' or a 'nothing'.

In the case of distraction, this means that there is a force in the mind that scatters the mind – a mechanism for dispersing attention, even a sort of will-to-distraction. Distraction is not merely something that happens to us; it is something we *do*. We seek it out, as a strategy for avoiding an uncomfortable confrontation with the way things are.

Restlessness, the second of the opponents to equanimity, is also an active force, but it differs from distraction. Both are forms of instability, but, whereas distraction means instability in one's choice of object, restlessness is instability in the nature of your relation to a chosen object. In other words, though you may sustain attention to a single object, restlessness makes your attitude to it fluctuate; you constantly think different things about it. This is a manifestation of craving: the mind can't settle because it is urgently looking for some pleasurable aspect in the object. It is, one might say, a restless and excitable hunger for pleasure but without quite knowing where to find it.

Like stagnation, restlessness appears in the classical list of hindrances to meditation, where it is linked with disquiet (*auddhatya-kaukṛtya*). We have already seen that disquiet can sometimes be skilful. Restlessness, in contrast, is always an affliction.

Because it does not make the mind flit between objects, restlessness is a rather more subtle affliction than distraction, and hence more difficult to recognize. You can, for instance, sit for hours in a state of restless fascination with some plan or idea, even when you are supposed to be meditating. This problem is compounded by the fact that restlessness is associated with the anticipation of pleasure, which (as we have already seen) is a factor that 'disguises' craving. You may well 'enjoy' being in a restless state: it feels lively, excited, and enthused. You may think that you are inspired or very creative because you are producing one idea after another. The restless mind jumps around eagerly, looking at the object from first one angle, then another – seeing one possibility after another. Conceit may arise with restlessness, because you can easily become intoxicated with your own cleverness and all the wonderful ideas you're producing.

Restlessness is implicit in all afflicted minds to some extent. A mind possessed by the afflictions is turbulent – constantly nosing out

Mind in Harmony

possibilities for advantage and pleasure in the things it encounters. This means we must learn to recognize this turbulence as soon as it shows its head, spotting its distinctive characteristics and identifying it before it takes too strong a hold, remembering that it is unskilful and the basis for further unskilfulness. It may have definite physical symptoms that you can learn to spot: you might feel a certain rising of energy to the head and even tingling in the limbs, for instance. Noting these when they arise can be a powerful generator of resistance to the affliction.

Restlessness and distraction make a two-pronged attack on our power to develop the positives. We must therefore learn to stabilize the mind in two distinct ways. Firstly, we overcome distraction by developing our capacity to attend steadily to a single object. Secondly, we overcome restlessness by steadying the mind in terms of its attitude to the object. This doesn't mean that we have to wait until we have overcome distraction before we can make a start on tackling restlessness. However, if we suffer badly from both afflictions, it makes sense to give at least a slightly greater emphasis to overcoming distraction first.

To some extent, this twofold plan of stabilization is already implicit in two fundamental Buddhist meditation practices. In the Mindfulness of Breathing[102] we discipline ourselves to focus the mind on one thing – the breath – thus subduing distraction. In the Mettā Bhāvanā or 'cultivation of loving-kindness'[103] we subdue restlessness by developing a consistent attitude towards a wide range of objects (all living beings), an attitude that is detached from the egoistic quest for pleasure. We train ourselves in this way through practising meditation, but for it to be effective we need to do this in the context of unifying our whole life around a solid purpose and meaning, and eliminating opportunities for being diverted from that. Stability of both object and attitude is what constitutes the positive known as equanimity, which is the very opposite of distraction and restlessness.

In Buddhist texts the word equanimity (upekṣā) is used in several senses, which though loosely related to one another are quite distinct. The equanimity that I am now referring to is a dhyāna factor that only manifests fully at a very high level of meditative absorption – the fourth dhyāna. As we have already seen, rapture (prītī) subsides when one enters the third dhyāna. However, there is another factor, bliss (sukha), that has been present in the first two dhyānas and continues in the third. Bliss subsides upon entry to the fourth dhyāna, and what replaces it is equanimity. Equanimity in this case does not mean (as it does in some contexts) a bland neutrality of feeling, but a lofty happiness that is beyond physical pleasure and pain, and even beyond joy and sorrow. We can only think of it as a calm so profound that it makes ordinary happiness seem troublesome. It is a completely serene and skilful state, free of even the slightest agitation or excitement.

However, we should not assume that we cannot taste equanimity to some extent until we experience the fourth dhyāna. Equanimity as a dhyāna factor is simply the perfection of a state that we can at least glimpse at lower levels of consciousness. Its essence is non-reactivity, so that you do not feel your sense of identity to be threatened or tempted by what it encounters and therefore stirred to hatred or craving, but you are not deadened and unresponsive; you are alive to what is before you, but not personally disturbed by it. This we can clearly make an effort to practise in the midst of our lives now – and we will find there are plenty of occasions for practice! For instance, if somebody says something unpleasant to you, even if you are reacting inside, you can choose not to let that influence your response, so you remain cool. And you can even take responsibility for the inner reaction, working to overcome it, especially by recognizing that whatever in you seems to be threatened is merely a conditioned construct and has no real existence.

Equanimity is ardour combined with contentment, goodwill, and clarity. A strong effort to realize and soak oneself in these positives can lead to a state in which the mind is completely free from the afflictions. The afflictions can't get a grip on your mind, because ardour is there, pushing you away from craving, hatred, and ignorance. Being so completely soaked in contentment, goodwill, and clarity, you don't react to anything. For example, if somebody insults or injures you, you don't react with rage. Similarly, you simply are not attracted to any of the things that people crave, and you don't fall into deluded views. You are left with your absorption in a higher calmness and even-mindedness. This is why equanimity is usually spoken of in terms of *balance*: if you have it, you are not impelled in one direction or another.

There are three levels of equanimity. First of all there is the 'equanimity of the balanced mind'. Here you have achieved this balance but quite a bit of effort is still required to maintain it. Perhaps you have started to get some experience of equanimity in meditation, but you constantly have to make an effort because your mind naturally tends to slip back into turbulence – into restlessness or distraction. But with effort – probably quite a lot of effort – you can maintain that balance.

The second level is the 'equanimity of the mind at rest'. Here, the mind begins to steady itself in a state of balance. It no longer requires

Mind in Harmony

a great effort to remain in it. You just have to make a little adjustment now and again, when old habits try to reassert themselves, or when difficult situations impinge on you.

Thirdly and finally, there is the 'equanimity of the spontaneous mind'. At this stage, you don't have to make any effort at all. Quite spontaneously – quite 'naturally', in a sense – you lack any emotional engagement in unskilful things. Nothing can shake your balance.

We need to develop equanimity in order to drive out distraction and restlessness. When we find ourselves experiencing distraction, it is helpful to think in terms of actively developing equanimity. Even if you haven't been meditating for very long yet, you probably have some sense of what it is like to be in a stable, balanced, pliable state of mind. If so, you can make an effort to turn yourself towards that state.

Similarly, we need to recognize restlessness for what it is and is not. It isn't truly a pleasant and inspired state; it is exactly what its name says – restless, unsettled, unsatisfied. Having seen what is going on and detaching ourselves from it, we have to allow ourselves to experience boredom, neither restlessly questing for pleasure nor idly seeking something to distract us. From that boredom, if we persist with it long enough and deeply enough, watching what is going on without being carried away by it, equanimity may begin to flower, and we may experience genuine inspiration arising within us. Neither distraction nor restlessness are 'natural' modes of functioning: they are neither inevitable nor 'normal' (in the sense of 'healthy' or 'acceptable'). We do not have to dwell in them.

Keeping equanimity in mind can help us to overcome other afflictions too. For instance, when we are reacting to some painful event with hatred or its secondary afflictions, such as resentment or envy, we need not just stoically endure that pain, although that may be useful as a starting point. We need to have a sense of something positive to replace the reaction, and we can get this by recalling the peace and beauty of the state of equanimity – at least to the extent that it is possible for us.

This brings us to a final and very important principle, one that is perhaps the key to Dharma practice from the point of view of redirecting the mind's current away from the afflictions. In most cases we will have the greatest success when we are able to call to mind, as a living experience or at least an echo of such an experience, the positive that corresponds to each affliction. Each of the three sets of mental events we have met in this chapter – ardour and inertia, serenity and stagnation, and equanimity and distraction and restlessness – represents a polarity that we all experience. There is a continuum from inertia to ardour, and we are always located at some point on that continuum. The same could be said of serenity and stagnation, and also of equanimity and its twin antagonists, distraction and restlessness. In each case, our spiritual task is to shift our position – if only an inch at a time – towards the pole of the positive.

Of the three, ardour is in practical terms the most important, because without it we would not take the steps necessary to develop serenity and equanimity. Accordingly, for many of us the cultivation of ardour is where we ought to focus our endeavour. We need to make more effort with effort. Of course, the task of cultivating ardour may require us to go back one stage and strengthen faith, for ardour is, in a sense, simply faith raised to critical mass, in so far as it is strong enough to actually change us. However, it may be that what we need is not so much to intensify faith as to learn how to nurture and use what we already have: to apply it through mindful self-discipline, and avoid dissipating it in distractions. In particular, we need to be conscious of what 'effort' means in our own experience, to learn to recognize and detect within ourselves both ardour and its enemy, inertia.

Chapter 12

....

Mindfulness and the mind

We have almost reached the end of our exploration of the unenlightened mind. Just one positive and three secondary afflictions remain to be dealt with: vigilance, together with inattentiveness, unawareness, and carelessness. However, I am going to change procedure and treat them in the context of a larger discussion, because the way in which the mental events are usually arranged does not, in my opinion, sufficiently bring out a very important aspect of training the mind: mindfulness. I am therefore going to deal with those mental events together with two more – attentiveness and awareness – since they then offer a complete picture of what mindfulness means. Attentiveness is found in the five intensifiers and has already been discussed in that connection. Awareness does not appear in the Abhidharma list as such, although its opposite, unawareness, is included among the secondary afflictions, together with the opposites of attentiveness and vigilance, which are inattentiveness and carelessness.

I am taking up this topic as the last step in our exploration of the fifty-one mental events partly because it links us back to our first list, the constants, the five structural elements that are present in every mind-moment. From this perspective we can get a clear idea of how we work with our immediate experience and how therefore we make best use of the system that we have been investigating.

What is mindfulness?

The way we talk about mindfulness is often rather vague. Of course, all Buddhists know that it is important to be mindful, but, if somebody said to you, 'Be mindful!', would you know precisely what sort of action was being urged upon you? It would be interesting to gather up readers' answers to this question and compare them. I am fairly sure that the ideas expressed would be relevant but quite varied. Consequently, I think it is useful to clarify and articulate how the various practices that we call 'mindfulness' fit together as a whole on the basis of this classical analysis of mind, so that we can get a more precise idea of how to be mindful.

To begin at the beginning, what is mindfulness in general terms? We can answer this question in two ways. Mindfulness may refer either to a particular quality of consciousness or to the effort to create that quality of consciousness in oneself. We can thus think of it either as a process or as the final product of that process. But, whether we are thinking of the product or the process, mindfulness clearly has to do with the highest possible lucidity and clarity of the mind.

To proceed further we need to refer back to our discussion about the nature of mind in Chapter 2. We learned then that mind is entirely momentary, being an unceasing flow of mind-moments (*citta*). At the same time, there is a certain consistency in the structure of each of these mind-moments. However they may differ from each other in other respects, they share a kind of regularity of pattern that makes the mind more knowable. According to the Abhidharma, each mind-moment consists of five factors or aspects – five constants that are always present whenever there is mind, indeed that together constitute mind. I am going to refresh our memory of these a little more fully, since they are one of the keys to understanding the full significance of the word mindfulness.

The five constants

The first constant is contact (*sparśa* in Sanskrit). Contact is the meeting of a sense-faculty with an object, together with the consciousness that arises from that meeting. For example, contact is the eye registering forms, or the ear hearing sounds. At this stage the mind has not yet identified the nature of those forms or sounds; nor has it developed an attitude towards them. Contact is said to be just the 'bare illumination' of the object, without understanding or response. Obviously, we experience many contacts in each mind-moment. They include not just the data that reaches us from the 'external world' via the physical senses, but also the memories, thoughts, and images that pop up into consciousness from some mysterious source within us, the mind itself being considered as an additional sense-faculty.

The next constant is feeling (*vedanā*) – a hedonic response that judges contact as pleasant or painful. (A third possibility, neutral feeling, is situated between the other two, really indicating minimal stimulation.) Pleasure and pain (*sukha* and *duḥkha*) are inherent in the nature of consciousness, and are part of the experience of all sentient life. In human beings they can take subtle mental forms for which the Buddhist texts reserve the terms joy and sorrow (*saumanasya* and *daurmanasya*). But whether feeling is physical or mental, consciousness always finds itself positioned somewhere on the spectrum of pleasure–pain.

Third comes interpretation (*saṃjñā*). This is the process whereby we fit the data of contact into the vast network of information stored in our memory. Interpretation is the mental act of picking out a particular object, recognizing its distinguishing features, and then assigning a label to it. Interpretation not only classifies the object but associates it with relevant previous experiences. Like the other constants, interpretation goes on all the time. Its accuracy and quality are very variable, but it is always at work, organizing the torrent of sense-impressions into an intelligible world around us.

Fourthly, there is will (*cetanā*). Will is the way we respond to contact, feeling, and interpretation, and it generally makes us move either towards the object or away from it. The choice mostly depends on the kind of feeling – pleasant or unpleasant – that the object evokes in us. (A neutral feeling tends to prompt indifference.) Within the broad category of will falls the whole range of human emotion and volition. However, we must remember that will is much more than the conscious will. In a sense, it is the whole movement of the mind towards the world, and most of that movement is instinctive and unconscious.

The fifth constant is attention (*manaskāra*). The function of attention is to 'bind together' the remaining constants. It is the act of *constructing* experience on the basis of the other four, for consciousness isn't simply a passive registering of experience. Attention could therefore be defined as the union of the four other constants in the 'act' of consciousness, an act that is performed afresh in every moment, and is cast in the form of a subject attending to an object.

The constants are, by definition, all present in each mind-moment. However, they also produce one another in a causal sequence, distributed over a number of mind-moments. We are at every moment experiencing new contacts, while also experiencing the feeling and so on produced by previous contacts.

This then recapitulates the five constants, in bare outline. In the present context, I have limited my reminder of them to what is necessary as a basis for my discussion of mindfulness. However, I still have a bit of memory-refreshing to do before embarking on that discussion. We need to relate the five constants to the principle of karma, with its two aspects of intentional action, which is what karma means, and its result for the agent (*karma-vipāka*).

Contact and feeling are karma-results, not karmas. When we pay attention to any sense-object we cannot determine what it looks like or whether it will feel pleasant or painful in an immediate sense. The act of attention itself is karmic, but how it appears and what impact that has on us is not in our immediate power to determine: if we shine a torch into a room, the torch does not decide what will be illumined. Of course, we can decide to attend elsewhere or to alter the appearance of the object in some other way, but not directly by way of contact and feeling themselves. They are, in this sense, passive. What is there is what contact senses and feeling feels.

Will, by contrast, is our emotional and volitional response to experience. Admittedly, it often seems to us that we cannot control such responses, but that impression just reflects our spiritual laziness and our unconsciousness of our own will. Sooner or later we have to face the fact that we are fully responsible, not just for our actions but also for our desires. We can't stop life producing pleasure and pain in us; we can't stop nettles from stinging painfully or chocolate from tasting good. Nevertheless, we *can* refrain from getting addicted to pleasures and chasing after them; and when something or someone hurts us, the choice is ours whether to respond with rage and resentment or with patience and understanding. We have a lot of control over this in the present moment. Will is therefore a matter of karma, and not of karma-result.

Interpretation is a more complex case. Here there are aspects that are karma-result and aspects that are karma. A lot of the basics of our interpretation are more or less given by our sense-organs and nervous system. Because we are human beings, the world appears to us in a certain way, and we share this level of interpretation with the animal kingdom. But there are 'higher' levels of interpretation that involve more complex inferences and judgements. Far from being neutral, the information we get from this level of interpretation can be very unreliable. For example, the judgement 'They're laughing at me' could be completely mistaken – and dangerous. This kind of interpretation is much more a matter of choice than the first kind. We can, then, distinguish between instinctual interpretation, which is broadly a karma-result that goes with simply having a human body, and the higher-level making of judgements about the world and coming to ideas and views about it that is clearly karmic.

Mind in Harmony

As we have seen, attention consists in drawing the other constants together and binding them to an object. This process is certainly not merely passive, although it may feel that way when one is drifting around in meditation. There is a powerful current all the time directing us to experience, usually not very conscious, but also susceptible to conscious direction. Attention is therefore karmic.

For the practical purposes of mindfulness, the constants thus divide into two kinds: contact and feeling are karma-results, while will and attention are karmas, and interpretation at the level of judgement is also karma. As we will see, these distinctions are very relevant to the following analysis of mindfulness.

In Buddhist discourse, there are three terms that together map the field of mindfulness: *smṛti*, *samprajanya*, and *apramāda* (to use their Sanskrit forms). Each of the three (particularly *smṛti*) is sometimes used generically (i.e. it can mean 'mindfulness' in a broad sense), but each one also has its own specific shade of meaning. To bring out that meaning, I will translate *smṛti* as 'attentiveness', *samprajanya* as 'awareness', and *apramāda* as 'vigilance'. Our next task is therefore to explore each of these three concepts, and see how they are related to the constants and the karma/karma-result process.

Attentiveness

Let's begin with attentiveness or *smṛti* (Pali *sati*). Of the three words, it is probably *smṛti* that crops up most frequently in Buddhist texts. It literally means 'memory' or 'recollection', but these definitions relate to *smṛti* as a generic word, rather than in the specific sense I now wish to define. In this sense, attentiveness is mindfulness applied to the bare facts of experience – that is, to contact and feeling. The practice of attentiveness consists literally in *attending* to that data in its raw form, before it starts to be processed by interpretation and will.

Attentiveness is thus, on the one hand, the effort to become more conscious of what your senses are telling you. On the other hand, attentiveness is also the effort to 'be in touch with' feeling. But remember that 'feeling' here means only the quantum of pleasure or pain (or joy or sorrow) produced by contact. It does not include the emotional/volitional response to that pleasure or pain. Attentiveness to feeling simply means knowing clearly whether your body is comfortable or uncomfortable, whether the taste in your mouth is nice or nasty, whether you find the colour of the wallpaper soothing or jarring, whether the words you have just heard spoken please or displease you, and so on.

Accurate knowledge of contact and feeling is extremely important, and we can't take such knowledge for granted. Precisely because each mind-moment arises as a single act of 'mind making', we usually fail to distinguish clearly its component elements of contact, feeling, interpretation, and will. Usually, as soon as contact and feeling arise, we quickly wrap them up inside our interpretation of them, without examining them carefully. Will then reacts to that. Consequently, we very often misjudge the raw data of our experience, and live our life on the basis of the secondary level of interpretation. In other words, we act from prejudice and habit, failing to see clearly what is in front of us.

Imagine, for instance, that you hear a loud knocking on your office door. Before you have even opened it, you know that it is X, and you immediately tense up for a scuffle, because you are sure that he is up to mischief. X is a very aggressive person, or so you think, and he rather despises you. The loud knocking just confirms his mood. You guess that he has discovered a certain error in your work – a gaffe, concealed until now, that has been troubling your self-esteem – and now he is going to enjoy taking you down a peg. You feel a pang of loathing for him, and wonder anxiously whether anyone else will be in the outer office to overhear the embarrassing scene that is about to ensue. Even before your hand has reached the doorknob, the words of a cutting riposte have begun to take shape in your mind.

Actually, the truth is that X isn't aggressive at all, just very open and forthright. And, in fact, he thinks quite well of you, although it's true he does tease you a bit (but no more than he does everybody else). In any case, when you open the door, you do not see X at all, but your boisterous friend from down the corridor, whose exuberant banging at the door expressed his enthusiasm to pass on some excellent news.

Very often, what we *think* we are hearing is very different from what we are actually hearing. Likewise, what we see is not what we think we see. Interpretation is constantly constructing around us a world of innumerable half-truths, and quite a few utter falsehoods. The function of attentiveness is to heighten our awareness of contact and feeling, so that a gap opens up between them and interpretation.

As we have seen, interpretation has two aspects. The primary level is the almost mechanical functioning of our perceptual apparatus. We may be able to let go of this level in very deep meditation, but in daily life it operates automatically. There is also, however, a higher, secondary level that is more conceptual and more tractable to the conscious will, and attentiveness in daily life consists in trying to hold this secondary level of interpretation in abeyance as much as possible. You can't entirely suppress it, but you can deprive it of fuel, so to speak, by keeping a firm hold on the raw data of contact and feeling, and discerning what that data does and does not contain. The Buddhist tradition – as represented for example by the *Satipaṭṭhāna Sutta* – generally recommends that we start by cultivating attentiveness to contact (focusing in particular upon bodily sensations).[104] As you get more in touch with contact, the scope increases for developing attentiveness to feeling.

Attentiveness is to be developed both in this general way, throughout one's daily comings and goings, and also in a more intensive way through meditation. In the Mindfulness of Breathing, for example, you attend to the sensations of the breath. In fact, you try to attend to them so minutely that you suspend or attenuate not only the secondary level of interpretation, but even the primary one. In other words, you may slip out of the habitual process through which you mentally label the breathing as 'breathing'. In this state, your sense of your surroundings, and even of your body, may recede to the periphery of your consciousness, as the breath itself becomes something fascinatingly unfamiliar. It becomes 'pure' in the sense that it has been stripped of its usual interpretative packaging. Instead of appearing as part of the routine furniture of a world shaped by appetite and ego, the breath can become something mysterious and indefinable, something that has escaped a little even from the framework of space and time.

The more experience we have of this intense, meditative form of attentiveness, the more we can bring a general attentiveness to bear upon our doings in everyday life. We can thus learn, at moments of emotional arousal or stress, to suspend our automatic habits of interpretation, and come back to the only thing that we securely 'know' – the bare data of experience-as-experience, as opposed to our secondary 'working up' of that experience into the fantasies and speculations of interpretation. To go back to my example, the practice of attentiveness allows us to hear a knock on the office door as simply a knock on the office door, and to surround that experience with a kind of openness. If the thought 'I am under attack!' arises at all, we will recognize its secondary, fabricated nature and treat it questioningly, putting our vigilance on the alert to protect us against the arising of unskilful states.

Attentiveness is the foundational aspect of mindfulness, but this doesn't mean that one must focus exclusively on attentiveness, postponing the practice of awareness and vigilance until 'later on'. In fact it is vital to practise all three forms of mindfulness as much as one can right from the start of one's spiritual life. However, until you have built up a strong capacity for attentiveness, your practice of awareness and vigilance won't have much power or delicacy.

Although attentiveness is not listed as a positive but as an intensifier, failure to be attentive is listed among the secondary afflictions as inattentiveness (*muṣitasmṛtitā*). This is characterized by a kind of vague forgetfulness, blundering, and awkwardness, not really knowing what is going on, losing things, failing to notice. No doubt it is sufficiently obvious to require no further explication. The drunkard might be the best image for it.

Awareness

Sometimes when one reads or hears discussions of mindfulness, one gets the impression that attentiveness – 'being in the present moment' – is the whole story. But we exist in a world with other beings, not in isolation. Consequently, while we can 'hold off' interpretation and will to some extent, we cannot function without them entirely. The more one thinks of mindfulness exclusively in terms of attentiveness, the more one risks weakening one's sense of the wider context of one's practice.

Very few people – even Buddhists – practise meditation as a full-time occupation. We may meditate at some point every day, and go on retreat from time to time, but at other times most of us have jobs to do, and many have families to look after as well. Consider the example of work. Let's say that your work involves loading boxes onto shelves. Will it really help you to believe that mindfulness consists of nothing but attentiveness to the sensations of the box in your hands – its weight and the smooth, hollow feel of the cardboard? I don't think so, because your relation to the box goes beyond that: you have to get it up onto the shelf! No doubt you will benefit if, at certain times, you try to bring a bit more attentiveness to the physical sensation of doing so. But if you take that practice so far that it leads to a ten per cent fall in the number of boxes you load, you may find that it brings you more troubles than blessings. Attentiveness therefore needs to be located within a wider frame of intelligent awareness. This wider frame is designated by the word *samprajanya*.

Samprajanya (or *sampajañña* in Pali) is formed from the root *jñā*, which expresses the idea of cognition or knowledge (both terms stem etymologically from the same Indo-European root). *Jñā* is related to *prajñā* ('wisdom') and *jñāna* ('knowledge') – words we may be more familiar with. It is also – significantly for the present discussion – related to *saṃjñā* (which I am calling interpretation). *Pra-* is an emphatic prefix, reinforcing the meaning of the main word, and *sam-* is a prefix that means 'together'. The meaning of *samprajanya* is therefore something like 'complete knowing' or 'knowing as a whole'. The English word 'comprehension' is often used to translate *samprajanya*. However, I think we need a word that suggests not only the idea of 'understanding' but also the idea of 'not-forgetting'. 'Mindfulness' would be appropriate, but we are already using that as our generic word. I will therefore render *samprajanya* as 'awareness'. According to the *Oxford English Dictionary*, to be 'aware' of something is to be 'informed, cognizant, conscious, sensible' of it.

Awareness is mindfulness as applied to the third constant, interpretation. Attentiveness can lead us to a sense of standing outside time, because we are focused on the bare sensation without labelling or contextualizing it, which means not drawing it under the heading of time; but the practice of awareness is more to do with maintaining mindfulness in or through time. It is the unceasing, moment-by-moment effort to bring our interpretation in line with reality.

Awareness operates on a hierarchy of levels. We can usefully distinguish five such levels, which I will designate as (i) functional awareness, (ii) awareness of purpose, (iii) awareness of means, (iv) awareness of practice, and (v) awareness of reality. I should mention that, while the last four are thoroughly traditional (they are to be found in the Pali commentarial tradition), the first is my own addition to the list.

By *functional awareness* I mean the ability to discern clearly what something is, and to label it correctly, within conventional terms. This includes being able to fit into the larger shared framework of space and time. This level is taken for granted (and therefore ignored) in the traditional accounts, but I find that it can be helpful to acknowledge it explicitly. I have met some earnest Buddhist practitioners who are strangely lacking in this 'functional awareness'. They have some capacity to bear their spiritual practice in mind, but can be utterly oblivious to the fact that they frequently disrupt other people's meditation by arriving in the shrine room late!

The second level – and this is where the traditional analysis begins – is *awareness of purpose*. This does not just refer to spiritual purposes; it includes all your mundane aims too. If you are the sort of person who sometimes walks into the kitchen or the garage only to realize that you have already forgotten what it was you came for, you probably need to do some work on this level of awareness. It is the faculty by which we are able to keep clearly in mind what we are trying to achieve, without getting sidetracked.

The third level – *awareness of means* (sometimes called 'awareness of suitability') – is very closely related to awareness of purpose. We need not only to keep in mind what we want to achieve, but also to be able to judge whether the means we are using is the best, or even whether it will achieve that end at all. At the most obvious level, if we want to get to the top of a mountain quickly, there is (usually) no point in walking in the opposite direction. We need to discover the most direct route and follow it. More significantly for the Dharma life, if we are trying to focus our minds in meditation, it is necessary to have a certain amount of regularity and even discipline in our lives, especially in the early days of our efforts. So cultivating a chaotic and distracted lifestyle is not likely to be a suitable means. It is essential to have a critical awareness of whether or not the methods we are using and the life we are living are really supporting our Dharma goals if we are to make any progress. High ideals are not enough.

Then, fourthly, there is *awareness of practice*. This assumes that you have a spiritual commitment, and that in order to fulfil that commitment you have chosen to live and behave in a certain way, and to do certain things, including formal spiritual practices such as meditation. In other words, you have decided to cultivate certain states of mind through certain means. Those states of mind are going to be the content of your meditation, but you will want them to pervade your consciousness, as far as possible, at other times too. Naturally, the specific content of this effort will change over time. At one time you may be focusing on reducing craving, for example, while at another you may be more concerned to develop loving-kindness. But at any time there is always something that is the spearhead of your attempt to develop yourself, something that you are trying to stay in touch with in every situation.

Traditionally, this aspect of awareness is called 'comprehension of the subject of meditation'. If, for example, your main meditation practice is currently the Mindfulness of Breathing, your awareness of practice will consist of the attempt to remember to bring attentiveness to your breath at frequent intervals throughout the day and to focus on it exclusively during your meditation sessions. But awareness of practice also goes a bit deeper than that. It should include a sense that you are doing the Mindfulness of Breathing not for its own sake, but in the service of some spiritual goal: perhaps to develop concentration (*śamatha*) and freedom from the hindrances. For spiritual life to be effective, there should always be a particular spiritual aim that you are pursuing.

That spiritual aim needs to be derived from some aspect of your *awareness of reality* (*amoha samprajanya*: literally, awareness of non-delusion, or clarity, in my nomenclature). This is the fifth and highest level of awareness. At the point of Stream Entry,[105] of course, awareness of reality begins to be direct, intuitive, and non-conceptual, but, until that point, it has to be expressed through some kind of representational system – what we could call a 'reality view'. Broadly speaking, a reality view consists of a set of ideas, a set of symbols, or some combination of the two. Such things are necessary to 'mediate' between your actual existence and your ideal. Buddhist *sādhanas* – visualizations of deities and recitation of mantras – are an instance of the symbolic kind of 'reality view'. In contrast, the Abhidharma systems on which this book is based are complex and sophisticated examples of the conceptual kind.

Whatever set of concepts or symbols you use, awareness of reality needs to be present in your life in some form, to direct and sustain your awareness of practice. When that happens, your awareness of practice can infuse and clarify your awareness of purpose and means, which in turn can permeate and strengthen your functional awareness. In this way, the whole range of your interpretation is gradually transformed by awareness, and so becomes more and more imbued with your understanding of the way things really are.

We therefore need to be as clear as possible about what our 'reality view' is. This doesn't mean neatly reducing it to a single formula, or trying to pin it down with legalistic and detailed precision. Our reality view should not be fixed, but evolving and deepening all the time, so it needs fluidity and flexibility, but these qualities are by no means the same as vagueness and incoherence. It is very important to have a relatively well worked-out 'reality view' as a framework shaping and informing one's practice, for that view will ultimately give one direct access to reality itself.

A lot could be said on the question of how to cultivate awareness: so much that it would be impractical to try to deal fully with such a vast topic here, and I will have to confine myself to briefly indicating a few things. Obviously, study of and reflection on the Dharma is vital to developing a 'reality view'. Making the effort to define (and periodically review) one's spiritual objectives is essential to awareness of practice, and solitary reflection and discussion with spiritual friends will usually be vital parts of that effort. In addition, there are many methods – the use of 'mindfulness triggers', for example – by which we can try to carry our sense of our spiritual purposes into all our routine activities.

Awareness is not explicitly enumerated anywhere in the list of fifty-one mental events, although it is implicit in a number of the other mental events. Its negative counterpart, unawareness (*asamprajanya*), is, however, in the list of secondary afflictions. Unawareness, in general, is a lack of clarity about where one is, what one is doing, why one is doing it, and how that relates to the larger issues of life. It is characterized either by a dreamy, drifty state of mind, disconnected from life around us, or by a preoccupation with immediate sensory stimuli and the needs of survival. One could even call this 'stupidity', because that is how it will appear to those who are rather more alert.

Vigilance

Finally then, we come to *apramāda* (or, in Pali, *appamāda*), the third of the three aspects of mindfulness. You may recognize this word if you have ever heard the Buddha's last utterance quoted in Pali: *appamādena sampādetha* ('with mindfulness, strive on'). That is perhaps an instance of the word being used in the generic sense, but, like the other two terms, *apramāda* also has a very specific meaning. It is formed from a root word (*māda*) that refers to drunkenness, intoxication, or even madness. (We come across this word in the last of the five precepts: *surāmeraya majja pamādaṭṭhānā – majja* being the Pali form of the Sanskrit *māda*.)[106] The literal meaning of *apramāda* is therefore something like 'non-intoxication' or 'non-heedlessness', and it indicates a state of being 'on watch' against spiritually dangerous mental states. I shall therefore translate *apramāda* as 'vigilance'. Vigilance is listed as a positive, and its opposite, *anapramāda*, 'lack of vigilance', which I translate as 'carelessness', is listed among the secondary afflictions.

Vigilance is the faculty that is awake to the moral quality of one's volitions, a steady receptivity to the messages delivered by conscience. It means being on guard against the arising of the *kleśa*s, the 'defilements' or 'afflictions' – unwholesome emotions that produce negative karma. In terms of the constants, vigilance is therefore concerned with will.

In the abstract, we 'know' that negative emotions like craving, rage, and resentment are the enemies of our spiritual goals. The trouble is that they so often take us off guard, and, once they have arisen, they are very hard to subdue, at least for a time. Prevention would be much better than cure, but all too often we simply don't see them coming, because we are not practising vigilance. How then do we develop vigilance? The main practice here is the very important one of confession. As well as confessional practice, however, one can also strengthen vigilance by cultivating the habit of asking oneself moral questions – for example, 'What is the moral quality of the mental state arising within me right now?'

Such then are the three forms of mindfulness: attentiveness, awareness, and vigilance. Attentiveness is the effort to discern, clearly and steadily, the actual content of contact and feeling, suspending the habitual patterns of interpretation that constrain and even distort them. Attentiveness therefore means 'being in the present moment', calmly but vividly. It is a discipline that restores freshness to our experience of everyday things, reinvesting existence with newness, even with aesthetic enjoyment.

Awareness is the cognitive dimension of mindfulness. It brings us from the timeless moments of attentiveness back into the flow of time, but equipped now with clarified understanding. While attentiveness seeks to put aside interpretation, or at least hold it at bay, awareness is the ongoing endeavour to educate and reconstruct interpretation in the light of our truest understanding of things. To practise awareness is to stay in touch with that understanding, so that it informs our actions in each moment of the day. By purifying interpretation, the ultimate function of awareness is to destroy ignorance and replace it with wisdom.

Vigilance operates within the framework of understanding created by awareness. It is like a protector, keeping guard over will (i.e. the emotional–volitional side of the mind). Its ultimate aim is thus to eliminate greed and hatred and replace them with compassion.

The value of the threefold model of mindfulness as comprised of attentiveness, awareness, and vigilance is that it relates the various dimensions of mindfulness to our understanding of the mind as a whole. As a result, the model also makes it clear that it is not enough to cultivate one of those dimensions alone: we need to make an effort to develop all three, and all three will be involved in eliminating and avoiding the afflictions, courting and cultivating the positives, and using the intensifiers finally to break through all the delusions about ourselves and our world that cause us so much pain and lead us to do so much harm.

When we have developed these three aspects of mindfulness to their highest degree, the mind is completely transformed and the analysis of the mind we have so painstakingly completed no longer applies. The minds of those who have attained to complete clarity pass completely beyond our normal understanding.

Part 5

The Enlightened mind

Chapter 13

··

The psychology of liberation

We now have a complete picture of the mind, in terms of the mental events of which it is constituted. However, it is only a picture of the *unenlightened* mind. We have from time to time caught glimpses of the Enlightened mind and what that is like, but we have not explored it at all comprehensively.

Of course, we know that the Enlightened mind does not contain any of the afflictions, or even the possibility of them. We could say therefore that it is made up of the positives. That is half right, in so far as it is certainly not a mere negation of the afflictions. However, even the positives cannot adequately describe its contents, although the positives at their superlative degree define the horizon over which the Enlightened mind disappears from our ordinary understanding. Each of the positives is represented in that mind in a form of such sublimity that words like contentment, faith, goodwill, even love and compassion, simply fail, because there is such a radical difference in kind between what we normally mean by them and the qualities of a Buddha.

The Buddha himself was very clear about this:

> *There is no measuring of man,*
> *Won to the goal, whereby they'd say*
> *His measure's so: that's not for him;*
> *When all conditions are removed,*
> *All ways of telling are removed.*[107]

Notwithstanding the inherent difficulty of trying to describe a mind that is so fundamentally different from our own, we can make some attempt to do so, but that requires us to do a bit more background exploration. So far we have looked at the unenlightened mind in terms of the states and processes that constitute our experience. What about the deeper structure of the mind? How does each moment of experience come to be an *unenlightened* moment? Once we understand that a little more deeply, it becomes easier for us to see in what way the Enlightened mind is different, because that difference lies not so much in its contents as in how it works.

We have seen that the unenlightened mind is actually a succession of mind-moments, each freshly constructed in each moment out of combinations of the fifty-one mental events in dependence on the events present in previous moments. The constant called attention is the pulling together of the other four constants in a single flash of subject-experiencing-object, that rich and complex moment of 'me here now', with all those tones and shades suggested by the variety of mental events we have so far studied. To us this appears as a stable, lasting self experiencing an enduring world.

This ever newly minted moment is always more or less distorted and is always somewhere on the continuum from unskilful to skilful. In the language of the Yogācāra, each moment of ordinary consciousness is cognitively obscured and ethically determined. That means that our normal way of seeing the world is to a greater or lesser extent fundamentally mistaken; and it means that our will, interpretation, and attention are always to some extent either skilful or unskilful.

If this was all there was to each mind-moment, the case would be hopeless, for an intrinsically distorted and ignorant mind could never be free from its ignorance. If it was intrinsically ignorant, it could not avoid the likelihood of falling back into unskilfulness, no matter how skilful it is for the present. There is hope, though, for the mind has deeper layers running beneath its ignorance and folly.

The three evolutions of mind

The Yogācāra sees each mind-moment as unfolding in a threefold 'evolution' – although one should perhaps not take this evolution as taking place in time: it is, so to speak, an evolution within each mind-moment, if that has any meaning. As always when we are talking about the mind, we must be vividly aware of the limitations of the language we are using. Our words are constructed out of the world of objects, initially as a kind of pointing, one could say. But the mind is not an object – indeed, it could be defined as whatever is non-object: it is subject, that which knows objects. The nature of our language naturally confuses our discussion of mind: when we start to talk about it, we seem to be speaking of an object, and, when we talk about how it works, it can seem as if it is a sort of machine. Yet, if we are to understand the mind at all beyond our direct involvement with it, we only have concepts and words to work with. So, when I refer to a threefold evolution, let it be understood that this is a metaphor that helps us to understand our immediate experience, but that does not literally describe it in a literal way.

The first evolution of the mind, the deepest layer within the mind-moment, is a pure spark of awareness, a flash of sentience that is, in itself, true and innocent, not ignorant or good or yet bad. It is, in technical language, neither cognitively obscured nor ethically determined. This is something like what the Buddha was getting at when he said, 'This mind is luminous, but is afflicted by adventitious afflictions.'[108] Mind itself is neither ignorant nor contaminated. So the first evolution of mind from the previous mind-moment is just mind, pure and simple.

It is very difficult to see what this means, apart from in deep meditation, because what we know as ordinary experience is already 'afflicted by adventitious afflictions' – it is already distorted by ignorance and contaminated by afflictions: the third evolution has already taken place. However, we can get some distant intimation of what the first evolution is like from a quite common occurrence. It happens from time to time when we awake from a deep sleep, especially if there is no pressure for us to jump out of bed, and perhaps when we are in an unfamiliar place. We lie there, fully awake, but, before we begin to engage our minds with the day that is to come, we simply rest in a kind of open awareness, without any particular focus or content. We are just aware, hardly knowing where we are – or even, perhaps, who we are – and hardly caring. This delicious state can carry on for quite a while, until life with its burdens and blessings begins to take shape around us again. Strangely, the most powerful experience of this kind I've had is on coming round from a fainting fit: as if dropping out of nothing into a completely open, unformed space, feeling no need to shape it in any way, attach labels and names to it, or work out who I was and what I was doing there. This state can be surprisingly blissful! These are but distant echoes, however, of the first evolution of mind. That initial layer of untrammelled awareness is even more open and innocent than this.

At the risk of tempting you to indolence, I can recommend deliberately courting this kind of experience. When you next wake up in the morning and can afford to experiment, simply hold off the full array of experience for a while and allow a kind of lazy investigation of what is going on. Even if you are not able to notice that open space, you can certainly experience the irresistible force that imposes me-in-my-world upon you again. I don't, however, suggest experimenting with deliberately fainting!

But of course that initial awareness does not remain innocent, as we know even from these examples. When you wake up or when you come round from that faint, sooner or later the world falls into place around you – and within you. You begin to remember who you are, where you are and what you are doing. All your predilections and prejudices slip from the shadows, ready armed for engagement with the world. In other words, through that open space of relatively open consciousness teems the conditioning power of past memory and habit. Me-in-my-world solidifies once again.

This process of coming back into the world reflects the second evolution within the mind-moment, following from that initial layer of pure sentience. In the second evolution, 'me' is identified as separate from 'my world'. That first flash has two aspects inherent in it, an inner and an outer, a perceiving and a perceived, although in the first evolution these are not discriminated. During the second evolution, the deep habit of self-clinging reasserts itself and seizes upon the inner dimension as 'me' and the outer as 'world'. This is ignorance, the inborn affliction, the most powerful of the shaping forces from the past, playing itself out in the present, structuring the mind into 'mine' and 'not mine' and forming the basis for all future egoistic interpretation.

This second evolution or transformation within the mind-moment colours and distorts with self-view and conceit all that emerges from it. This is not merely a cognitive step: the self that is discriminated is grasped with the tremendous grip of self-attachment. Ignorant as this renders us, however, at this level we are still innocent. Nothing has been done. There is as yet no question of skilfulness or unskilfulness. This layer is therefore said to be cognitively obscured but still ethically undetermined.

Needless to say, having divided experience into 'I' and 'world', we begin to populate it with the 'ten thousand things', as Chinese tradition puts it. This is the third evolution of mind: the manifestation of the full array of 'me-in-my-world', here and now – precisely as it is happening for you, the reader, and me, the writer, at this very moment. The bias that cognitive obscuration gives to interpretation quickly gives a further twist to the plot. We interpret our experience on the basis of our ignorant self-clinging and thus we contaminate it. We see not the objects of experience as they are, but our contaminated and egoistic distortions of them. And then we begin to act on the basis

Mind in Harmony

of our contaminated and egoistic interpretations. We crave and grasp at what we believe will secure our self-identity and give it satisfaction, and we hate and fight against what we believe threatens us. Thus the twenty-six afflictions come into play, according to their various natures and conditions. Of course, it is not only the unskilful that is triggered in the third evolution. We also have the possibility of skilful action. When we begin to sense some identity *with* the world around us, rather than *against* it, then we respond skilfully and the eleven positives come into play.

It is thus primarily the third layer or evolution of each mind-moment that we have been learning about in examining the fifty-one mental events, although we have had more than a little glimpse of this deeper structure. This fuller picture of the mind in terms of the three evolutions or transformations within the mind-moment helps us to know how we get out of the unenlightened state, with its cognitive obscuration and ethical determination, its ignorance and its potential for unskilful action – and therefore its pain and lack of fulfilment and true satisfaction. And it then helps us to understand better what the Enlightened state is like as liberation from the afflictions and especially from ignorance, the ultimate source of suffering. It gives us the basis for attempting a psychology of liberation.

Peeling the onion

The problem of cognitive obscuration or ignorance begins with the second evolution: the emergence of a sense of self and world as independent and real, with its inevitable powerful attachment to self-identity. From that ignorance the third evolution takes place: the unfolding of a world of contaminated and egoistic objects, distorted by interpretation, within which we have the possibility, even inevitability, of falling into unskilful actions that are themselves suffering and from which suffering then follows in accordance with the principle of karma.

But the mind-moment does not have to evolve in this way. It can avoid both cognitive obscuration and even the possibility of unskilfulness. The clue is in that first layer of the mind, that pure flash of sentience, which is cognitively unobscured and ethically undetermined. If the mind could somehow remain at that level or could bring that level to bear on the construction of experience, then we could avoid obscuration and contamination. However, we cannot attain that in a single bound, although we can have shorter or longer periods of experiencing that freedom. The power of our past ignorance is too strong. We have to undo the threefold evolution piece by piece, starting at the outermost evolution, which is the world and self as we know them right now. We have to peel away the layers of the onion.

If we are to peel the onion, though, we need to see where to start. So where does the essence of the problem lie? It lies with karma. It is karma that drives the evolutions of mind in each moment. The habit of ignorance reasserts itself again and again within the open space of mind that is the first evolution. But it does so more or less powerfully. The strength with which that habit comes back into play depends upon how we have acted in the past. If we have performed a great deal of unskilful karma, the habit of self-clinging will be very strong and will reassert itself with an irresistible force, brushing through that space with hardly a pause. Our unskilful action strengthens our self-clinging and our self-clinging generates our unskilfulness. Round and round it goes.

At some point, however, some people wake up, at least for a moment or two. They realize the situation they are in and, if they are fortunate, they come to recognize that there is an escape. And the means of escape lies within those very fifty-one mental events that are the product of the ignorance that causes our bondage and suffering. By working with those mental events we can gradually use karma to our advantage and so peel the onion of the mind, getting back to its basic state before we distort and contaminate it.

The first step in our escape is the arising of faith. We find ourselves responding to virtue, beauty, and the truth. We are drawn to end our suffering in the bliss of release. On that basis, our conscience is aroused in the form of scrupulousness and reverential shame, and so vigilance and ardour are stirred into action. We work to eliminate the afflictions from our minds and prevent them from arising again; and we try to develop the positives and bring them to perfection. This is the stage of ethics in the threefold path of ethics, meditation, and wisdom, that presentation of the path that was the Buddha's main subject of teaching during his last few months of life. The more we work to eradicate the afflictions and cultivate the positives, the weaker the habit of self-clinging becomes. This stage of practice mainly consists in working on one's actual behaviour, especially by applying the precepts, but we need to get deeper into the underlying mental states. This is the task of meditation.

Meditation calls in the aid of the intensifiers. Through systematic practice we learn to move from emotional engagement, to resolve, to attentiveness, and to absorption. We are even able for a while to refine or suspend to some degree the action of that habit of self-clinging, and to experience thereby higher states of consciousness – higher here meaning freed to some degree from that powerful inborn habit, so that we taste something of the first layer of mind, pure, innocent, and blissful. However, at the stage of meditation, such higher states can only be temporary. As soon as we cease to exercise the intensifiers, we fall back into egoistic interpretation, and thus a strong tendency to contaminating the objects of our attention with the afflictions.

It is only when we enter the stage of wisdom or penetration that we are able to see through and then destroy ignorance. We gradually recognize the falsity of the step taken in the second layer of the mind-moment's evolution, wherein the inner and outer dimensions of experience are interpreted in terms of a fixed and independent 'me' in an independent world 'out there'. Wisdom penetrates this illusion. We recognize its artificial and constructed nature, and consciousness is revolutionized in its very basis. In fact, it turns outside in.

This is how we escape. We reverse the process of the three evolutions of the mind-moment by means of ethics, meditation, and wisdom. The three evolutions of mind take us from that initial pure and innocent spark of awareness, through seizing onto its inner dimension as 'me', to the egoistic distortion and contamination of the objects of experience. It is those distorted and often contaminated objects that we take as real and on the basis of which we shape our lives. In this process we become increasingly disconnected from the true nature of mind and experience because we cover over mind's fundamental innocence with egoistic cognitive obscuration and then ethical contamination. As we follow the path of ethics, meditation, and wisdom, we undo the contaminated interpretation of experience by means of ethics and meditation; and we undo the egoistic distortion through wisdom.

Once that has happened, our mind works in an entirely different way: it is turned upside down and outside in. We no longer live trapped in the cognitive distortions and ethical contaminations of ignorance. Of course, while we have a body, our senses and nervous system will continue to present experience that has an inner and an outer dimension, but we never lose touch with the initial freedom and openness of mind and are never again tempted to interpret our experience in terms of 'me' and 'my world' as fixed and opposed polarities.

But what is that marvellous state like?

The five constants and the five gnoses

It could be briefly stated that, instead of consisting of the five constants, the five gnoses now form the structure of the Enlightened mind. But this doesn't yet tell us what the state is like. For that we require a little more explanation. The fifty-one mental events are the constituents of the unenlightened mind. The basic building blocks of that mind, around which all the others arrange themselves, are those five constants: contact, feeling, interpretation, will, and attention. Since they emerge on the basis of ignorance, the essential structure of the unenlightened mind is set up for egoistic distortion. The constants collectively discriminate 'me-in-my-world'.

Once wisdom has penetrated the fundamental delusion brought about in the second evolution of mind, the mind transforms itself. It no longer takes the subjective, inner side of experience as a self separate from the moment of experience, and it no longer reads the objects of outer experience as belonging to an ultimately real world. Now that pure, clear, luminous awareness, which is the mind's deepest layer, is the basis of all experience, without a trace or possibility of clinging.

All the contents of the mind are transformed by this revolution, and in particular the constants are dissolved. Contact, feeling, interpretation, will, and attention no longer form the basic structure of experience. This does not mean that the sensory world does not appear to the Enlightened mind. In so far as there is still a body associated with it, trees remain trees, and mountains mountains. But they are illumined now by that essential, luminous character of mind. The pure and shining awareness that now knows reality cannot be analyzed in the neat categories of Abhidharma psychology. However, to help us get some sense of what it is like, we could say that the five constants are replaced by the five gnoses.

The Sanskrit word that I am here translating as 'gnosis' is *jñāna*, with which it is etymologically connected. I have used this perhaps rather obscure term to translate *jñāna* because I want to emphasize the radical difference implied by this mode of awareness/knowledge. Normal English words like knowledge, even wisdom, simply won't do. Gnosis is a word of Greek derivation. It is used in English in connection with a mystical religious current that ran parallel to Christianity in its early days to indicate a kind of direct knowledge or wisdom that was not derived from the senses or the intellect. The word is sufficiently unusual to ensure we do not mistake it for 'mere knowledge', and its established meaning is very close to what I wish to indicate, even if in a very different context and at an even loftier level. It here indicates a way of being aware that is integral and direct, involving no concepts to arrive at truth. It is intuitive wisdom or imagination, but at the highest possible pitch, completely without delusion or even the possibility of being deluded.

The five gnoses that replace the constants are the fundamental characteristics of a mind that is entirely free from self-clinging, so hearing about these five will give us a taste, at least, of what such a mind is like. We will examine them briefly, one by one, seeing how each gnosis relates to the constant that it replaces.

Contact is the function of the unenlightened mind that brings together in consciousness each sense-organ with its sense-object. Because contact is already conditioned by ignorance from preceding mind-moments, it presents a strong basis for egoistic distortion, in the sense that even at such a functional level there is an implicit separation between the organ, the object, and the consciousness that perceives the object. This is fertile ground for the distortions of interpretation. Now, once this revolution in the mind is complete, contact is replaced by the mirror-like gnosis.

The metaphor of a mirror is very expressive, as we have already seen: whatever is put before a mirror, assuming it is free from imperfections, it simply reflects, without distortion. In the same way, the mirror-like gnosis simply perceives what is before it without adding to or taking away from it, and without altering it in any other way. Of course, this refers to the most obvious accuracy of perception: seeing shapes and colours, hearing sounds as they present themselves to the sense-organs, and so on – and it should be noted that an Enlightened person who is colour blind will still be unable to distinguish red from green, for instance. But, much more significantly, it means that the structure of perception will not be mistaken for reality in itself. The way it appears will be simply as a moment arising in dependence on conditions, without any fixed nature independent of that moment, whether internally or externally. This is now directly seen. The very act of perception will reveal itself as relative. This is perhaps what William Blake meant when he said, 'I look through [my corporeal eye], and not with it.'[109] The mirror-like wisdom watches the productions of time like smoke, twisting and curling in the breeze.

The function of the constant of feeling is to register hedonic response to the stimulus of contact: whether of pleasure/happiness, pain/suffering, or lack of stimulation/indifference. Feeling is always underlain by ignorance because, beyond the level of immediate bodily responses, our sense of happiness or suffering is conditioned by our attachment to self – and even physical pleasure and pain are affected by our clinging to the body. Without ignorance, feeling ceases and the gnosis of equality arises.

But what is the inequality of our normal feeling that is now transcended? Of course, our distinction between pleasure and pain is a kind of inequality, but it goes further than that. We feel the relative intensity of pleasure and pain in accordance with their significance for us – in other words, in dependence on our self-identity. My own pains are deeply felt, whilst I might hardly register those of another. The gnosis of equality makes no such distinctions. Though my body registers my pain and pleasure more immediately, the suffering and joys of all are felt equally. The gnosis of equality is therefore empathy at its highest level.

But the matter goes further still, beyond response to pleasure and pain. One can perhaps best understand it in terms of aesthetic perception. Most commonly we experience an aesthetic response to particular objects under particular circumstances, such as viewing a painting in a gallery or hearing music in a concert hall. But there are moods in which aesthetic sensibility is awakened without special objects or circumstances. In that heightened state, we perceive beauty in everything, because we have somehow got into a mood of detached sensitivity to the whole world around us. Even things we might previously have found ugly now seem beautiful – or rather we can see the beauty in them. The gnosis of equality is this kind of aesthetic feeling raised beyond its highest possible power. This reminds me of the words of the seventeenth-century poet and divine Thomas Traherne:

> You never enjoy the world aright, till the Sea itself floweth in
> your veins, till you are clothed with the heavens, and crowned
> with the stars...[110]

Interpretation takes the data of contact and feeling, identifies and labels it, fitting it into an overall pattern of knowledge. This conceptualizing, reasoning power of the unenlightened mind is the most immediate source of egoistic distortion of experience, twisting its objects in the perspective of self-clinging. On that basis, it readily contaminates them with the afflictions. With the ceasing of interpretation, the discriminating gnosis arises.

Here again the artist's eye might help us to understand something of this gnosis. The artist who paints still life, for instance, sees his or her subject in all its minute particularity – indeed, sees its unique essence far more penetratingly than the ordinary observer cares to do – yet, at the same time, in that act is quite unconcerned about what it is for or even what it is ordinarily called. The discriminating gnosis, similarly, attends to its object without conceptualizing it. There is no interest in it as an object of utility – even perhaps to identify it by a label. It is simply there, in all its unique glory. Above all, the object is not viewed at all from the perspective of self-clinging. We might even say that this kind of appreciative, aesthetic awareness at the highest possible level 'loves' its objects, since it views them with a deep sense of affinity and empathy. For, though the object of awareness is not viewed egoistically, but is even, one could say, seen with detachment, it is not a cold, alienated searchlight picking out the object for scrutiny. It is a loving gaze, and all the more loving when it is directed to a person who is capable of responding.

Will is transcended by the action-accomplishing gnosis. Whereas will drives action of body, speech, or mind on the basis of an egoistic interpretation of the intrinsically biased data of contact and feeling, the action accomplished by this gnosis has no selfish motivation. There is simply a spontaneous creative response. What needs to be done is done without the intervention of any self-identity or even a conceptual process. We have some distant echo of such action in creative acts such as the composition of a poem: the poem sometimes seems to write itself and the poet is almost like a scribe, writing down what comes from completely beyond self. Even in our ordinary lives we experience moments of spontaneous generosity or compassion, when we simply *do* without premeditation, responding to the need as soon as it appears. These are prefigurations of that mysterious suprapersonal force, the action-accomplishing gnosis, that moves through the Enlightened mind without any sense of self, always for the greater benefit, always finding the creative means of liberation.

Attention focuses all the other mental events that are in play in a single moment of me-in-my-world. Similarly, the gnoses focus around the gnosis of the realm of reality. This is best understood by referring back to the idea of the three worlds accessible to the unenlightened mind: the sense-world, the world of pure form, and the formless world (*kāma-*, *rūpa-*, and *arūpaloka*). We saw that, as interpretation becomes more subtle, we find ourselves inhabiting progressively more refined and beautiful dimensions of experience, each of which works according to its own laws of appearance – for instance, time may expand and new dimensions open up in ways that our sense world cannot know. We are most likely to experience the world of pure form and, much more rarely, that of formlessness in intensive meditation. However, no matter how lofty and refined our experience may become as we move up through these states, it is always underlain by self-clinging. That ceases with Enlightenment so that all experience becomes the realm of truth, liberated as we now are from the fundamental distorting delusion of a separate 'I'. Whatever the objects of awareness, whatever the circumstances and situation, the Enlightened mind sees reality. The Enlightened are always at home.

These five gnoses thus entirely replace the five constants together with their attendant mental events. However, such a psychological analysis of the Enlightened mind seems doomed to miss the point. The very enterprise of classification is an aspect of interpretation and therefore egoistically distorted. There are not really five separate gnoses like five cogs in a machine. In truth, this particular teaching tells us only that those five constants are transcended and that the mind now works in a quite different way, free from self-clinging. Concepts can only bring us a little way towards non-conceptual understanding. For that reason, the Yogācāra linked the five gnoses to an image, or an arrangement of images: the mandala of the five Buddhas.

The advantage of image, myth, and symbol is that they speak to the imagination and liberate us from the constrictions of the intellect, which is bounded by the limitations of concepts. We know that an image is not to be taken literally or to be defined in a single way. Because it is a symbol, we can intuit for instance that there are not really five Buddhas, as separate individuals, and they are not at all different from each other – and yet we can understand something by contemplating this image that an exposition of the five gnoses can hardly tell us. Let me conclude by describing the mandala rather simply, hoping that you will try to see the Buddhas in your own mind's eye, without interpretation.

We must picture the mandala as appearing in the midst of the infinite blue sky of imagination, each figure shining from within, radiant with exquisite coloured light of the greatest delicacy and beauty. The figures of the five Buddhas are arranged in a circle of perfect balance and harmony, one at each of the four cardinal points and one at the centre.

In the eastern quarter, where the sun rises, sits the deep blue figure of Akṣobhya, the Imperturbable, who embodies the mirror-like gnosis, the transformation of the constant of contact. He sits with his right hand touching the earth before him in a gesture that communicates his unshakeable certainty. His left hand is in his lap and holds a golden thunderbolt (vajra), the symbol of indestructible power. The blue lotus he sits on as a throne is supported by two mighty elephants. He could be called the Buddha of truth.

Ratnasambhava, the Jewel-Born, sits in the south, where the sun is at its zenith. His colour is the golden yellow of freshly ripened wheat and he embodies the transformation of the constant of feeling into the gnosis of equality. He holds his right hand at his knee with the palm facing outwards in the gesture of giving. In his left hand he cups a shining jewel. His golden lotus is supported by two horses, richly caparisoned. He is the Buddha of beauty.

Amitābha, Infinite Light, glows the deep red of the setting sun in the west. His gnosis is the discriminating, the transformation of the constant of interpretation. His hands are folded in his lap for meditation, cradling a red lotus blossom, and he sits on a red lotus throne, supported by a pair of magnificent peacocks with their tails unfurled. He is the Buddha of love.

The northern realm of mysterious night is Amoghasiddhi's, the green Buddha. His name means 'Infallible Success', as befits one who embodies the action-accomplishing gnosis, which is the transformation of the constant of will. His right hand is raised, palm towards us, in the gesture of fearlessness and he holds a golden double-vajra in his left palm. His lotus throne is supported by two celestial musicians, eagle from the waist down, human from the waist up. He is the Buddha of creativity.

In the centre sits Vairocana, the Illuminator, who transforms the constant of attention into the gnosis of the sphere of reality. His body is the purest white, combining all colours, and he sits on a throne supported by lions, the kings of the jungle. His hands are held at his chest, turning a dazzling wheel of the Dharma, signifying teaching the truth. He could be called the Buddha of fulfilment.

Many more correlations and symbols can be added to this composite image, filling out and enriching its meanings: female consorts, attendant Bodhisattvas, connections with the *skandhas* or the elements or poisons.[111] But the main outlines have been drawn here and they give us the essence of it. It is enough to contemplate these. It is the image of the mind in its ultimate harmony.

Appendix

The fifty-one mental events (*caitta dharmas*)

This appendix lists the mental events in the traditional order of the Yogācāra Abhidharma. The author's term is given first in **bold**, the Sanskrit second in *italic*, and the translation used by Sangharakshita in *Know Your Mind* third in roman (occasionally there is none, as the author's translation is the same as Sangharakshita's).

The five constants, *sarvatraga caitta dharma*s, the omnipresent mental events
1. **Feeling**, *vedanā*, feeling-tone
2. **Interpretation**, *saṃjñā*, recognition
3. **Will**, *cetanā*, directionality of mind
4. **Contact**, *sparśa*
5. **Attention**, *manaskāra*, egocentric demanding

The five intensifiers, *viniyata caitta dharma*s, the object-determining mental events
6. **Emotional engagement**, *chanda*, interest
7. **Resolve**, *adhimokṣa*, intensified interest which stays with its object
8. **Attentiveness**, *smṛti*, inspection (or mindfulness or recollection)
9. **Absorption**, *samādhi*, intense concentration
10. **Penetration**, *prajñā*, appreciative discrimination

The eleven positives, *kuśala caitta dharma*s, the positive mental events
11. **Faith**, *śraddhā*, confidence-trust
12. **Scrupulousness**, *hrī*, self-respect (or shame)
13. **Reverential shame**, *apatrāpya*, decorum (or respect for wise opinion)

14. **Contentment**, *alobha*, non-attachment
15. **Goodwill**, *adveṣa*, non-hatred
16. **Clarity**, *amoha*, non-deludedness
17. **Ardour**, *vīrya*, diligence (or energy in pursuit of the good)
18. **Serenity**, *praśrabdhi*, alertness (or tranquillity)
19. **Vigilance**, *apramāda*, concern or non-heedlessness
20. **Equanimity**, *upekṣā*
21. **Compassion**, *avihiṃsā*

The six afflictions, *mūlakleśas*, the six basic emotions
22. **Craving**, *rāga*, cupidity-attachment
23. **Hatred**, *pratigha*, anger
24. **Conceit**, *māna*, arrogance
25. **Ignorance**, *avidyā*, lack of intrinsic awareness
26. **Vagueness**, *vicikitsā*, indecision
27. **Views**, *dṛṣṭi*, opinionatedness

The twenty secondary afflictions, *upakleśas*, the proximate factors of instability
28. **Rage**, *krodha*, indignation (or rage)
29. **Resentment**, *upanāha*
30. **Concealment**, *mrakṣa*, slyness-concealment
31. **Spite**, *pradāśa*, defensiveness
32. **Envy**, *īrṣyā*
33. **Avarice**, *mātsarya*, acquisitiveness
34. **Deceit**, *māyā*, pretence
35. **Pretence**, *śāṭhya*, dishonesty
36. **Inflation**, *mada*, mental inflation (or self-intoxication)
37. **Malice**, *vihiṃsā*
38. **Unscrupulousness**, *āhrīkya*
39. **Shamelessness**, *anapatrāpya*, lack of sense of propriety
40. **Stagnation**, *styāna*, gloominess
41. **Restlessness**, *auddhatya*, ebullience
42. **Lack of faith**, *āśraddhya*, non-faith
43. **Inertia**, *kausīdya*, laziness
44. **Carelessness**, *pramāda*, unconcern (or heedlessness)
45. **Inattentiveness**, *muṣitasmṛtitā*, forgetfulness (or unrecollectedness or unmindfulness)
46. **Unawareness**, *asamrpajanya*, inattentiveness (or purposelessness)
47. **Distraction**, *vikṣepa*, desultoriness

The four variables, *aniyata caitta dharma*s
48. **Sleepiness,** *middha,* drowsiness (or torpor)
49. **Disquiet,** *kaukṛtya,* worry
50. **Thinking of,** *vitarka,* initial application of mind
51. **Thinking about,** *vicāra,* sustained application of mind

Notes

Preface

1 See the Appendix (pp.219–21) for a complete list of Sanskrit terms along with their translations.

2 Sangharakshita, *Know Your Mind*, Windhorse Publications, Birmingham 1998.

3 *The Necklace of Clear Understanding* is by Yeshe Gyaltsen (1713-1793), a Tibetan Buddhist of the Gelug school.

4 The terms 'skilful' and 'unskilful' are discussed in Chapter 2.

5 Buddhists with a basis in Sangharakshita's teaching will be more familiar with the term 'spiritual life'. Since 'spiritual' can have many other connotations than those implied by Sangharakshita, here the less ambiguous 'Dharma life' (i.e. a life lived based on Dharmic principles) is used. 'Spiritual life' is sometimes used elsewhere in the book.

6 For a further introduction see for example Sangharakshita's *What Is the Dharma? The Essential Teachings of the Buddha*, Windhorse Publications, Birmingham 1998.

7 One such introduction to the Buddhist path can be found in Sangharakshita's *A Guide to the Buddhist Path*, Windhorse Publications, Cambridge 2011.

Chapter 1

8 Founded in England in 1968 by Sangharakshita, it was called the Western Buddhist Order. In the following decades the order spread to many parts of the globe. In India in particular the order grew quickly as followers of the great Buddhist convert Dr Ambedkar became involved with this new Buddhist movement. (In India the order was known as the Trailokya Bauddha Mahasangha.) In 2010 it was given a new name suitable for both the Indian and the 'Western' wings. It became the Triratna Buddhist Order. (Triratna means 'the Three Jewels', these being the Buddha, Dharma, and Sangha, representing what is most precious in a Buddhist life.) The order is open to any man or woman who wishes and is able to undertake the training – which includes learning how to effectively train one's own

mind. Ordination ceremonies take place in the course of a long retreat, where possible a three- or four-month retreat. During the ceremony ordinands undertake to practise ten ethical precepts (including three mind precepts) and are given a new name (in Sanskrit or Pali) signifying their birth as a spiritually committed Dharma practitioner.

9 Sangharakshita began handing on responsibilities for conferring ordinations to a number of senior men and women disciples in the late 1980s. In 1993 he formed a college of public preceptors to whom he handed on his remaining responsibilities as head of the order. For further reading, see Vajragupta's *The Triratna Story: Behind the Scenes of a New Buddhist Movement*, Windhorse Publications, Cambridge 2010, pp.119–21.

10 *Kosambīya Sutta, Majjhima Nikāya* 48. See *The Middle Length Discourses of the Buddha: A Translation of the Majjhima Nikāya*, trans. Bhikkhu Ñāṇamoli and Bhikkhu Bodhi, Wisdom, Boston 1995, pp.419–23.

11 The Buddha's teachings were collected together in what is traditionally known as the Tripiṭaka (lit. 'three baskets'): the Sūtra Piṭaka, the Abhidharma Piṭaka, and the Vinaya Piṭaka. The Pali canon is one version of the Tripiṭaka, with the distinction of being the oldest complete record of the Buddha's teachings that has survived in the original language.

12 The Buddha's last words are from the *Mahāparinibbāna Sutta, Dīgha Nikāya* 16, and have been variously translated. See *The Long Discourses of the Buddha: A Translation of the Dīgha Nikāya*, trans. Maurice Walshe, Wisdom, Boston 1995, p.270.

13 See for example Sangharakshita's *The Buddha's Noble Eightfold Path*, Windhorse Publications, Birmingham 2007.

14 *Dvedhāvitakka Sutta, Majjhima Nikāya* 19.2–7, in Ñāṇamoli and Bodhi, op. cit., pp.207–8.

15 Ibid., 19.8, p.208.

16 Dhyāna is the technical term for meditative absorption. Some thought processes are present in the initial stages but these gradually fade, leaving an experience characterized by physical pleasure and mental happiness. The most refined dhyānic states are said to be characterized by a one-pointed equanimity. There is more on this topic in Chapters 7 and 11. See also Kamalashila's *Buddhist Meditation: Tranquility, Imagination and Insight*, Windhorse Publications, Cambridge 2012.

17 Asaṅga (*c.* AD 310–90) was founder (or co-founder) of the Yogācāra school, one of the two main philosophical schools of Mahāyāna Buddhism. He is recognized as the author of a number of great treatises and it is to him that authorship of the *Abhidharmasamuccaya* is attributed. This is a key text in which the author shows how the older Abhidharma tradition links to the Mahāyāna developments in which Asaṅga played a central role.

18 Vasubandhu (*c.* AD 320–400) was the brother of Asaṅga and renowned author of the *Abhidharmakośa*, a commentary on the earlier renderings of the Abhidharma. According to tradition he was later converted to his

brother's Yogācāra viewpoint and came to be regarded as co-founder of the Yogācāra tradition.

19 Xuanzang (also rendered Hsüan Tsang) (c. AD 600–64) is famed as a pilgrim who travelled to India to bring the Buddhist scriptures back to China (the story *Monkey* is based on his adventures). On his return he was instrumental in bringing about the translation of many of these texts as well as writing a definitive commentary on one of Vasubandhu's works, which became the root text for the Faxiang school founded by Xuanzang. For further reading see for instance Kulananda's *Teachers of Enlightenment*, Windhorse Publications, Birmingham 2000, pp.199–205.

20 See for instance the *Bhayabherava Sutta*, *Majjhima Nikāya* 4, in Ñāṇamoli and Bodhi, op. cit., pp.102–7.

21 See for instance Sangharakshita's *A Survey of Buddhism*, 9th ed., Windhorse Publications, Birmingham 2001.

22 The five *skandha*s comprise *rūpa* (form), *vedanā* (sensation), *saṃjñā* (perception), *saṃskāra* (volition), and *vijñāna* (consciousness). For an accessible introduction see Subhuti, *The Buddhist Vision: A Path to Fulfilment*, Windhorse Publications, Birmingham 2001, chapter 6.

23 In Buddhism ethical action is said to be not 'good' or 'bad' but rather skilful or unskilful depending on whether it brings about happiness or suffering in the lives of oneself and others. This is discussed in detail in Chapter 2. The Buddha taught that, as well as one's words and deeds, one's thoughts and states of mind also carry ethical consequences – thus the triad of body, speech, and mind. For further reading on Buddhist ethics and ethical precepts see for instance Sangharakshita's *The Ten Pillars of Buddhism*, Windhorse Publications, Cambridge 2010.

24 *Śamatha* and *vipaśyanā* are used to describe two aspects of, or approaches to, meditation. The first (*śamatha*) is to calm the mind by developing skilful mental states that lead to the experience of dhyāna (see note 16); the second (*vipaśyanā*) is to reflect on the true nature of existence and so to develop insight or wisdom. It is said that only with a basis in *śamatha* is it possible to gather enough concentrated and purified energy to really penetrate into the nature of existence in a way that permanently alters one's outlook and experience of life.

25 'Mindfulness' has become a popular term in recent times. However, its use is by no means always equivalent to what is meant by mindfulness in the context of the Buddha's teaching of the path to Enlightenment. The term is discussed more fully in Chapter 12.

Chapter 2

26 *Dhammapada*, trans. Sangharakshita, Windhorse Publications, Birmingham 2001, p.13, verses 1–2.

27 *Dvedhāvitakka Sutta*, *Majjhima Nikāya* 91, in Ñāṇamoli and Bodhi, op. cit., pp.207–10.

28 Ibid., 2.
29 Ibid., 3–5.
30 Ibid., 3.
31 Ibid., 7.
32 Ibid., 8–10.
33 Ibid., 12.
34 Ibid., 6, 11.
35 *Dhammapada*, op. cit., p.14, verse 3.
36 For an introduction to spiritual friendship as inherent to spiritual life, see Subhuti with Subhamati, *Buddhism and Friendship*, Windhorse Publications, Birmingham 2001.
37 *Devadaha Sutta, Majjhima Nikāya* 101.23, in Ñāṇamoli and Bodhi, op. cit., p.834.
38 For an overview of theories of the relationship between the brain and the mind, see chapter 1 of *The Mind and the Brain: Neuroplasticity and the Power of Mental Force* by Jeffrey M. Schwartz and Sharon Begley, Harper Perennial, New York 2004.
39 For example in 'The shepherd's search for mind', in *The Hundred Thousand Songs of Milarepa*, vol.1, trans. Garma C.C. Chang, Shambhala, Boston 1962, chapter 12.

Chapter 3

40 See note 22.

Chapter 4

41 For a more detailed exposition of the *niyāma*s see Sangharakshita's *What Is the Dharma?*, op. cit., pp.164–5, and Subhuti and Sangharakshita, *Revering and Relying Upon the Dharma*, available at http://subhuti.info/sites/subhuti.info/files/revering_and_relying_upon_the_dharma.pdf, accessed on 28 November 2014.
42 A reference to the first three of the *viparyāsa*s, or 'topsy-turvy views'.

Chapter 5

43 *The Hundred Thousand Songs of Milarepa*, vol.2, trans. Garma C.C. Chang, Shambhala, Shaftesbury 1962, p.591.
44 From the *Mahāsaccaka Sutta, Majjhima Nikāya* 36.34–9, in Ñāṇamoli and Bodhi, op. cit., pp.340–1.
45 See for instance the *Kevaddha Sutta, Dīgha Nikāya* 11, in Walshe, op. cit., pp.175–80.

46 For more on the 'three worlds' and the 'six realms' into which (according to Buddhist tradition) beings may be reborn, see Subhuti, *The Buddhist Vision*, op. cit.

47 George Stubbs (1724-1806) was a British painter who specialized in equine portraits (though he also once painted a kangaroo). *Whistlejacket* was commissioned by the second marquess of Rockingham and acquired by the National Gallery in 1997.

48 See, for instance, the horses painted by Picasso in his *Guernica* (1937).

49 The five hindrances to meditative absorption are craving for sense experience, ill-will, restlessness and anxiety, sloth and torpor, and doubt. See Kamalashila, op. cit., pp.54–8.

50 Access concentration is the precursor to full absorption or dhyāna (see note 16), arising as the five hindrances (see note 49) fall away. See Kamalashila, op. cit., pp.86–8.

Chapter 6

51 The Mindfulness of Breathing is one of the oldest meditation techniques of the Buddhist tradition, and still practised today by Buddhists all over the world. Precise instructions may vary but the essentials are the same. The natural breathing process becomes the object of one's interest and attention until one becomes more and more deeply absorbed. In the Triratna Buddhist Community, a four-stage Mindfulness of Breathing meditation is taught. At first one counts one's breaths as an aid to concentration, then gradually counting is dropped, allowing one to become ever more absorbed in the experience of breathing itself. See Kamalashila, op. cit., chapter 1.

52 In the Buddhist tradition a mantra is a string of syllables, usually in Sanskrit, with or without intelligible meaning, that evoke a spiritual quality such as wisdom or compassion. Repeating a mantra over and over is a way of both guarding the mind's wandering attention and encouraging it towards the quality the mantra symbolizes. A mantra is often associated with an archetypal form. For example, the well-known mantra *oṃ maṇi padme hūṃ* (which means 'the jewel in the lotus') is the mantra of Avalokiteśvara (known as Chenrezig to the Tibetans), the archetypal embodiment of compassion. Such archetypal forms (known as Bodhisattvas) may be called to mind or visualized as a type of meditation. Today such practices are most widely associated with the Tibetan Buddhist tradition. The ten *kasiṇas* or devices for concentrating the mind are the elements earth, water, fire, and air; the colours blue, yellow, red, and white; space and consciousness. See Sangharakshita, *A Survey of Buddhism*, op. cit., p.180, or Kamalashila, op. cit., pp.98–9.

53 The Buddha, who lived around 480–400 BC (the dates are disputed), is the historical founder of the Buddhist tradition. After some years of search and struggle he gained Enlightenment while still a relatively young man

and spent the rest of his long life teaching the Dharma so that others, too, could know the happiness and freedom that were his. See Vishvapani Blomfield's *Gautama Buddha: The Life and Teachings of the Awakened One*, Quercus, London 2011, and Sangharakshita's *Who Is the Buddha?*, 2nd ed., Windhorse Publications, Birmingham 2002.

54 Traditionally the Buddha is regarded as fully Enlightened while the Bodhisattvas, though highly evolved, are still on the path to Enlightenment. For more on Bodhisattvas, see notes 52 and 78.

55 A rendering of *Dhammapada*, verse 204. Compare Sangharakshita's translation in *Dhammapada*, op. cit., p.73: 'Nirvana is the supreme happiness'.

56 The afflictions are mentioned in Chapter 1 and discussed in detail in Part 4. The technical name is *kleśa*. The *kleśa*s include all the unwholesome mental states that arise from the greed, hatred, and delusion inherent in the unenlightened mind. Sangharakshita translates the term as meaning both 'that which torments' and 'that which defiles' (see *Know Your Mind*, op. cit., p.161).

57 For Xuanzang, see note 19.

58 The Mettā Bhāvanā is a meditation practice that was taught by the Buddha himself (see the *Mettā Sutta* of the *Sutta Nipāta*, e.g. trans. H. Saddhatissa, Curzon Press, London 1985). Its essential character is the development of a mind or heart that desires the well-being and security of all, for mettā is the opposite of hatred and cruelty. In the Triratna Buddhist Community the practice is taught in five stages, in which one develops mettā or loving-kindness towards oneself, a good friend, a neutral person, and an enemy, and then, having tried to balance the mettā so it is equally felt for all four persons, one universalizes it by radiating loving-kindness to all corners of the universe. See Kamalashila, op. cit., pp.21–31.

59 For *vipaśyanā* and *śamatha*, see note 24. Here the reference is to the three *lakṣaṇa*s or characteristics of conditioned existence that can be objects of contemplation in *vipaśyanā* meditation: conditioned existence is impermanent (*anicca*), ultimately unsatisfactory to our ego desires (*dukkha*), and without fixed 'being' (*anattā*).

60 See also Chapter 5. For a description of the four lower and four higher or formless dhyānas, see for instance Sangharakshita's *A Survey of Buddhism*, op. cit., pp.187–92.

61 See note 16 and note 59 above.

Chapter 7

62 See note 49.

63 *The Age of Anxiety: A Baroque Eclogue* is a long poem in six parts by W.H. Auden (1907-1973), published in 1948. It deals with the search for identity in an increasingly industrialized world. The poem inspired

Leonard Bernstein's Symphony No. 2, also called *The Age of Anxiety*. The writer Alan Watts, more widely known for *The Way of Zen* (1957), called the first chapter of his *Wisdom of Insecurity* (1951) 'The age of anxiety'.

Chapter 8

64 Xuanzang, *Ch'eng Wei-Shih Lun: Doctrine of Mere Consciousness*, trans. Wei Tat, Ch'eng Wei-Shih Lun Publications Committee, Hong Kong 1973, p.389. See also note 19.

65 Sangharakshita, *Know Your Mind*, op. cit., p.119.

66 Shinran founded the Jōdo Shin school of Pure Land Buddhism, which today is the largest of the Japanese branches of Mahayana Buddhism. His teaching emphasized the salvific efficacy of complete trust in the Buddha Amitābha since any effort on one's own part to achieve Enlightenment would always be egoistic. For Shinran's most eloquent account of faith see *Kyō Gyō Shin Shō: The Teaching, Practice, Faith, and Enlightenment*, trans. H. Inagaki, Ryokoku University, Kyoto 1983. See also Kulananda, op. cit., pp.220–4.

67 See the *Kālāma Sutta*, *Aṅguttara Nikāya* 65, called *Kesaputtiya* in *The Numerical Discourses of the Buddha: A Translation of the Aṅguttara Nikāya*, trans. Bhikkhu Bodhi, Wisdom, Boston 2012, p.280.

68 *The Perfection of Wisdom in Eight Thousand Lines and Its Verse Summary*, trans. Edward Conze, Four Seasons Foundation, San Francisco 1983, p.10.

69 *Hesiod and Theognis*, trans. Dorothea Wender, Penguin, London 1976, p.65.

70 The disciples of the Buddha who made up the early sangha consisted of laymen and laywomen who lived with their families in towns and villages, as well as men and women who had 'gone forth' from the home life into homelessness, people who lived as wandering ascetics practising meditation and begging for alms. These latter were known as bhikkhus (men) and bhikkhunīs (women), and are often – though rather misleadingly – referred to by contemporary writers as 'monks' and 'nuns'. In time the bhikkhus and bhikkhunīs formed settled communities and Buddhist monastic life flourished for many centuries in many parts of the East.

71 *Paradise Lost*, book 4, line 110, in John Milton, *The Complete English Poems*, ed. Gordon Campbell, David Campbell Publishers, London 1992, p.225.

Chapter 9

72 Buddhist cosmology describes existence as a 'triple world' of ever-increasing refinement from the *kāmaloka* or sense-world, through the *rūpaloka* or world of archetypal form, to the *arūpaloka* or formless world (or rather, a world of extremely refined form). The last two both belong to the angelic realms of existence where subjective experience is one

of unalloyed happiness and pleasure. But subtle craving may still
be present, as well as delusion, and eventually, through the natural
workings of karma, angels, if they are not practising the Dharma –
Buddhist tradition does speak of 'angels of the path' – will come to the
end of their lifespan in the higher realm and find themselves reborn in a
lower realm of existence. See also note 46.

73 *Dīgha Nikāya* 1, in Walshe, op. cit.

74 Scrooge is the central character in Charles Dickens' *A Christmas Carol*
(1843).

75 From Walter Scott's *Marmion: A Romance*, VI.xvii.332–3, in *Sir Walter
Scott's Poetical Works*, ed. Rev. George Gilfillan, James Nichol, Edinburgh
1857, p.179.

76 Buddhaghoṣa distinguished three types: the greed type, the hate type,
and the deluded type. See *The Path of Purification: Visuddhimagga*,
Buddhist Publication Society Pariyatti Editions, Seattle 1991, p.104,
chapter 3, paragraph 86.

77 In the Boin-Webb translation of the *Abhidharmasamuccaya* we find anger
characterized as 'supplying a basis to violence, the use of weapons
and sticks, etc.' See Asaṅga, *Abhidharmasamuccaya: The Compendium of
the Higher Teaching*, trans. Sara Boin-Webb, Asian Humanities Press,
Fremont, CA 2001, p.15.

78 In the Mahāyāna Buddhist tradition there are many archetypal forms of
Buddhas (fully Enlightened beings) and Bodhisattvas (highly developed
beings striving to gain Enlightenment for the sake of all). These figures
are depicted as having a certain colour, hand gesture, and so on, and
are associated with a particular aspect of Enlightenment. Associated
with love and compassion are, for example, Amitābha, the Buddha of
Infinite Light, and Avalokiteśvara (see note 52) and Tara, Bodhisattvas of
compassion. See also Chapter 13. For further reading see Vessantara, *A
Guide to the Buddhas*, Windhorse Publications, Birmingham 2008, and *A
Guide to the Bodhisattvas*, Windhorse Publications, Birmingham 2008.

79 See Asvaghoṣa's *Buddhacarita*, trans. E.H. Johnston, Motilal Banarsidass,
Delhi 1984, chapter 13, 'The defeat of Mara'.

80 See note 58.

81 The brahma-vihāra meditations or meditations of the sublime abodes are
described in Kamalashila, op. cit., pp.139–48.

82 For the Bodhisattva as the embodiment of compassion, see
Sangharakshita's *The Bodhisattva Ideal: Wisdom and Compassion in
Buddhism*, Windhorse Publications, Birmingham 1999.

Chapter 10

83 From John Lennon's (1940–80) bestselling song 'Imagine' (1971).

84 These four are: denial of cause; denial of effect; denial of oneself
as an ethical agent; and denial of the attainments of the Buddhas

and Bodhisattvas, i.e. denial of the possibility of liberation. See Sangharakshita, *Know Your Mind*, op. cit., pp.197–202.

85 See Subhuti and Sangharakshita, *A Suprapersonal Force*, available at http://subhuti.info/sites/subhuti.info/files/pdf/A-Supra-Personal-Force.pdf, accessed on 28 November 2014.

86 For further elucidation see Sangharakshita's *What Is the Dharma?*, op. cit., or Subhuti and Sangharakshita, *Revering and Relying Upon the Dharma*, op. cit.

87 *Brahmajāla Sutta, Dīgha Nikāya* 1, in Walshe, op. cit., pp.67–8.

88 See Sangharakshita's 'Religio-nationalism in Sri Lanka', in *Alternative Traditions*, Windhorse Publications, Glasgow 1986.

89 See the *Cetokhila Sutta, Majjhima Nikāya* 16.2–7, in Ñāṇamoli and Bodhi, op. cit., pp.194–5. Here the Buddha enumerates five 'wildernesses of the heart' which are doubt in the teacher, in the Dharma, and in the Sangha, as well as doubt in the training, and anger and resentment towards companions on the path. In the Buddha's own time Buddha and teacher were one, of course, whereas subsequently there was the Buddha and the personal, living teacher – making for six wildernesses of the heart or six kinds of doubt.

90 See for instance Sangharakshita, *The Purpose and Practice of Buddhist Meditation: A Source Book of Teachings*, Ibis Publications, Ledbury 2012, p.173.

91 This is the traditional Theravādin view based on the Abhidhamma classification – see Sangharakshita's discussion in *Living with Kindness: The Buddha's Teaching on Metta*, 2nd ed., Windhorse Publications, Cambridge 2008, pp.132–7.

92 A rendering of the *Pabhassara Sutta* of the *Aṅguttara Nikāya* I.vi.51–2. Bhikkhu Bodhi's translation refers to 'adventitious defilements' (see Bhikkhu Bodhi, op. cit., p.97).

Chapter 11

93 This is Sangharakshita's translation of Śāntideva's 'the endeavour to do what is skilful'. See Śāntideva's *The Bodhicaryāvatāra*, trans. K. Crosby and A. Skilton, Oxford University Press, Oxford 1995, p.67, and Sangharakshita, *Know Your Mind*, op. cit., p.141.

94 *Mind in Buddhist Psychology: A Translation of 'The Necklace of Clear Understanding'*, trans. Herbert V. Guenther and Leslie S. Kawamura, Dharma Publishing, Berkeley, CA 1975, p.94.

95 *The Jewel Ornament of Liberation*, trans. Khenpo Konchog Gyaltsen Rinpoche, Snow Lion, New York 1998, p.215.

96 *Troilus and Cressida*, V.ii.

97 Sangharakshita, *Peace Is a Fire: A Collection of Writings and Sayings*, 2nd ed., Windhorse Publications, Birmingham 1995, p.31.

98 *Hamlet*, III.iii.

99 See Sangharakshita, *The Purpose and Practice of Buddhist Meditation*, op. cit., pp.262–3.

100 The Bodhisattva ideal has been described by Sangharakshita as 'one of the sublimest spiritual ideals mankind has ever seen' ('The endlessly fascinating cry: an exploration of Śāntideva's *Bodhicaryāvatāra*', unedited seminar, http://www.freebuddhistaudio.com/texts/read?num=SEM063, accessed on 28 November 2014 (also available from www.lulu.com). It is the ideal of a life dedicated to the attainment of Enlightenment for the sake of all living beings. The Bodhisattva practises the six pāramitās or perfections: giving, morality, patience, energy (ardour), meditation, and wisdom. See Sangharakshita's *The Bodhisattva Ideal*, op. cit.

101 The true origin of this well-known Zen maxim, sometimes attributed to Zen master Baizhang, is not established.

102 See note 51.

103 See note 58.

Chapter 12

104 *Satipaṭṭhāna Sutta, Majjhima Nikāya* 10, in Bodhi, op. cit., pp.145–55.

105 The Buddha spoke of entering the stream of the Dharma as being that point on the path when the first three of the ten fetters of the mind have been broken: the fetters of belief in a fixed self, dependence on rites and rituals as ends in themselves, and sceptical doubt (see Sangharakshita's *The Taste of Freedom: Approaches to the Buddhist Path*, 2nd ed., Windhorse Publications, Birmingham 1997, pp.28–32, where he discusses them under the terms of habit, superficiality, and vagueness). When these three fetters are broken, one's Dharma life becomes irreversible; one cannot but move forwards even though, traditionally, it may take up to seven more lifetimes to reach Enlightenment. Stream Entry is also described as 'the opening of the Dharma eye' (i.e. it is when direct insight into the nature of existence arises) or as real going for refuge to the Three Jewels. See Sangharakshita *Going for Refuge*, Windhorse Publications, Birmingham 1983.

106 See note 23.

Chapter 13

107 *Sutta Nipāta* 1076, trans. E.M. Hare, in *Woven Cadences of Early Buddhists*, Oxford University Press, London 1945, p.155.

108 *Aṅguttara Nikāya*, I.vi.51–2.

109 From William Blake's 'A vision of the last judgment', in *Blake's Poetry and Prose*, Nonesuch Press, London 1941, p.652.

110 Thomas Traherne, *Centuries of Meditation*, Faith Press, London 1960, 'First century', section 29.

111 See Vessantara's *A Guide to the Buddhas*, op. cit.

Select bibliography
and further reading

Asaṅga, *Abhidharmasamuccaya: The Compendium of the Higher Teaching*, trans. Sara Boin-Webb, Asian Humanities Press, Fremont, CA 2001.

Bhikkhu Bodhi (trans.), *The Numerical Discourses of the Buddha: A Translation of the Aṅguttara Nikāya*, Wisdom, Boston 2012.

Bhikkhu Ñāṇamoli and Bhikkhu Bodhi (trans.), *The Middle Length Discourses of the Buddha: A Translation of the Majjhima Nikāya*, Wisdom, Boston 1995.

Guenther, Herbert V., and Leslie S. Kawamura (trans.), *Mind in Buddhist Psychology: A Translation of 'The Necklace of Clear Understanding'*, Dharma Publishing, Berkeley, CA 1975.

Kamalashila, *Buddhist Meditation: Tranquility, Imagination and Insight*, Windhorse Publications, Cambridge 2012.

Kulananda, *Teachers of Enlightenment*, Windhorse Publications, Birmingham 2000.

Sangharakshita, *The Bodhisattva Ideal: Wisdom and Compassion in Buddhism*, Windhorse Publications, Birmingham 1999.

Sangharakshita (trans.), *Dhammapada*, Windhorse Publications, Birmingham 2001.

Sangharakshita, *Know Your Mind*, Windhorse Publications, Birmingham 1998.

Sangharakshita, *The Purpose and Practice of Buddhist Meditation: A Source Book of Teachings*, Ibis Publications, Ledbury 2012.

Sangharakshita, *A Survey of Buddhism*, 9th ed., Windhorse Publications, Birmingham 2001.

Sangharakshita, *What Is the Dharma? The Essential Teachings of the Buddha*, Windhorse Publications, Birmingham 1998.

Subhuti, *The Buddhist Vision: A Path to Fulfilment*, Windhorse Publications, Birmingham 2001.

Subhuti and Sangharakshita, *Revering and Relying Upon the Dharma*, available at http://subhuti.info/sites/subhuti.info/files/revering_and_relying_upon_the_dharma.pdf, accessed on 28 November 2014.

Subhuti and Sangharakshita, *A Suprapersonal Force*, available at http://subhuti.info/sites/subhuti.info/files/pdf/A-Supra-Personal-Force.pdf, accessed on 28 November 2014.

Walshe, Maurice (trans.), *The Long Discourses of the Buddha: A Translation of the Dīgha Nikāya*, Wisdom, Boston 1995.

Vessantara, *A Guide to the Bodhisattvas*, Windhorse Publications, Birmingham 2008.

Vessantara, *A Guide to the Buddhas*, Windhorse Publications, Birmingham 2008.

Xuanzang, *Ch'eng Wei-Shih Lun: Doctrine of Mere Consciousness*, trans. Wei Tat, Ch'eng Wei-Shih Lun Publications Committee, Hong Kong 1973.

Index

ordinary 34, 206
quality of 190
transcendental 41
visual 42
constant of feeling 213,
217
constants, five, *see* five
constants
consumerism 157
contact 40–5, 50–1, 56–7,
190–5, 212–13, 215–16,
219
attention conditioning
57
conditioning
interpretation 57
data of 40, 191, 195, 214
visual 42
contaminated feeling 63–5
contaminated
interpretation 82, 211
contaminated objects 90,
145, 211
contamination 64–5, 89,
209, 211
contentment 123, 125,
127–31, 133–5, 137,
186, 220
continuous effort 12
control 50, 54, 62, 99, 103,
192
cosmology, Buddhist 65,
67–8, 229
courage 83, 109, 179
cowherds 24–6
craving 22–5, 64–6, 89–91,
123–32, 134–5, 147–8,
186
objects of 124, 128
critical awareness 61, 198
critical mass 97, 188
crops 24, 26, 193
cruelty 16, 21–4, 28, 82,
140–1, 228
cultivation 10, 16, 80, 161,
169–70, 180, 188
culture 9, 14–15, 116, 118,
148, 152, 161
cupidity-attachment 220

cynicism 97, 108, 115, 176
inertia of 176

daily meditation 3, 7, 11
dāna 160
dangers 12, 15, 21, 23, 31,
58, 65
dark states 30–1
darkness 111, 167
death 109, 125–6, 140–1,
157
decay 125, 148, 153–4
deceit 131–4, 220
deep faith 110–11
deep interpretation 54–6,
67
deep meditation 194, 207
deeper structure 205, 209
defilements 23, 90, 200
degradation 23
delight 30, 111, 128, 139,
141, 178
deluded belief 65–6
delusions 65, 90, 170, 201,
213, 228–9
fundamental 183, 212
denial 107, 156–7, 159, 230
dependence 5, 89, 146, 155,
157, 206, 213–14
depression 66, 95, 97,
180–1
desire, sensual 22
despair 115, 175
ardour that does not
178
destructive inertia 176
detachment 128–30, 215
development, spiritual 64,
114, 118
devotion 112, 117
Dhammapada 19, 21, 28, 50,
225–6, 228
Dharma 76–7, 82–4,
109–11, 117, 159–66,
170, 231–2
communities 77, 83,
164–6
friends 77, 81
law 156

life 76–9, 81–2, 97, 101,
129, 156–7, 163
practice 74, 77–9, 83–4,
168–9, 177, 187
processes 156–7
Dharmic efforts 78, 81,
83, 163
Dharmic values 109
dhyāna 12, 65, 108, 178,
182–3, 185–6, 224–5;
see also meditative
states
first 104, 178
dhyāna, rūpa 126
dhyāna
second 104
third 182–3, 185
dignity 55, 127, 130
moral 97
dirt 167–70
disappointments 22, 151
disciples 10–11, 13, 63–4,
229
discipline 78–9, 164, 198,
201
discord, lessons of 7–10
discriminating gnosis
214–15
disgust 43–4, 55, 86
disharmony 8–9, 165
disputes 9–10
disquiet 93, 96–101, 117,
184, 221
false 98
feelings of 86, 96, 99,
120
functional 98–100
distortions 61, 124, 167,
213
distraction 7, 75, 78, 85–6,
94, 183–8, 220
dithering 83, 162
dogmatism 159–61
doubt 53, 83–4, 117, 131,
161–7, 196, 231–2
doubting frame of mind
165–6
dṛṣṭi 102, 220
drugs 117, 145, 176
dukkha 90, 228

neutral feeling 40, 43, 62, 190–1
nibbāna 23–4
nihilism 41, 126, 154–5, 157, 163
noble eightfold path 10, 177
non-being 152, 154–5
non-clarity 167
non-craving 123, 127
non-cruelty 16, 21–2
non-existence 126, 128
non-faith 114, 220
non-harm 141
non-heedlessness 200, 220
non-ill-will 16, 21–2
non-intoxication 200
norms, social 9, 160
nostalgia 129
nothing 184

object-determining mental events 16, 73, 219
object-perception 43–4
objects 33–5, 40–8, 52–9, 87–91, 123–7, 183–5, 211–16
    contaminated 90, 145, 211
    craved 124
    of craving 124, 128
    of experience 208, 211
    experience of 62, 82
    hated 136, 140
    meditation 76, 78–9, 85, 87, 91, 103–4
    mental 47, 76, 123–4
    new 47, 58
    pleasant 123
    single 47, 184–5
    unreal 53, 77, 90, 126–7, 135, 145, 173
    world of 33–4, 206
obscuration, cognitive 208–9, 211
one-pointed equanimity 224
one-sidedness 153, 155, 160
onion, peeling 209–10

openness 183, 195, 211
opposites 28, 31, 93, 101, 108, 123, 128
opposition 28, 128, 182
ordinary consciousness 34, 206
ordinary mind 86, 113, 138
other-awareness 9
'out there' 46–7, 124, 211
outgrowth 134–5, 146, 157

pain 43–4, 126–7, 129, 139–42, 186–7, 192–3, 214
    absence of 43
    of loss 63–4
pain-power 124, 128
pairings 107–8
Pali canon 8, 14, 127, 167, 224
parents 61, 98–9, 115–16, 147
passivity 52, 161, 192–3
path 3, 16, 30, 44, 122, 225, 231–2
    Buddhist 155, 223, 232
patterns 15, 27, 29, 45, 190, 214
peace 52, 128, 187, 231
peach 40, 45, 54, 62
penetration 67, 74–6, 89–91, 95, 161, 169–71, 219
perception 10, 44, 67, 213, 225
perfection 186, 210, 232
permanence 90, 146
personal conscience 116, 120
personal experience 84, 179
philosophies 45, 151, 155, 163
phone 57–9
physical body, *see* body
physical energies 80, 180
physical exercise 80, 181
physical feeling 43
physical inertia 174

physical pleasure 186, 214, 224
physical senses 41, 190
plants 49, 153, 171
pleasant feeling 25, 58, 64, 112
pleasant objects 123
pleasure 22, 43–4, 81–2, 124–6, 139–41, 184–5, 214
    highest 82
    physical 186, 214, 224
pleasure-power 124, 128
pliancy, mental 181–2
poems 74, 215, 228
poets 113, 215
polarity 140, 187
Portrait of the Artist as a Young Man 98
positive emotional engagement 77
positive mental events 16, 119, 123, 219
positives 107–8, 123, 173–8, 180, 185–6, 205, 209–10
potentiality 49, 126, 156, 168
power 48, 50, 53, 101–2, 141, 148, 150
    sticking 47, 73
pradāśa, see spite
praiseworthy states 28–9, 32
prajñā, see penetration
pramāda, see carelessness
praśrabdhi, see serenity
pratigha, see hatred
precepts 117, 120, 210
    ethical 6, 224–5
    moral 112, 117
prejudices 100, 151, 194, 208
prema, see selfish affection
pretence 14, 131–4, 220
pride 32, 96, 149–50
private moments 121, 133
procrastinating inertia 176–7

sense-organs 124, 152, 192, 213
sense-world 67, 69, 88, 126, 128–9, 145, 229
sensitivity 97, 117, 139
sensual desire 22
sensuous longing 173
separate identity 139–40
separate self 138, 143, 149
sequence 40, 51, 58
serenity 108, 173, 180–3, 187–8, 220
sex 98, 100, 125
sexual feelings 100
Shakespeare, William 175
shallow interpretation 54–7
shame 59, 99, 219
  and faith 107–22
  kinds of 116–22
  reverential 116–22, 130, 132, 210, 219
shamelessness 120–1, 220
shrine room 132, 197
silence 118, 154
singleness 12, 25
skandhas 16, 217, 225
skilful actions 16, 156, 158, 209
skilful behaviour 28–9
skilful choices 156
skilful form 110, 112
skilful mental events 107, 118
skilful mental states 16, 30, 96, 108, 113, 178
skilful states 29, 96, 107–8, 177, 186
skills 28–9, 149, 151
sleep 11, 93–4, 174, 179
sleepiness 93–6, 101, 180, 221
sloth 93, 95, 97, 180, 227
slyness-concealment 220
smell 33, 42
smṛti, see attentiveness
social media 85, 141
social norms 9, 160
society 29, 137, 159, 181
solvent abusers 67

sorrow 43–4, 57, 129, 186, 191, 193
space 33, 59, 68, 103, 170, 195, 197
  open 128, 207–8, 210
sparśa, see contact
speech 8, 16, 53, 215, 225
spiritual ardour 173–4, 220
spiritual community 4, 6–9, 129, 134, 136, 176, 178–9
spiritual development 64, 114, 118
spiritual efforts 4–5, 10–12, 151, 175–6, 179
spiritual friends 97, 100, 133–4, 165–6, 199
spiritual friendship 7, 29, 121, 226
spiritual goal 112, 160, 198, 200
spiritual growth 3, 30, 99, 150
spiritual ideals 5, 114, 176, 232
spiritual laziness 192
spiritual life 3–4, 6–7, 11, 29–30, 121–2, 161–2, 175–80
spiritual map and compass 12–18
spiritual path 3–4, 41, 161–2, 169, 178
spiritual practice 4–5, 10, 24, 41, 62, 100, 130
spiritual progress 5, 104, 162
spite 135–6, 138, 220
śraddhā, see faith
stagnation 180–4, 187–8, 220
state of meditative absorption 25, 88
states 23–4, 26–8, 30–1, 63–6, 178, 181–4, 186–7
  cold 63, 131
  concentrated 78, 89
  dark 30–1
  high 29–30
  light 30–1
  low 29–30

positive 128, 130
praiseworthy 28–9, 32
skilful 29, 96, 107–8, 177, 186
unskilful 16, 23, 31–2, 93–4, 108, 112, 177
unwholesome, see unwholesome states
wholesome, see wholesome states
sticking power 47, 73
story 23, 52, 57, 63–5, 133, 196
strategy 7, 61–2, 154, 183–4
Stream Entry 133, 199, 232
structure 46, 86–7, 138, 161, 190, 212–13
  deeper 205, 209
styāna, see stagnation
subafflictions 107
subsidiary afflictions 107, 132
substantiality 90, 146
subtle objects of meditation 80, 103
suffering, and unwholesome states 22–4
sukha, see bliss
superficiality 80, 232
suprapersonal feeling 63, 65–6
survival 68, 79, 147, 200
Sutta Nipāta 228
symbols 77, 199, 216–17
sympathetic joy 137, 142
sympathies 30, 66, 149

taste 24, 33, 42, 183, 193, 211, 213
teachers 8, 15, 83, 98, 116, 163–6, 231
teachings 13, 109, 111, 163–4, 216–17, 224–5, 229
technical language 69, 124, 207
technology 10, 12, 85
temperament 136, 152, 162
temptations 5, 7, 176
tensions 8, 12, 23, 165, 182

WINDHORSE PUBLICATIONS

Windhorse Publications is a Buddhist charitable company based in the UK. We place great emphasis on producing books of high quality that are accessible and relevant to those interested in Buddhism at whatever level. We are the main publisher of the works of Sangharakshita, the founder of the Triratna Buddhist Order and Community. Our books draw on the whole range of the Buddhist tradition, including translations of traditional texts, commentaries, books that make links with contemporary culture and ways of life, biographies of Buddhists, and works on meditation.

As a not-for-profit enterprise, we ensure that all surplus income is invested in new books and improved production methods, to better communicate Buddhism in the 21st century. We welcome donations to help us continue our work – to find out more, go to www.windhorsepublications.com.

The Windhorse is a mythical animal that flies over the earth carrying on its back three precious jewels, bringing these invaluable gifts to all humanity: the Buddha (the 'awakened one'), his teaching, and the community of all his followers.

Windhorse Publications
169 Mill Road
Cambridge CB1 3AN
UK
info@windhorsepublications.com

Perseus Distribution
210 American Drive
Jackson TN 38301
USA

Windhorse Books
PO Box 574
Newtown NSW 2042
Australia

THE TRIRATNA BUDDHIST COMMUNITY

Windhorse Publications is a part of the Triratna Buddhist Community, which has more than sixty centres on five continents. Through these centres, members of the Triratna Buddhist Order offer classes in meditation and Buddhism, from an introductory to a deeper level of commitment. Members of the Triratna community run retreat centres around the world, and the Karuna Trust, a UK fundraising charity that supports social welfare projects in the slums and villages of South Asia.

Many Triratna centres have residential spiritual communities and ethical Right Livelihood businesses associated with them. Arts activities and body awareness disciplines are encouraged also, as is the development of strong bonds of friendship between people who share the same ideals. In this way Triratna is developing a unique approach to Buddhism, not simply as a set of techniques, but as a creatively directed way of life for people living in the modern world.

If you would like more information about Triratna please visit www.thebuddhistcentre.com or write to:

London Buddhist Centre
51 Roman Road
London E2 0HU
UK

Aryaloka
14 Heartwood Circle
Newmarket NH 03857
USA

Sydney Buddhist Centre
24 Enmore Road
Sydney NSW 2042
Australia

Know Your Mind:
The Psychological Dimension of Ethics in Buddhism

Sangharakshita

'The mind is its own place, and of itself can make a heaven of hell, a hell of heaven' -
Milton, *Paradise Lost*

Know Your Mind is an accessible introduction to traditional Buddhist
psychology, offering a clear description of the nature of mind and how it
functions.

Sangharakshita guides us expertly through the Abhidharma classification
of positive and negative mental states and shows us how we can work
with them. In exploring the part we play in creating our own suffering and
happiness, he elucidates the relationship of the mind to karma and rebirth,
and stresses the ethical, other-regarding nature of Buddhist psychology.

According to the Buddha's teaching, there is no limit to the human mind,
nothing is beyond its reach: *Know Your Mind* is essentially a practical guide
that can help us unlock that potential.

ISBN: 9780 904766 79 0
£18.99 / $29.95 / €22.95
304 pages

From *Know Your Mind*:

Because mind in Buddhism refers to something that is experienced by direct
perception, every point made in this book is verifiable from personal experience,
provided we are prepared to examine our experience honestly. The inner
tranquillity, clarity, and insight that can be developed through meditation
practice is not merely helpful to this process of examination, but absolutely
necessary to it. From a Buddhist point of view, to try to philosophize, or even
think clearly, without getting one's negative mental states out of the way is
going to be a flawed enterprise. Whatever efforts one makes to come to a true
understanding of reality, if one has not given attention to the mental state with
which one approaches the matter, one will inevitably see things in terms of one's
own craving, hatred, fear, and delusion. In Buddhism, therefore, there is no
philosophy without meditation. One has to rise above one's limited, personal,
or individual standpoint, at least to some extent, and be relatively free from
negative mental states, in order to see the truth.

   This book has two aims: to present the picture of mind and mental events
that centuries of Abhidharma scholarship brought into focus, and to act as a
practical guide to mental states for meditators, showing how the various mental
events may be recognized, and which are to be eradicated and which cultivated
so that psychological health, spiritual insights, and ultimately transcendental
knowledge may be attained.

The Three Jewels series

Sangharakshita

This set of three essential texts introduces the Three Jewels which are central to Buddhism: the *Buddha* (the Enlightened One), the *Dharma* (the Buddha's teachings), and the *Sangha* (the spiritual community).

Who is the Buddha?

ISBN 9781 899579 51 8
£11.99 / $18.95 / €15.95
188 pages

What is the Dharma?

ISBN 9781 899579 01 3
£12.99 / $20.95 / €15.95
272 pages

What is the Sangha?

ISBN 9781 899579 31 0
£9.99 / $19.95 / €12.95
288 pages

Satipaṭṭhāna: The Direct Path to Realization

Anālayo

This best-selling book offers a unique and detailed textual study of the Satipaṭṭhāna Sutta, a foundational Buddhist discourse on meditation practice.

This book should prove to be of value both to scholars of Early Buddhism and to serious meditators alike. – Bhikku Bodhi

. . . a gem . . . I learned a lot from this wonderful book and highly recommend it. – Joseph Goldstein

An indispensible guide . . . surely destined to become the classic commentary on the Satipaṭṭhāna. – Christopher Titmuss

Very impressive and useful, with its blend of strong scholarship and attunement to practice issues. – Prof. Peter Harvey, author of *An Introduction to Buddhist Ethics*

ISBN 9781 899579 54 9
£17.99 / $27.95 / €19.95
336 pages

Perspectives on Satipaṭṭhāna

Anālayo

As mindfulness is increasingly embraced in the contemporary world as a practice that brings peace and self-awareness, Bhikkhu Anālayo casts fresh light on the earliest sources of mindfulness in the Buddhist tradition.

The Satipaṭṭhāna Sutta is well known as the main source for Buddhist teachings on mindfulness and its place in the Buddhist path. Ten years after Anālayo's acclaimed study of the Sutta, his current work, *Perspectives on Satipaṭṭhāna*, brings a new dimension to our understanding by comparing the Pali text with versions that have survived in Chinese. Anālayo also draws on the presentation of mindfulness in a number of other discourses as they survive in Chinese and Tibetan translations as well as in Pali.

The result is a wide-ranging exploration of what mindfulness meant in early Buddhism. Informed by Anālayo's outstanding scholarship, depth of understanding and experience as a practitioner, this book sheds fresh light on material that is central to our understanding of Buddhist practice, bringing us as close as we can come to the mindfulness teachings of the Buddha himself.

'*Anālayo builds on his earlier ground-breaking work,* Satipaṭṭhāna: The Direct Path to Realization. *The brilliance of his scholarly research, combined with the depth of his meditative understanding, provides an invaluable guide to these liberating practices.*' – Joseph Goldstein

'*He offers us a work of great scholarship and wisdom that will be of immense benefit to anyone who wants to seriously study or to establish a practice of mindfulness.*' – Sharon Salzberg

'*A treasury of impeccable scholarship and practice, offering a wise, open-minded and deep understanding of the Buddha's original teaching.*' – Jack Kornfield

ISBN: 9781 909314 03 0
£15.99 / $24.95 / €19.95
336 pages

The Buddha on Wall Street: What's Wrong with Capitalism and What We Can Do about It

Vaḍḍhaka Linn

After his Enlightenment the Buddha set out to help liberate the individual, and create a society free from suffering. The economic resources now exist to offer a realistic possibility of providing everyone with decent food, shelter, work and leisure, to allow each of us to fulfil our potential as human beings, whilst protecting the environment. What is it in the nature of modern capitalism which prevents that happening? Can Buddhism help us build something better than our current economic system, to reduce suffering and help the individual to freedom? In this thought-provoking work, Vaḍḍhaka Linn explores answers to these questions by examining our economic world from the moral standpoint established by the Buddha.

'An original, insightful, and provocative evaluation of our economic situation today. If you wonder about the social implications of Buddhist teachings, this is an essential book.' – David Loy, author *Money, Sex, War, Karma*

'Lays bare the pernicious consequences of corporate capitalism and draws forth from Buddhism suggestions for creating benign alternatives conducive to true human flourishing.' – Bhikkhu Bodhi, editor *In the Buddha's Words*

'Questions any definition of wellbeing that does not rest on a firm ethical foundation, developing a refreshing Buddhist critique of the ends of economic activity.' – Dominic Houlder, Adjunct Professor in Strategy and Entrepreneurship, London Business School

ISBN 978 1 909314 44 3
£9.99 / $16.95 / €12.95
272 pages